MARVEL

RISE OF THE SUPER HEROES

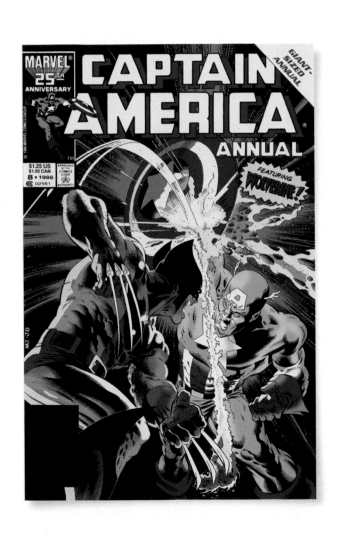

CONTENTS

THE MODERN AGE YEAR BY YEAR

MODERN AGE COMIC BOOK ART

THE MODERN AGE

1986–

THE MID-1980s SAW a change in storytelling. Led by creators such as Alan Moore and Frank Miller, writers and artists started to explore darker, more adult themes in their comics. Alongside this, creator-owned comics came to the fore through the rise of publishers such as Image, Dark Horse, and Marvel's own Epic and Icon Imprints. This period also saw the rise of the X-Men. By the 1990s Marvel's mutants were not only a part of a best-selling comic, but also a huge franchise, with countless X-Men-related books in print.

A whole new generation of artists also burst onto the comic-book scene. Jim Lee, Marc Silvestri, Alan Davis, Carlos Pacheco, David Aja, and others started to push the boundaries of the art forward once again, creating some amazing covers along the way. By the 21st century, comics were becoming increasingly part of mainstream culture, with many top movies in Hollywood being based on Marvel heroes. The rise of digital publishing also gave readers a new way of reading comics. Publishing was changing, and Marvel was at the forefront of that change.

THE NEW AVENGERS #1 ▶

January 2005
Artist: David Finch
(Cover shown in full on p162)

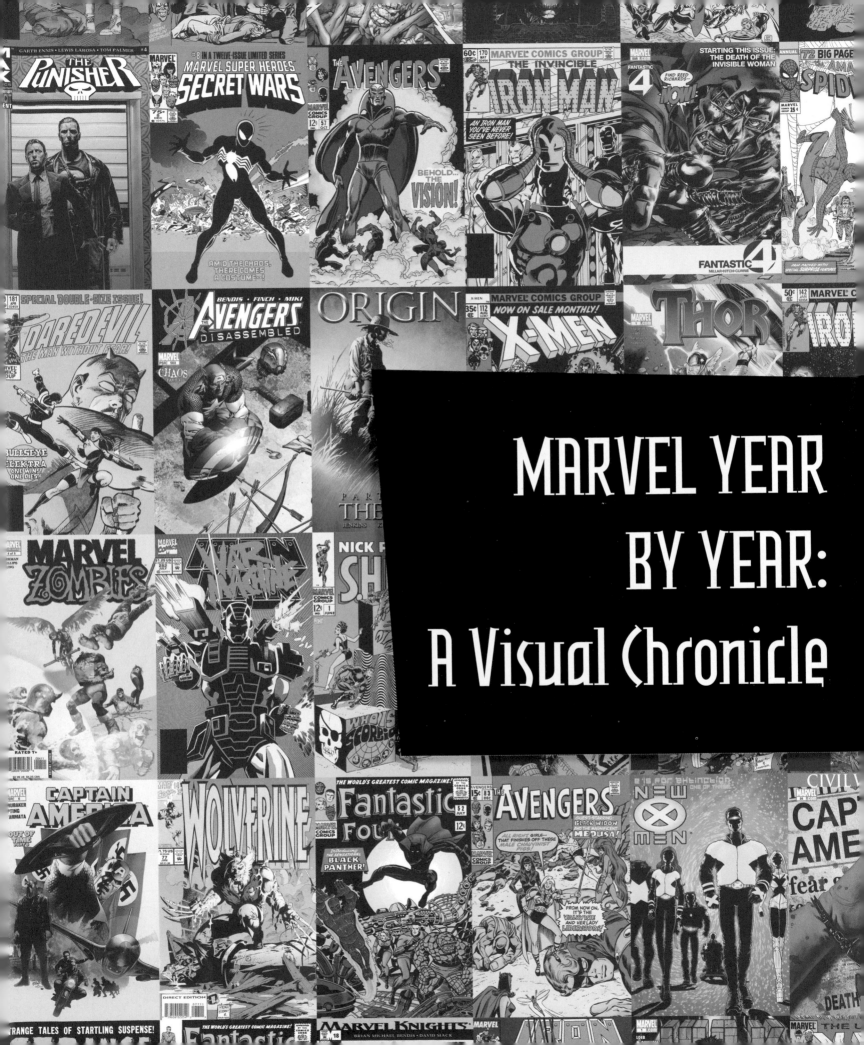

MARVEL YEAR BY YEAR:

A Visual Chronicle

1986

NEW WORLD AND A NEW UNIVERSE

The year 1986 was the twenty-fifth anniversary of the Marvel Universe, which had begun with *The Fantastic Four* #1 in November, 1961. Jim Shooter decided all November-dated books would mark the occasion with a portrait of the title's main character. He also embarked on his most ambitious project: he would celebrate the birth of one universe by creating a brand new one.

Appropriately dubbed the New Universe, the new comics were built around the idea of real people gaining superhuman powers. These new titles would inhabit a world that looked and behaved exactly like the one outside the reader's window. There would be no aliens, no magic, and no fictional technology. The titles would also operate in real time and characters would age with their readers.

In 1986, Marvel Comics was purchased by New World Pictures, a major film and television production company that had been established in 1970 by the legendary producer/director Roger Corman. New World Pictures planned to create a series of major films starring the Marvel characters. They produced *The Punisher* (1989) starring Dolph Lundgren, the direct-to-video *Captain America* (1990) with Matt Salinger, an unaired pilot of a television series based on the Power Pack, and three made-for-television *Incredible Hulk* movies.

A SON FOR CYCLOPS AND MADELYNE PRYOR

• *The Uncanny X-Men* #201

Nathan Christopher Summers was born to Scott "Cyclops" Summers and his wife, Madelyne Pryor, in this issue. He seemed to be a normal baby boy at first. But little did he know that his mother was actually a clone of the deceased Jean Grey and that she had been created for the specific purpose of conceiving him. Mister Sinister carefully arranged Nathan's birth because he knew the child would have great powers—powers that Sinister planned to use to destroy Apocalypse. Unfortunately, Apocalypse learned of Sinister's plan and infected Nathan with a techno-organic virus that would slowly kill him. Rachel Summers arrived from the future as an old woman and promised Cyclops that she could use technology from her era to save Nathan, so he sent him with her in *X-Factor* #68 (July, 1991).

Nathan Summers left the present as a baby to go into the future with Rachel Summers. In The New Mutants *#87 (March, 1990) he appeared as the adult called Cable.*

DAREDEVIL IS BORN AGAIN

• *Daredevil* #227

Born Again was a seven-issue story arc that appeared in *Daredevil*, from issue #227 to #233 (Feb.–Aug., 1986) by writer Frank Miller and artist David Mazzucchelli. Karen Page, Matt Murdock's former girlfriend, had become a drug addict and revealed Daredevil's secret identity to someone in the Kingpin of Crime's employ in exchange for drugs.

The Kingpin proceeded to wage a secret war against Murdock. He used his contacts to freeze the lawyer's bank accounts and foreclose on his house. Murdock was also disbarred when a crooked cop testified that he had paid a witness to perjure himself. Realizing that the Kingpin was destroying his life, Daredevil struck back and publicly exposed the Kingpin's underworld connections, ruining his image as an honest businessmen. No longer a high-priced attorney, Murdock was literary reborn as the protector of Hell's Kitchen.

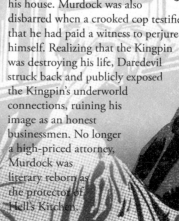

FEBRUARY

THE ORIGINAL FIVE X-MEN ARE BACK

"Ironic isn't it, Iceman? Garbed as mutant hunters, we're welcomed with open arms! Garbed as mutants, we become Public Enemy #1!"

• *X-Factor* #1
Time had changed the X-Men. Professor X had gone into outer space to be with his girlfriend Lilandra, leaving his former enemy Magneto in charge of the New Mutants. Storm now led the main X-Men team, which consisted of Kitty Pryde, Nightcrawler, Rogue, Colossus, Wolverine, and Rachel Summers. Like many older fans, writer/artist Bob Layton longed for the good old days. He missed the original five X-Men and wanted to do a book that featured Cyclops, Angel, Beast, Iceman, and Marvel Girl. Unfortunately, Jean Grey, the original Marvel Girl, had died at the conclusion of the Dark Phoenix Saga in *X-Men* #137 (Sept., 1980). Marvel writer Kurt Busiek offered a solution: what if Jean Grey had never been Phoenix? What if Phoenix had been a different entity and Jean Grey was still alive in Jamaica Bay?

In *The Avengers* #263 (Jan., 1986), the team detected a cocoon at the bottom of Jamaica Bay. The same month, Reed Richards examined the cocoon in *Fantastic Four* #286 and was startled to discover Jean Grey inside. The original X-Men gathered in *X-Factor* #1 by Bob Layton and artist Jackson Guice and learned that Jean had been inside the cocoon since she had been exposed to cosmic rays in *X-Men* #100 (Aug., 1976)—the issue before Phoenix's first appearance. Even though it meant leaving his new wife and child, Cyclops joined with the others to set up their new team in New York City. Based on the concept used in the *Ghostbusters* movies, X-Factor posed as mutant hunters and publicly advertised their services. When called to deal with a mutant menace, they didn't harm the mutants they captured. Instead, unknown to their employers, they secretly trained the mutants in how to hone their skills so that they could fit into society.

During the course of Born Again, Daredevil realized that he had a responsibility to protect the innocent when he battled Nuke—a Rambo-like, drug-addicted member of America's Super-Soldier program who did not hesitate before killing anyone in his way.

MAY

WEDDING BELLS

• *The Incredible Hulk* #319
Dr. Bruce Banner first met Betty Ross in *The Incredible Hulk* #1 (May, 1962) and finally married her in issue #319, by John Byrne. Temporarily separated from the Hulk, Banner raced to the wedding altar while Dr. Samson and the Hulkbusters battled his alter ego. Betty's father, a furious General "Thunderbolt" Ross, tried to stop the ceremony, but he only succeeded in shooting Banner's sidekick Rick Jones, who insisted the wedding continued.

JUNE

INTRODUCING APOCALYPSE AND HIS ALLIANCE OF EVIL

"You shall soon provide all mutantkind with a source of unlimited might—a race of super-mutants! And I shall lead them to war against the puny infection called—man!"

• *X-Factor* #5
Writer/artist Bob Layton intended to use Daredevil's foe, the Owl, as X-Factor's main villain. But Louise Simonson wanted X-Factor to battle someone new, so when Layton left the title with *X-Factor* #5, she had the final page redrawn, adding a shadowy figure named Apocalypse. Simonson liked the idea of introducing a Darwinian character who would initiate disasters to help stimulate humanity's evolution, by forcing people and mutants to keep evolving to higher and higher levels.

In *X-Factor* #6 (July, 1986), readers learned that Apocalypse had hired a mutant team called the Alliance of Evil, which consisted of Frenzy, a mutant with steel-hard skin and superhuman strength; Tower, who could increase his size; Stinger, who could project electrical blasts; and Timeshadow, who could teleport so fast that  he appeared to be in several places at once. Apocalypse sent the Alliance to capture Michael Nowlan/Source, a mutant who could enhance other mutants' powers.

Apocalypse had been born nearly six thousand years ago and had been a slave of Rama-Tut, a previous identity of the time-traveling Kang. Virtually immortal, Apocalypse was one of the most powerful mutants ever born. He could alter his body's molecular structure at will and so could become as strong as he desired or assume any appearance he wanted. He was able to physically interface with technology and could generate force-fields and project concussive blasts of energy. Although he had apparently been killed on several occasions, Apocalypse always found a way to revive himself.

ELEKTRA'S OWN SERIES

• *Elektra: Assassin* #1
Produced by Frank Miller and illustrated by Bill Sienkiewicz, *Elektra: Assassin* was an eight-issue limited series. Because its mature content was inappropriate for children, it was published by Marvel's Epic Comics imprint. The story was illustrated with a series of individual panels that were painted in watercolors rather than by the traditional method of pencilling and inking.

Elektra learned that a Presidential candidate intended to launch a nuclear war as soon as he was elected. Battling cyborgs, monsters, and SHIELD agents, she tried to prevent him from being elected. Although she failed, she did manage to stop the war by transferring the mind of a good man into the new President's body.

THE MUTANT MASSACRE

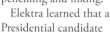

• *The Uncanny X-Men* #210
Although he had co-created the Morlocks in *The Uncanny X-Men* #169 (May, 1983), Chris Claremont did not like the idea of so many mutants living beneath New York City. He conceived a story line that would solve the problem and also introduce a new team of villains for the X-Men.

The Mutant Massacre was an eleven-issue story that ran from October, 1986, through *The Uncanny X-Men* #210–213, *The New Mutants* #46, *The Mighty Thor* #373–374, and *X-Factor* #9–11. Working for Mister Sinister, the Marauders—a team of mutant mercenaries—raided the Alley and callously slaughtered most of the Morlocks.

 *G.I. Joe* proved so popular that a second title, *G.I. Joe Special Missions* #1, was launched.

 Spider-Man guest-starred in *Top Dog* #10 in the first very crossover between characters from Marvel and Marvel's imprint Star Comics.

INTRODUCING THE SUPER-PATRIOT

• *Captain America* #323
John Walker worshipped his older brother and was devastated when he was killed in Vietnam. To honor his brother's memory, John enlisted in the military. He later heard about Curtiss Jackson, the Power Broker, and signed up with him to gain superhuman strength. Walker was going to join the Unlimited Class Wrestling Federation until he met Ethan Thurm in *Captain America* #323, who suggested that Walker become a corporate-sponsored Super Hero. Thurm later organized a rally to criticize Captain America. Taking the name Super-Patriot, Walker believed that the American people should be able to decide who wore the uniform of Captain America and he began to campaign for the job. The Super-Patriot came to fame when he killed a terrorist to prevent him from detonating a nuclear warhead in Washington D.C..

A MARVEL MOVIE

• *Marvel Super Special* #41
This issue adapted the story line of *Howard The Duck*, the first major motion picture based on a Marvel character. The comic showed Howard plucked from his home on Duckworld and taken to Cleveland, Ohio, where he met a young singer named Beverly. When Howard discovered that an alien Dark Overlord was planning to invade the Earth, he stopped the invasion by destroying the only device that could send him home. Produced by Lucasfilm and Universal Pictures, the film starred Lea Thompson and Tim Robbins.

A NEW UNIVERSE TITLE

• *D.P.7* #1
Created by editor Mark Gruenwald and artist Paul Ryan, *D.P.7* was published under the New Universe imprint. The title stood for the seven Displaced Paranormals—ordinary people with super powers—who met in a clinic where they had gone to learn how to deal with their new superhuman powers.

PROUDSTAR FORMS THE PSI-FORCE

• *Psi-Force #1*

This title was part of the New Universe imprint and lasted thirty-two issues. Created by editor Archie Goodwin and artist Mark Texeira, it focused on teenagers with psionic powers. Former CIA agent Emmett Proudstar had gained his powers from the mysterious "White Event" that had suddenly created paranormals—ordinary people with super powers—in the New Universe. His dreams led him to gather a group of teenagers who had various psionic powers. After Proudstar was murdered, the teens formed the powerful entity called the Psi-Hawk.

The Psi-Hawk possessed all the powers of the members of Psi-Force, but magnified to a much greater degree. The whole was far more powerful than the sum of its parts.

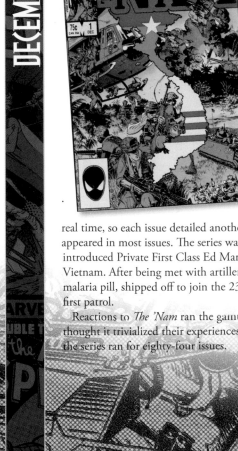

A NEW VIETNAM WAR COMIC

"Yeah, the perfect replacement. Green as grass and just stupid enough to fit in. Welcome to the jewel of Southeast Asia."

• *The 'Nam #1*

Oliver Stone's movie *Platoon* had already been released to critical acclaim when Editor-in-Chief Jim Shooter walked into editor Larry Hama's office one day. He carried a *G.I. Joe* cover with a new logo on it. The logo simply said "The 'Nam." Shooter asked Hama if he was interested in developing a new title that was set during the United States' war with Vietnam. Hama immediately called Doug Murray, a veteran who had served in Vietnam. Murray had written a feature about Vietnam called "The 5th Of The 1st" for Marvel's black-and-white magazine *Savage Tales #1* (Oct., 1985) and *Savage Tales #4* (April, 1986). Hama also called artist Michael Golden to draw the new title. Working together, Murray and Golden produced *The 'Nam #1*, the first of a twelve-year limited series It was their intention to produce one issue for every month the United States had been in Vietnam. They also planned for the book to occur in real time, so each issue detailed another month in the characters' lives. A glossary that explained military slang also appeared in most issues. The series was set from the average soldier's point of view. The first issue introduced Private First Class Ed Marks as he was saying goodbye to his family before flying to Vietnam. After being met with artillery fire as he landed in Saigon, Marks was handed a malaria pill, shipped off to join the 23rd Infantry, assigned to his squad, and sent on his first patrol.

Reactions to *The 'Nam* ran the gamut. Some veterans were pleased, others thought it trivialized their experiences. Sales, however, were excellent and the series ran for eighty-four issues.

Although Ed Marks was rotated out of the title when he completed his twelve-month tour of duty with The 'Nam #12, Doug Murray had intended to bring him back as a reporter who covered the war, although this never happened.

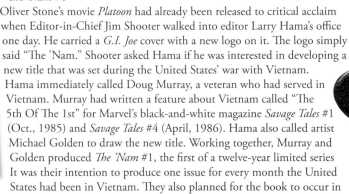

1987
A NEW ORDER BEGINS

Jim Shooter used January's *Bullpen Bulletins* to apologize for a television interview with Stan Lee about Marvel's twenty-fifth anniversary. The interview had edited out any mention of Jack Kirby, Steve Ditko, Larry Lieber, and all the other creators who had helped launch the Marvel Universe in the 1960s. Shooter used the following month's *Bulletins* to describe the lesson he had learned about responsibility from reading *The Amazing Spider-Man*. It would be the last *Bullpen Bulletins* he ever wrote.

On April 15, 1987, a day when most Americans were thinking about their taxes, Tom DeFalco was informed that he had become Marvel's Editor-in-Chief. Where Shooter had deliberately put a spotlight on himself, DeFalco took a more low-key approach. He had always considered himself a freelancer who was only masquerading as a staff person and he never thought the job would last. DeFalco appointed Mark Gruenwald as executive editor. They initially wrote the *Bullpen Bulletins* together, but did not sign it. DeFalco could already foresee the day when his responsibilities would prevent him from working on it. He and Gruenwald immediately began formulating a publishing plan that would slowly increase the number of titles over the next five years. Marvel was on the move, again.

JANUARY

A NEW TYPE OF COMIC

• *Spider-Man Comics Magazine* #1
While working for Archie Comics in the 1970s, Tom DeFalco had spearheaded a line of highly successful digest-sized comics. Measuring about five by seven inches, they fitted into the racks for magazines like *Reader's Digest* and *T.V. Guide* that were displayed near cash registers in supermarkets across America. DeFalco introduced a similar line at Marvel that featured Spider-Man, G.I. Joe, the Transformers, Alf, and a general Star Comics anthology.

🅜 *Defenders Of The Earth* #1 featured the famous comic strip heroes Flash Gordon, the Phantom, and Mandrake the Magician.

FEBRUARY

THE COMET MAN DEBUTS

• *The Comet Man* #1
Bill Mumy and Miguel Ferrer were writers, actors, and musicians who created this six-issue limited series. Astrophysicist Dr. Stephen Beckley was on a space mission when he was exposed to radiation. As a new Super Hero, he could rocket through the air, teleport himself, project his mind into others, and read peoples' thoughts.

THE LOST IN SPACE-TIME STORY BEGINS

• *The West Coast Avengers* #17
This issue began a seven-part story line called Lost In Space-Time that sent the Super Heroes Hawkeye, Iron Man, Tigra, Wonder Man, and Mockingbird into the past. Part of the team ended up in the old west and others were sent to ancient Egypt.

MARCH

DUNPHY BECOMES DEMOLITION MAN

• *Captain America* #328
Dennis Dunphy was a wrestler who gained superhuman strength thanks to the Power Broker. He worked for the Unlimited Class Wrestling Federation where he met Ben Grimm in *The Thing* #28 (Oct., 1985). He became Demolition Man—or D-Man—and teamed up with Cap to investigate the Power Broker's criminal activities. He stayed on as Cap's partner until he was frozen in a block of ice in issue #384 (April, 1991).

THE SUPER-PATRIOT TAKES OVER AS CAPTAIN AMERICA

"I cannot represent the American government: the President does that. I must represent the American people. I represent the American Dream, the freedom to strive, to become all that you dream of being. Being Captain America has been my dream."

• *Captain America* #332

This issue began a nineteen-part story arc called Captain America No More! The US President appointed a Commission on Superhuman Activities to supervise Americans with superhuman powers. When it ordered Captain America to work directly for the government, Steve Rogers turned in his shield and costume. The Commission appointed John Walker, the Super-Patriot, as the new Captain America.

Walker was trained in this new role by the Taskmaster and was partnered with a new Bucky—Lemar Hoskins—who later changed his name to Battlestar. Walker did his best to replace Rogers, but he was far more brutal than his predecessor and the job was not everything he had hoped. Walker's former friends became jealous of his success and turned on him. When a neo-Nazi group learned of his secret identity and murdered his parents, Walker flew into a rage and exacted a terrible revenge.

Meanwhile, a high-ranking member of the Commission was secretly working for the evil Red Skull, Cap's longtime enemy. The Skull had masterminded everything to destroy his old foe's reputation: he had deliberately forced Rogers into a corner, knowing he would quit. Mission accomplished, the Skull planned to kill Walker. When Steve Rogers learned that Walker had been captured by the Skull, he raced to his rescue. That was the moment John Walker finally realized that he was not ready to replace Cap. He soon resigned and allowed Rogers to resume his identity as the true Captain America.

Ⓜ *The Flintstone Kids* #1 showed the famous television characters—Fred, Wilma, Barney, and Betty—as young children.

Ⓜ Walter Simonson and Sal Buscema ended their popular run with *The Mighty Thor* in issue #382, which celebrated the 300th appearance of Thor. The Thunder God commemorated the occasion by breaking Loki's arm with his enchanted hammer.

MISTER SINISTER APPEARS

• *The Uncanny X-Men* #221

Although he had been mentioned as early as issue #212 (Dec., 1986), Mister Sinister did not appear until this issue. Nathaniel Essex discovered Apocalypse lying in suspended animation. Apocalypse made him superhumanly strong and virtually immortal as Mister Sinister. A scientist interested in Darwin's Theory of Evolution, Essex had worked for the Nazis during World War II and was obsessed with studying mutant children. He tested the young Charles Xavier and, later, Scott Summers. He also hired the Marauders to massacre the Morlocks because he believed they would weaken mutantkind's ability to evolve.

MARVEL PUBLISHES WORK BY MOEBIUS

• *Moebius* #1

The French comic book artist Jean Giraud, who signed his work Moebius, allowed Marvel's Epic Comics imprint to translate his work and publish it as a series of graphic novels. These included his *Blueberry* western series as well as many of his science-fiction fantasies.

SPIDER-MAN AND KRAVEN MEET IN FEARFUL SYMMETRY

• *Web Of Spider-Man* #31

J.M. DeMatteis had an intriguing idea. What if a villain put a hero in suspended animation and took over his costumed identity? He first tried this with the Grim Reaper and Wonder Man. When that didn't sell, he rewrote it to star Batman. When that failed, he substituted Spider-Man and a new villain. Finally, deciding the story would work better with a classic villain, he rewrote it a fourth time with Spider-Man and Kraven the Hunter.

The six-issue story arc, Fearful Symmetry, drawn by Mike Zeck and Bob McLeod began in this issue and ran through all the Spider-Man titles for two months, climaxing in *The Spectacular Spider-Man* #132 (Nov., 1987).

SPIDER-MAN'S WEDDING

"I will take this man—this very special man—to be the most important thing in my life. Because that's exactly what I realize he already is."

• *The Amazing Spider-Man Annual* #21
In 1977, Stan Lee had begun writing a syndicated newspaper comic strip that starred Spider-Man. Realizing that adults were the primary market for newspapers, Lee tailored the strip accordingly, focusing on the soap-opera elements of Peter Parker's life and downplaying the superheroics. He wanted Parker to marry Mary Jane Watson in the comic strip and he mentioned the idea to Jim Shooter at a comic book convention. Shooter turned to the audience and asked their opinion. The shouts of approval convinced Shooter to approve the marriage.

Peter Parker had asked Mary Jane to marry him on at least two occasions, but, being a child of divorce, Mary Jane was afraid of committing to anyone for the rest of her life. She refused, but later realized that it was time to stop running away and accepted.

Neither Peter nor Mary Jane arrived on time for their wedding. Their friends feared neither would show up, but they did. Surrounded by their friends and family, Peter and Mary Jane were married on the front steps of City Hall.

The wedding occurred in *The Amazing Spider-Man Annual* #21, which sported two different covers: one with Peter Parker beside Mary Jane and one with Spider-Man in his place. The wedding was also recreated with actors in front of a live audience at New York's Shea Stadium on June 5, 1987 and was celebrated in the newspaper strip on June 21.

Mary Jane's wedding dress was created especially for her by the renowned fashion designer Willi Smith, who died unexpectedly before any of these ceremonies took place.

MARVEL MASTERWORKS

Tom DeFalco had barely moved into his new office as Editor-in-Chief when he was informed of a crisis. The New Universe comics had not sold as well as expected and the company needed to make up the budgetary difference. DeFalco had to create some new titles quickly or come up with another idea. His solution was *Marvel Masterworks*—a line of hardcover books that reprinted the earliest Marvel comics. He started with three titles: *The Amazing Spider-Man* #1–10, *The Fantastic Four* #1–10, and *The X-Men* #1–10. The sales department was thrilled with the idea and many different titles have been published as *Marvel Masterworks* ever since.

INTRODUCING MICROCHIP

• *The Punisher* #4
Linus "Microchip" Lieberman first appeared in this issue by writer Mike Baron and artist Klaus Janson. Inspired by Q from the James Bond films, Microchip had been secretly providing Frank Castle—the Punisher—with weaponry and technology for years and had even helped build the Punisher's battle van. Linus had a son named Louis who was also introduced in weapons technology. Nicknamed Microchip Jr., Louis was killed while aiding Castle in *The Punisher* #8 (May, 1988).

STEVE ROGERS CARRIES ON

• *Captain America* #335
Although he had resigned as Captain America in August, Steve Rogers resumed his superheroic duties as Cap in this issue, wearing a black version of his famous costume. He continued to be a member of the Avengers and even set up an interim team when the Earth's Mightiest Heroes temporarily disbanded.

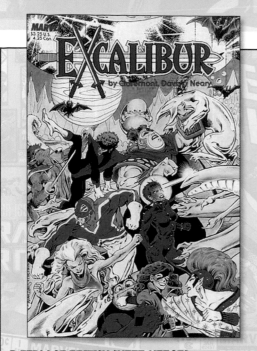

A TEAM OF BRITISH SUPER HEROES

• *Excalibur Special Edition*

Captain Britain had been created by Chris Claremont and Herb Trimpe for Marvel's London office and he first appeared in the weekly *Captain Britain* #1 (Oct. 13, 1976). Claremont always had a fondness for the character, as did Alan Davis, who had drawn many of his adventures. So it was only natural that they produced *Excalibur Special Edition*, a graphic novel about a team of Super Heroes based in England. It featured Captain Britain, Meggan (his shape-shifting girlfriend), the former X-Men members Nightcrawler and Phoenix (Rachel Summers), and Kitty Pryde and her pet dragon Lockheed. A regular *Excalibur* title was soon published that ran for 125 issues.

ARMOR WARS BEGIN

• *Iron Man* #225

Although actually called Stark Wars, the story arc that became known as Armor Wars began in this issue and ran until June, 1988. Written by David Michelinie and Bob Layton and drawn by Mark Bright, Tony Stark was horrified to learn that a mercenary called FORCE was using his own technology against him. Fearing other villains would do the same, Stark journeyed around the world to disable every armored suit that was using his stolen technology.

THE NORSE GODS MEET THE CELTIC GODS

• *The Mighty Thor* #386

While Thor was pursuing a dangerous beast, he crossed a dimensional rift that led him to Avalon, the home of the Celtic Gods, where he confronted Leir, the God of Lightning and the Spear. Leir later journeyed to Thor's homeland, Asgard, where he challenged Thor for the hand of Lady Sif. However, he was sent packing when Sif defeated him in a fair duel.

A SPLIT BOOK FOR THE 1980s

• *Solo Avengers* #1

Harkening back to the split books of the 1960s, *Solo Avengers* #1 was launched to fulfill two goals: it would give Hawkeye a regular eleven-page feature and it would also provide Marvel with a second eleven-page slot that could be used to try out new talent or to tell stories with the Avengers characters who did not have their own series. The backup story in issue #1 starred Mockingbird and was drawn by Jim Lee, who achieved fame drawing the X-Men. Backups in other issues featured Moondragon, the Swordsman, and Starfox. The title was changed to *Avengers Spotlight* with its twenty-first issue.

Captain America #332 (Aug., 1987) *Written by Mark Gruenwald, cover pencilled by Mike Zeck and inked by Klaus Janson.*

Mark Gruenwald was born in Oshkosh, Wisconsin on June 18, 1953 and bought his first comic book—The Fantastic Four #8—when he was nine years old. He became a serious fan and soon started drawing his own stories. He moved to New York City and got an editorial job at Marvel, where he wrote titles like Marvel Two-In-One, The Spider-Woman, D.P.7, Quasar, and, of course, Captain America. He is also famous for having spearheaded The Official Handbook Of The Marvel Universe. He died unexpectedly on August 12, 1996, and was named the patron saint of Marvel in 2006.

1988

ONE UNIVERSE ENDS, OTHERS BEGIN

Marvel's editorial staff continued to evolve in 1988. Editors Larry Hama and Ann Nocenti left to pursue careers as full-time writers and were replaced by Bob Harras, Bobbie Chase, and Terry Kavanagh. Jim Novak resigned from his post as production department supervisor and was succeed by Virginia Romita (the wife of John Romita Sr.), whose skills as art traffic manager had assured that the comics all came out on time.

The *Bullpen Bulletins* congratulated Doug Murray, writer of *The 'Nam*, for winning the prestigious Veterans Achievement Award For Entertainment from BRAVO—the Brotherhood Rally of All Veterans Organization. And Marvel even used the pages to salute their distinguished competition—DC Comics—on Superman's fiftieth anniversary.

The New Universe came to an end with three graphic novels, *The Pitt*, *The Draft*, and *The War*. The city of Pittsburgh was destroyed, all the paranormals were drafted into the army, and nuclear war was barely averted by a Star Child, who took responsibility for protecting the world.

Marvel increased its number of monthly titles, adding a new one every month. In addition, the company expanded some of its already popular lines with two new X-Men-related titles (*Excalibur* and *Wolverine*), *The Punisher War Journal*, and *G.I. Joe European Missions*.

JANUARY

SHARON IS THE SHE-THING

• *Fantastic Four #310*
While returning from a space mission, Sharon Ventura/Ms. Marvel and the Thing were exposed to cosmic rays. The Thing's second exposure caused him to mutate even further and Sharon became a hideous She-Thing. Unable to cope with her appearance, she suffered a mental breakdown and was cared for by the adventurer Wyatt Wingfoot.

THE RETURN OF THE SIN-EATER

• *The Spectacular Spider-Man #134*
Obsessed with destroying anyone who sinned, the Sin-Eater had first appeared in issue #107 (Oct., 1985). Haunted by his crimes, he returned for a three-issue story that climaxed when he committed "suicide by cop" by threatening a child with an unloaded gun.

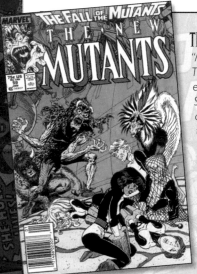

THE FALL OF THE MUTANTS

"Mutants are not inhuman monsters! They are people who are born with extraordinary abilities. That's all. Some are good. Others become criminals. But they, like you, deserve to be judged as individuals."

• *The New Mutants #59*
"Do you know what your child is?" Small cards with this question began appearing in comic-book stores as Marvel geared up its advertising campaign for The Fall Of The Mutants twelve-issue story arc that ran through *The New Mutants #59–61*, *The Uncanny X-Men #225–227*, and *X-Factor #24–26*. *Captain America #339*, *Daredevil #252*, *Fantastic Four #312*, *The Incredible Hulk #340*, and *Power Pack #35* also tied into to the story. Against the backdrop of growing fear and suspicion of mutants, the government was considering a Mutant Registration Act, which would require all mutants to register themselves, as if they were dangerous weapons. (A similar law for those with superhuman powers was the basis for the 2007 company-wide crossover *Civil War*.)

The Fall of the Mutants was actually three separate stories—one in each of the X-Men titles. In *The Uncanny X-Men*, the team battled the government-sponsored Freedom Force and sacrificed themselves to banish a monster from their plane of existence. A goddess took pity on the team and restored them to life, but made them invisible to surveillance equipment so that the world would still think they were dead. In *X-Factor*, Apocalypse had turned the now-wingless Angel into a murderous cyborg and planned to unleash his Four Horsemen on New York City. X-Factor drove off the Horsemen and rescued their former teammate, now called Archangel. In *The New Mutants* the team tried to help semi-sentient creatures who were being abused. In the course of battle, Cypher was killed, and Magneto blamed his death on humanity.

THE DARKNESS THAT BLANKETS THIS CITY IS NOTHING! *NOTHING!* NOT COMPARED TO THE SHROUD THAT SPIDER-MAN PULLED OVER *ME!*

HE STOLE MY LIFE... SHATTERED IT...THEN CAST IT ASIDE LIKE YESTERDAY'S NEWS!

SO IT IS ONLY FITTING, ONLY *FAIR*, THAT I DO THE SAME TO *HIM!*

AND I WILL

SOON!

SPIDEY'S ALIEN COSTUME IS BACK!

"You may call me Venom—for that's what I'm paid to spew out these days! I'm your victim, Spider-Man—I'm the innocent you ruined!"

• *The Amazing Spider-Man* #298

The alien costume that Spider-Man had obtained in *Marvel Super Heroes Secret Wars* #8 (Dec., 1984) and that was later revealed to be a sentient symbiote was back. And it wanted revenge!

Daily Globe reporter Eddie Brock thought he was destined for a Pulitzer. The Sin-Eater had just begun his first murder spree when Brock received a call from someone claiming to be him. He revealed the Sin-Eater's identity and was the *Globe*'s star reporter... for about an hour. Then Spider-Man caught the real Sin-Eater and Brock's source was exposed as a fake. Brock was fired and began a downward spiral, his hatred of Spider-Man growing in proportion to how far he fell. Unable to go on, Brock went into a church to ask for guidance. As it turned out, this was the same church where the alien symbiote had allegedly perished during its final battle with Spider-Man in *Web Of Spider-Man* #1 (April, 1985). Sensing a kindred spirit, the symbiote bonded with Brock. The two became one. And that one was called Venom.

Since he could not be detected by Peter Parker's spider-sense, Venom's first act was to push Parker in front of a subway car in this issue by David Michelinie and Todd McFarlane, although all readers saw of him was his hand. In the next issue, he terrorized Mary Jane and issue #300 revealed his origin and showed his first battle with Spider-Man. Stronger and larger than the webhead, Venom honestly believed that Spider-Man was a monster and that it was his responsibility to protect other innocents from the wall-crawler.

THE FIRST APPEARANCE OF GATEWAY

• *The Uncanny X-Men* #227

The Australian Aborigine known as Gateway, who first appeared in this issue by writer Chris Claremont and artist Marc Silvestri, had the ability to open teleportation gateways. After being forced to aid the super-criminal cyborgs called the Reavers, he assisted the X-Men when they established a temporary base in the Australian outback.

Ⓜ Written by Michael Gallagher and drawn by Dave Manak, *Alf* #1 was based on the popular television show and ran for fifty issues.

Ⓜ *Captain Justice* #1 featured New World Pictures' television hero.

INTRODUCING ERIC MASTERSON

• *The Mighty Thor* #391

Eric Masterson was an architect working on a construction site in this issue by Tom DeFalco and Ron Frenz. He never wanted to be a hero. He just wanted to do his job, raise his son, and live a normal life. But fate decreed otherwise. When Thor and Spider-Man battled the Mongoose, Eric was injured as he pushed a coworker out of the way of falling debris. Eric and Thor became friends and when Eric was fatally injured, Thor merged himself with the human to save his life in issue #408 (Oct., 1989). Eric proved so worthy that Odin awarded him his own enchanted mace in issue #459 (Feb., 1993).

THREE MARYS IN ONE

• *Daredevil* #254

Mary was first introduced in *Daredevil* #254 by editor Ann Nocenti and artist John Romita Jr. Mary could be quite contrary. That tended to happen when you had three distinct personalities: Mary Walker was timid; Typhoid Mary was adventurous; and Bloody Mary was sadistic.

All of them possessed telekinetic powers and the ability to mentally start fires. As Mary Walker, she fell in love with Matt Murdock. But as Typhoid Mary, she worked as an assassin for the Kingpin and often tried to kill Daredevil, and as Bloody Mary, she would torture him.

JULY

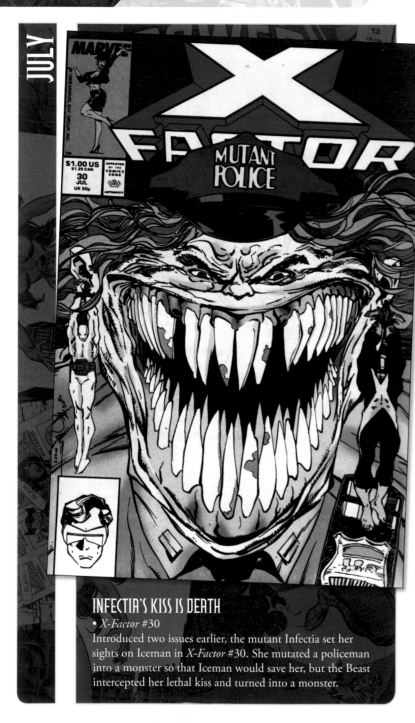

INFECTIA'S KISS IS DEATH
• *X-Factor* #30
Introduced two issues earlier, the mutant Infectia set her sights on Iceman in *X-Factor* #30. She mutated a policeman into a monster so that Iceman would save her, but the Beast intercepted her lethal kiss and turned into a monster.

SEPTEMBER

A NEW SPLIT BOOK
• *Marvel Comics Presents* #1
This new comic came out twice a month and contained four stories that were eight pages each. Two of the stories featured popular characters and two were reserved for new talent or characters without their own titles. It ran for 175 issues.

◪ *Akira* #1 was based on a 2,000-paged manga by Katsuhiro Otomo. The original *Akira* had been printed in black and white and was designed to be read from right to left. Epic Comics colored their version and made the art read from left to right.

SEPTEMBER

SPEEDBALL GETS HIS OWN TITLE
• *Speedball* #1
Editor-in-Chief Tom DeFalco thought Marvel should publish more titles starring teenagers because they comprised the majority of Marvel's audience at that time. He wrote the basic scenario and character descriptions for a new series and hired Steve Ditko to design it. Accidentally exposed to energy from another dimension, Robbie Baldwin gained the ability to bounce like a living rubber ball. He first appeared in *The Amazing Spider-Man Annual* #22 in early 1988 and then in September in his own title. *Speedball* only lasted ten issues, but the character came back as a member of the New Warriors in 1989.

A MULTI-ANNUAL CROSSOVER
• *The Avengers Annual* #17
The Evolutionary War was a new kind of crossover. It was an eleven-part story that was told across the 1988 Annuals, including titles as diverse as *The Punisher Annual* #1 and *The Uncanny X-Men Annual* #12. It began with *X-Factor Annual* #3 and ended with *The Avengers Annual* #17 when the High Evolutionary attempted to jumpstart humanity's evolution by releasing a "Genetic Bomb."

OCTOBER

MUTANT APARTHEID
• *The Uncanny X-Men* #235
Intended to criticize South Africa's policy of apartheid, Genosha was a fictional island located off the east coast of Africa that first appeared in this issue by writer Chris Claremont and artist Rick Leonardi. Genosha had a high standard of living thanks to its mutant population, which was considered the property of the state and was enslaved. David Moreau, the Genegineer, could modify mutants so that their powers could better serve the state. Seeing the potential of the X-Men, the Genegineer ordered their kidnap—a mistake that ultimately caused the collapse of his government.

THE LOBOS BECOME WEREWOLVES
• *The Spectacular Spider-Man* #143

Created by writer Gerry Conway and artist Sal Buscema, Carlos and Eduardo Lobo possessed the mutant ability to transform into werewolves. They used this ability to become major crimelords and started a gang war with the Kingpin.

◪ *Excalibur* #1 by Chris Claremont and Alan Davis was launched as a monthly series based on the group of British Super Heroes.
◪ *The Mutant Misadventures Of Cloak And Dagger* #1 was Marvel's second attempt to give the popular duo a regular title.

NOVEMBER

WOLVERINE HEADLINES HIS OWN TITLE

• *Wolverine #1*

When Tom DeFalco asked writer Chris Claremont and editor Bob Harras to produce a monthly Wolverine title, Claremont objected. He thought the character would be better served by a run of limited series, each marketed as a big event. Fearing that these series would never materialize, DeFalco scheduled *Wolverine #1*, which ran for 189 issues.

◩ Marvel published *Count Duckula #1*, based on the popular animated series.

◩ *Doctor Strange, Sorcerer Supreme #1* propelled the master of mysticism on his longest running series.

DECEMBER

A NEW WAR COMIC

• *Semper Fi #1*

Since the war comic *The 'Nam* was selling so well, Marvel created *Semper Fi #1*. The title—"always faithful" in Latin—was taken from the official motto of the United States Marine Corps. The comic focused on the Whittier family whose members had been Marines in various wars from 1777 to the present day. Each issue contained two stories written by Michael Palladino. John Severin, Andy Kubert, and Sam Glanzman provided the artwork.

Inspired by the comic strip Terry And The Pirates *and the film* Casablanca, *Chris Claremont set the new* Wolverine *series in the fictional country of Madripoor.*

MEANWHILE IN 1988...

PERESTROIKA: RESTRUCTURING BEGINS

Under President Gorbachev, the USSR begins a program of economic reforms that introduces private ownership, market economics, and foreign investment and brings a thaw in relations with the West.

TERRORIST EXPLOSION OVER LOCKERBIE

Pan Am flight 103 crashes over Scotland after Libyan intelligence agents place a bomb on board. All 259 passengers and eleven people in the Scottish town of Lockerbie are killed.

USSR FORCES LEAVE AFGHANISTAN

After eight years of conflict between Marxist and Mujahideen insurgents, the Red Army begins to withdraw from Afghanistan.

NASA RESUMES SPACE FLIGHTS

America's program of space travel begins again with the launch of Discovery, the first voyage since all flights were grounded after the Challenger disaster in 1986.

FIRST WOMAN PRIME MINISTER IN PAKISTAN

Benazir Bhutto wins the first democratic election in eleven years and becomes Prime Minister.

NEARLY ONE TV PER HOUSEHOLD

Ninety-eight per cent of American households now have at least one television set.

OPTICAL FIBERS UNDER OCEAN

TAT-8 is the eighth transatlantic telephone cable under the sea, but it represents a landmark in telecommunications because it is the first to use optical fibers.

CDS OUTSELL RECORDS

For the first time, music compact discs (CDs) are now outselling vinyl records.

FIRST "FAIRTRADE" LABEL

The first label promoting ethical standards in agriculture is brought to mainstream consumers thanks to an initiative with Mexican coffee producers. This move marks the beginning of increased consumer awareness of the impact of trade on the developing world.

AND AT THE MOVIES...

Die Hard, Bruce Willis's one-man-army gets his shirt off in this taut thriller about a skyscraper taken over by terrorists; Who Framed Roger Rabbit, this comedy-noir whodunit plays the sexy Jessica Rabbit opposite Bob Hoskins' wisecracking PI in this flawless integration of animation and live-action; Rain Man, selfish yuppie (Tom Cruise) discovers he has a brother with Asperger's syndrome (Dustin Hoffman) and they set off on a road trip, which begins with financial motivations, but becomes a touching journey of discovery for both of them.

EVIL IS A REAL FORCE AND IT'S GOING TO HAVE ITS WAY WITH SOME PEOPLE.

1989

A PRESIDENT READS AND A PERELMAN BUYS

As the decade drew to a close, Marvel received some rather unexpected publicity—President Ronald Reagan confessed that the first thing he read in the newspaper every morning was the syndicated *Spider-Man* comic strip.

Spider-Man was already an active spokesman for the National Committee to Prevent Child Abuse and in 1989 he was made an honorary chairperson for UNICEF's Halloween fundraising campaign.

Tom DeFalco and Mark Gruenwald began weekly "Assistant Editor Classes," in which they revealed the secrets of the comic book industry and taught the craft of visual storytelling to the next generation of editors.

In the June-dated comics, *Stan Lee's Soapbox* returned to the *Bullpen Bulletins* after an absence of nearly nine years. Along with its line of hardcover *Marvel Masterworks*, the company increased its production of trade paperbacks and actively distributed them to bookstores.

Having owned Marvel for three years, New World Entertainment sold it to a holding company owned by billionaire investor Ronald Perelman. Believing that Marvel had the potential to become as big as Disney, Perelman's people began to acquire other companies. For the first time in its history, Marvel was owned by someone who could afford to invest in its future, a future that suddenly seemed brighter…

MARCH

VISION QUEST COMMENCES

• *The West Coast Avengers* #42
Writer/artist John Byrne produced the story arc that came to be known as Vision Quest that ran through *The West Coast Avengers* #42–45. The Scarlet Witch awoke one morning to discover that her husband, the synthozoid Vision, was missing. He had been kidnapped by a consortium of intelligence agents from various governments, which viewed the Vision as a threat to world security because of his ability to infiltrate any computer network. The consortium dismantled him and erased his programming. Hank Pym managed to reassemble the Vision, but only in an all-white body that had lost all his emotions.

THE SUPER NOVA SAGA

• *The Avengers* #301
The solo survivor of a ravaged planet, Super Nova streaked toward Earth on a mission of vengeance in the story arc that ran through *The Avengers* #301–303 by editor/writer Ralph Macchio, writer/artist Bob Hall, and artist Rich Buckler. Mistakenly believing that the woman who had destroyed his world was an Avenger, he planned to incinerate the entire planet, but the Avengers stopped him.

DAMAGE CONTROL TO THE RESCUE!

• *Damage Control* #1

Has a spaceship crashed into your building? Are inhabitants from an underworld civilization ruining your lawn? Did the Hulk smash your house to smithereens? Call Damage Control! Created by writer Dwayne McDuffie and artist Ernie Colan, Damage Control was a construction company that specialized in the removal and repair of property damaged by anything out of the ordinary. It first appeared in the 1988 *Marvel Age Annual* and then in *Marvel Comics Presents* #19 (May, 1989). This four-issue limited series was followed by two others: *Damage Control: The Movie* (1991) and *World War Hulk Aftersmash: Damage Control* (2008).

INTRODUCING JUBILEE

"Rock'n'rude, that's Jubilee—especially with folks who torture my friends! So clear the road, Jack—before I cut loose my Fourth of July."

• *The Uncanny X-Men* #244

Jubilation Lee was a talented Chinese American gymnast. She appeared destined for the Olympics until her parents were murdered, when she ran away and lived in the Hollywood Mall. One day, while escaping mall security, she discovered that she had the mutant ability to generate explosive bursts of light like "fireworks" on the Fourth of July.

Frustrated by their inability to catch her, mall security hired a team of mutant hunters. In this issue, written by Chris Claremont and illustrated by Mark Silvestri, a group of X-Men happened to be shopping at the Mall and helped Jubilee to escape. She followed them into a portal that teleported her to their secret base in the Australian outback and, without their knowledge, hid in the tunnels that surrounded their base. The super-criminal cyborgs, the Reavers later attacked, capturing and torturing Wolverine. After Jubilee nursed him back to health, she became his unofficial sidekick, travelling the world with him and helping him on various missions. Professor Xavier later persuaded her to join a new team of young mutants called Generation X-Men, which was being instructed by Banshee and the recently reformed Emma Frost.

Jubilee lost her mutant powers in the mega-crossover *House Of M* (2005). After briefly running a halfway house for former mutants, she acquired a pair of gauntlets that gave her superhuman strength and, in 2008, she joined the regrouped New Warriors, using the name of Wondra.

Ⓜ *The Sensational She-Hulk* #1 by writer/artist John Byrne took a tongue-in-cheek approach to superheroics.

A NEW TEAM OF CRIME-FIGHTERS

• *The West Coast Avengers* #46

When Craig Hollis discovered that he could not die, he decided to fight crime as Mr. Immortal. He advertised for other would-be crime-fighters and assembled the Great Lake Avengers: Dinah Soar, a winged creature who never spoke; Big Bertha, a model who gained superhuman strength by mentally becoming obese; Flatman, who could stretch his body thinner than paper; and Doorman, who could teleport. Squirrel Girl later joined the team, a mutant with squirrel-like powers—writer/artist John Byrne took a tongue-in-cheek approach to superheroics.

BLACKHEART DEBUTS

• *Daredevil* #270

In 1658, a woman was brutally murdered on a hill. Her blood soaked the ground and attracted a flock of crows. Over time, other crimes occurred on the same hill and strange plants began to grow. Finally, in *Daredevil* #270 by editor Ann Nocenti and artist John Romita Jr., a grotesque creature emerged, a creature formed by the demon Mephisto to be his son. Mephisto sent Blackheart to explore the world of men and he soon found himself battling Daredevil and Spider-Man. He later fought Wonder Man and was ultimately destroyed by Ghost Rider. He appeared as the major villain in the film *Ghost Rider* (2007).

A HERD OF SUPER HERO ELEPHANTS

• *Power Pachyderms* #1

Originally entitled *Adult Thermonuclear Samurai Elephants*, *Power Pachyderms* #1 was a parody of Mirage's *Teenage Mutant Ninja Turtles* comic, which, itself, was a parody of Marvel's *The Uncanny X-Men* and Frank Miller's version of *Daredevil*.

◪ Based on the success of the *Nick Fury Vs. SHIELD* limited series, Marvel launched a second volume of *Nick Fury, Agent Of SHIELD*.

◪ In October, Marvel published *Freddy Krueger's A Nightmare On Elm Street* #1, a black-and-white magazine for adults based on the 1984 horror film franchise that inspired six sequels.

INTRODUCING CROSSBONES

• *Captain America* #360

Captain America was in a race against Baron Zemo in this issue by editor Mark Gruenwald and artist Kieron Dwyer. Cap and the Baron were on an Indiana Jones-like hunt for fragments of the Bloodstone—a jewel that bestowed immortality. Determined to steal the Bloodstone for himself, the Red Skull sent his most trusted operative, the dangerous Crossbones, to steal it. The deadly Crossbones snuck aboard Captain America's ship, kidnapped his girlfriend Diamondback, and destroyed the jewel fragments to prevent them from falling in the hands of the Skull's enemies.

QUASAR DEBUTS

"I'm still not sure what to make of these wristbands, whether they're safe or not. I'm going to some remote unpopulated area to work on controlling them. If I succeed in mastering them, I'll be back. If I don't, well, let me apologize in advance for ruining your project."

• *Quasar* #1

Wendell Vaughn did not seem destined to be a Super Hero. He joined SHIELD, but was not deemed good enough to be a field agent. Instead, he was assigned to protect a pair of alien wristbands that had once been worn by Atlas Comics' Marvel Boy. Marvel Boy had returned to Earth in the 1970s and battled the Fantastic Four, but he lost control of his wristbands and was disintegrated. The wristbands were confiscated by SHIELD and when agent William Wesley was asked to test them, he, too, lost control and was disintegrated.

When AIM attempted to steal the wristbands in *Quasar* #1, an issue by Mark Gruenwald and Paul Ryan, Vaughn instinctively donned them and used their power to repel the attack. Fully expecting to suffer the same fate as Marvel Boy and Wesley, Vaughn flew into space. Nothing happened. He had somehow managed to keep control of the wristbands. He went on to call himself Quasar.

Although this issue finally revealed the origin of Quasar, the character had first appeared in *Captain America* #217 (Jan., 1978), using the name Marvel Boy. He occasionally guest-starred in *Captain America* and *Marvel Two-In-One* until he was awarded his own series, which ran for sixty issues. *Quasar* #1 predated all these appearances and *Quasar* #2 occurred after them. Later, Quasar joined the Avengers and in October, 2006, he was killed by Annihilus in *Annihilation: Nova* #4.

PUNISHER COMES TO LIFE

• *The Punisher Magazine* #1

This three-issue limited series adapted the *Punisher* film, starring Dolph Lundgren and Louis Gossett Jr. In this version of the story, Frank Castle was an ex-cop who, since the murder of his wife and children, lived in the sewers and served as judge, jury, and executioner to the city's criminals. Directed by Mark Goldblatt (*X-Men: The Last Stand*, 2006) and written by Boaz Yakin (*Conan The Barbarian*, 2008), the movie was, unfortunately, a box-office failure.

◪ *Police Academy* #1 adapted the animated series that was based on the popular film franchise.

◪ *Marvel Comics Presents* #31 printed the first of an eight-part *Excalibur* serial by Michael Higgins and newcomer Erik Larsen.

SPIDEY'S COSMIC ADVENTURES

• *The Spectacular Spider-Man* #158
Spider-Man was a friendly neighborhood Super Hero. What if that changed? What if he was now powerful enough to take on Magneto or flatten the Hulk with a single blow? These were the questions that led to a scientific accident that temporarily super-charged Spidey. Spider-Man: The Cosmic Adventures story line began in *The Spectacular Spider-Man* #158. It ran through all three Spider-Man titles for two months and climaxed in *The Spectacular Spider-Man* #160.

THE ACTS OF VENGEANCE CROSSOVER

• *Avengers Spotlight* #26
Acts Of Vengeance was a company-wide crossover that appeared in most of Marvel's Super Hero titles between December, 1989, and February, 1990. Loki, the Norse God of Mischief, gathered together the villains Dr. Doom, the Kingpin of Crime, Magneto, the Mandarin, the Red Skull, and the Wizard. He had a simple plan—instead of fighting their regular foes, everyone would fight a hero who was unfamiliar with their powers and abilities, for example Spider-Man fought Magneto from the X-Men titles. Unlike previous crossovers, it was not necessary to read other titles to get the gist of the story.

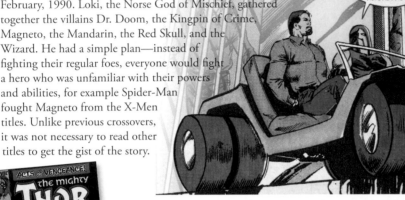

YUPPIES FROM HELL

• *Sex, Lies, And Mutual Funds Of The Yuppies From Hell*
Written and illustrated by cartoonist Barbara Slate, this was a graphic album for older readers that contained short stories about finding true love in New York City, a theme that foreshadowed television shows like *Sex And The City*.

THE NEW WARRIORS DEBUT

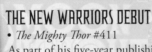

• *The Mighty Thor* #411
As part of his five-year publishing plan, Tom DeFalco had intended to launch a team of teenage Super Heroes in 1990, but an opportunity came along in 1989. All he had to do was come up with a team. He made a list of every teenage Super Hero in the Marvel Universe and he learned from Marvel's newsstand distributor that the best-selling magazines among teenagers were those about skateboarding. Armed with this information, he assembled his team. The New Warriors consisted of the cosmic adventurer Nova; Angelica Jones, the mutant called Firestar; crime-fighter Speedball; Vance Astrovik as Marvel Boy; and a new character—Night Thrasher, who rode a motorized skateboard.

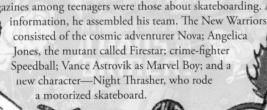

The West Coast Avengers #46 (July, 1989) Written and pencilled by John Byrne and inked by Mike Machlan.
John Byrne was born in West Bromwich, England on July 6, 1950 and settled in Canada when he was eight. His first exposure to Super Heroes was George Reeves in The Adventures Of Superman *television show. He broke into comics in 1974 when he started freelancing for Charlton Comics. He later moved to Marvel, where he worked on titles like* Iron Fist, The Champions *and* Marvel Team-Up *and, later on,* The X-Men *and* Fantastic Four. *Having established himself as both a writer and a penciller, Byrne would go on to revamp* Superman *for DC Comics with the best-selling* Man Of Steel *limited series and ries like* John Byrne's Next Men *and* Danger Unlimited. *Byrne has also written three novels:* Fear Book, Whipping Boy, *and* Wonder Woman: Gods And Goddesses.

1990s

Comics were selling in the millions. The 1990s saw the peak of the direct market, as fans bought dozens of their favorite issues, hoping to see a return on their investment years later. Crossovers began to be commonplace, taking characters from their usual world and comic book title and placing them into the lives and titles of other heroes in order to birth massive team-up stories or unexpected battles. It was a time of superstar artists, flashy splash panels, and multi-issue epics where character development was often shelved in favor of violence and action. But that is not to say there weren't diamonds hidden in the heaps of cubic zirconium. As in any era of comics, groundbreaking works appeared, stunning a complacent audience, or at times even coming in beneath their radar. It was a decade that birthed criticism, records, and legends. And as always, Marvel was at the forefront of it all.

> BUT I'VE GOT TO TELL YOU, WHEN IT COMES RIGHT DOWN TO IT, I CAN BE PRETTY AWESOME IF I WANT.

1990
BIRTH OF THE IMAGE AGE

By 1990, the era of the comic book superstar artist had begun. Todd McFarlane, Jim Lee, and Rob Liefeld had been amassing hoards of fans with their dramatic drawing styles in the pages of their respective titles Amazing Spider-Man, The Uncanny X-Men, and The New Mutants. Indeed, the artists had begun to enjoy such creative freedom that the writers at each title seemed to be taking a back seat. However, this new approach to comics was clearly working, and sales were hitting record highs. This culminated with Todd McFarlane's new monthly series, titled simply Spider-Man, which sold over 2.5 million copies, thanks in part to variant cover editions.

In 1990, Marvel enjoyed unparalleled success with the comics that McFarlane, Lee, and Liefeld created, with fans purchasing several copies of their favorite comics as a future investment of sorts. This resulted in mammoth sales figures that would only be exceeded in the year to follow. In recent years, Marvel had bred its own superstar artists, but by 1992, the comic company would lose them as McFarlane, Lee, and Liefeld went on to cofound Image Comics, along with four other Marvel luminaries: Erik Larsen, Whilce Portacio, Jim Valentino, and Marc Silvestri. But as of 1990, the stars were shining brighter than ever before, and the future looked just as brilliant.

FEBRUARY

HULK QUELLS THE RIOT SQUAD
• *The Incredible Hulk #366*
Continuing his legendary Hulk run, writer Peter David, along with artist Jeff Purves, created the Riot Squad, a team of super-powered villains intent on bringing down the Hulk. The team was under the employ of the Hulk's arch-foe the Leader, and included the aptly-named Rock, the heavily armed Redeemer, the telekinetic Jailbait, the fire-projecting Hotshot, and the bestial Ogress.

The fierce Ogress could nearly match the Hulk's physical strength and savagery.

🅜 The Mutant Liberation Front, a team of terrorist mutants, debuted in the pages of *The New Mutants #86* by writer Louise Simonson and penciller Rob Liefeld.

MARCH

CABLE VS. STRYFE
• *The New Mutants #87*
When the newly formed Mutant Liberation Front (MLF) staged an attack on a secret energy research station, writer Louise

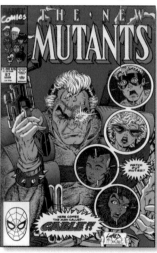

Simonson and penciller Rob Liefeld introduced one of the hottest stars of the 1990s, the mysterious mutant known only as Cable. Displaying an impressive array of telekinetic abilities, and toting a gun nearly as large as he was, Cable hunted the mutant terrorists for reasons solely his own. Also introduced in this issue was the evil leader of the MLF, Stryfe, whose past was as enigmatic as the man stalking him, and who seemed to share a common bond with his pursuer.

APRIL

NAMOR'S NEW LEASE
• *Namor The Sub-Mariner #1*
Comics superstar John Byrne revamped the classic Marvel character Namor in this new series that he both wrote and drew. The comic saw the avenging son of Atlantis meet Dr. Caleb Alexander, who had deduced that Namor had a blood imbalance that created fluctuations in his personality, explaining some of Namor's past fits of rage. With Dr. Alexander's help, Namor founded Oracle, Inc., a large corporation intent on saving the planet.

🅜 Hulk's future teammates, the Pantheon, made their debut in a few panels of The Incredible Hulk #368.

GHOST RIDER RIDES AGAIN

• *Ghost Rider #1*

Popular writer Howard Mackie and penciller Javier Saltares had a sensation on their hands when they created Daniel Ketch, the second man to wear the mantle of the supernatural Ghost Rider. Accidentally wandering onto the scene of an underworld deal gone bad in a junkyard one night, Danny and his sister Barb hid underneath a mountain of junked cars, Barb bleeding badly from having been shot with an arrow by one of the criminals. With his hands covered in the blood of his innocent sister, Danny touched a glowing gas cap of a mysterious motorcycle and was transformed into the avenging Ghost Rider.

THE GUARDIANS RETURN

• *Guardians Of The Galaxy #1*

Marvel's 31st-century heroes finally received an ongoing series thanks to writer/artist Jim Valentino. The series featured the adventures of super-powered teammates Starhawk, Major Vance Astro, Charlie-27, Yondu, Nikki, and Martinex.

NEW WARRIORS AND OLD FAVORITES

"Is it just me… or is this an incredibly dramatic and emotional turning point in our lives?"

• *The New Warriors #1*

Billed as "Heroes for the 90's--!", *The New Warriors* was the brainchild of writer/editor Tom DeFalco, who first debuted the team in the pages of *The Mighty Thor #411* in December of the previous year. In this ongoing series, writer Fabian Nicieza with former Marvel Tryout art contest winner and future *Spider-Man* superstar Mark Bagley chronicled the tales of a team that not only thrived in this brave new decade, but continued to make an impact in the Marvel Universe over the years. *The New Warriors* lasted a solid seventy-five issues, perhaps enticing a generation of readers that wanted a young team they could get on board with from the beginning. The series also inspired two later follow-up series and a miniseries of the same title.

An eclectic bunch, the New Warriors consisted of Firestar, a character created for the popular *Spider-Man And His Amazing Friends* animated TV series; street-tough newcomer Night Thrasher; the young powerhouses Marvel Boy (later Justice) and Kid Nova (later Nova); Atlantian cousin of the Sub-Mariner, Namorita; and Steve Ditko's classic comic relief character, Speedball. Funded and organized by Night Thrasher's guardians' fortune, the New Warriors set up shop in a midtown Manhattan high-rise after Night Thrasher sought out Nova, Firestar, and Marvel Boy individually, deducing their secret identities one by one. Namorita and Speedball were not recruited, but joined as the team banded together for an impromptu fight against the earth-moving villain Terrax at the site of an outdoor genetic research study in Queens, solidifying the New Warriors' roster.

GAMBIT GUEST-STARS

• *The Uncanny X-Men #266*

When the X-Men's Storm attempted to break free from the home of the Shadow King, she encountered one of the most popular X-Men of the 1990s, the enigmatic thief called Gambit. Created by legendary X-scribe Chris Claremont and artist Michael Collins, Gambit's Southern charm, thick Cajun accent, and ability to supercharge objects with kinetic energy for explosive results won over the readers. He soon became a full-fledged member of the X-Men, forming an on-again/off-again romance with Southern belle member, Rogue.

The New Warriors featured such talents as Speedball, Firestar, Namorita, Marvel Boy, Kid Nova, and Night Thrasher.

TODD McFARLANE'S SPIDER-MAN

"The witch bleeds. Life drains from her—but she is blinded to it all. Consumed with an image that must be obliterated, cleansed from her mind. An image of—the spider."

• *Spider-Man #1*

Fan sensation Todd McFarlane was previously established only as an artist but finally got his chance at more creative freedom when he wrote, pencilled, and inked the new series created just for him—the adjective-free *Spider-Man*. Feeling restless in his role of penciller on *The Amazing Spider-Man* and wanting a new challenge, McFarlane spoke to his editor Jim Salicrup about the possibility of working on a title that he could both write and draw. Not wanting to lose the popular creator, Salicrup instead offered him his own new Spidey title, and McFarlane jumped at the chance. The result was Torment, McFarlane's first story arc that ran through the pages of the first five issues of *Spider-Man*, beginning in August.

Torment told the story of a mind-controlled Lizard lurking in Manhattan's sewers and on a mad killing rampage. Following a set of clues that revealed that Dr. Curt Connors was behind the recent string of murders, Spider-Man finally defeated the Lizard. He also managed to defeat the voodoo-wielding witch that was manipulating him, a woman who had been a former lover of Spider-Man's old foe, Kraven.

Famous for his depiction of Spidey's webs, McFarlane's art was given the foil treatment with three variant cover editions: silver, gold, and card-stock platinum.

This sequence shows Peter Parker's optimism and upbeat attitude, traits that kept him going as his surroundings grew ever darker.

Featuring a dark and moody tale, *Spider-Man* was printed on a high grade of paper stock, previously unavailable to McFarlane on *The Amazing Spider-Man*, and one that allowed the details of his artwork to really be displayed for the first time. The series proved to be such a hit that McFarlane left the book after fifteen issues to found his own comic company, Image Comics, with other well-known creators.

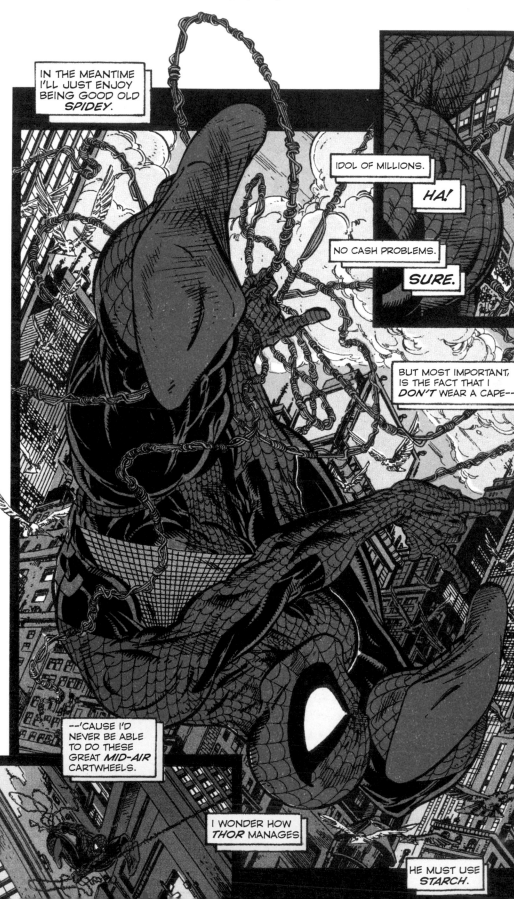

THE X-TINCTION AGENDA

"Goodbye, Selfriend. We're going to miss you."

• *The Uncanny X-Men* #270
With a marketplace primed for flashy event-oriented stories, the X-Men titles took full advantage with their epic crossover, "X-Tinction Agenda". The story line originated in November in issue 270 of *The Uncanny X-Men* and continued into *The New Mutants* and *X-Factor*. The powers that be at Marvel saw not only the selling potential of uniting their vast multitude of X-Men characters, but also the power of linking many of their popular creators on one narrative. Among those industry giants that helped craft this larger-than-life crossover story were writers Chris Claremont and Louise Simonson, and artists Jim Lee, Rob Liefeld, and Jon Bogdanove. The story featured the team-up of all three X-Men teams, allowing the fan favorite X-Men founders to mingle with the new class of super-popular heroes, a formula Marvel revisited a year later, when the titles were revamped.

The X-Tinction Agenda story line began when X-Factor's foe Cameron Hodge successfully survived decapitation at the hands of winged Archangel. He then kidnapped several members of the New Mutants and held them on Genosha, a small island nation off the coast of Africa, preparing to execute them for past crimes. In an attempt to free their friends, the remaining New Mutants and X-Factor members journeyed to the island, encountering the slave-like mutates that served as the bottom rung of society in this segregated nation. With the help of the X-Men, the teams rescued their captured friends and defeated Hodge, but at the cost of the life of New Mutant member Warlock.

The X-Tinction Agenda also saw the brainwashed former X-Men member Havok lead an attack on Storm and the New Mutants.

THE LOOSE-LEAF MARVEL HANDBOOK

• *The Official Handbook of the Marvel Universe* #1
Having released two series of guides to their characters' powers and histories in a standard comic book format, Marvel debuted this thirty-six-issue series. The handbook was in a loose-leaf format and could be stored in three ring binders, providing its readers with easy updating potential.

DAYS OF FUTURE PRESENT

• *Fantastic Four Annual* #23
With the success of the now-classic X-Men story Days of Future Past, where mutants were held in concentration camps in an alternate future, the similarly titled Days of Future Present story line crossed over into four of the annuals of the 1990s and continued into *X-Factor*, *The New Mutants*, and *The Uncanny X-Men*. This first part, written by Walter Simonson, with art by Jackson Guice, marked the debut of Ahab, a denizen from the alternate future, preparing to travel back in time to the present in pursuit of the missing Rachel Summers.

MARVEL MIGNON EDITION
$3.95 US
$5.25 CAN

THE OFFICIAL HANDBOOK OF THE ① MARVEL UNIVERSE

CONTENTS		
ANACONDA	JUGGERNAUT	RONAN
BLUE SHIELD	LLYRA	SPIDER-MAN
CORSAIR	MIDNIGHT SUN	STARFOX
COUNTERWEIGHT	MODAM	STRANGER
DORMAMMU	MOONBOY	TRICKSHOT
FOXFIRE	NEBULON	TYPHOID
GORGON	ONEG THE PROBER	WATCHDOG
HARKNESS, AGATHA	PUCK	ZURAS

MEANWHILE IN 1990...

NELSON MANDELA FREED
After twenty-seven years of imprisonment in South Africa, Nelson Mandela is released from prison.

MILITARY DICTATOR OF PANAMA SURRENDERS TO US
Having fled after the American invasion of Panama in December, Manuel Noriega surrenders to US troops.

REUNIFICATION OF GERMANY
East Germany and West Germany officially reunify into a single country after fifty-five years of separation.

LEANING TOWER OF PISA CLOSES
Following safety concerns about its structural condition, the Leaning Tower of Pisa, which leans at an angle of 3.97 degrees, is closed to the public.

FIRST MCDONALD'S IN RUSSIA
The first McDonald's restaurant opens in Moscow in Pushkin Square.

AMERICANS WITH DISABILITIES ACT SIGNED
President George H.W. Bush signs legislation intended to protect disabled Americans from discrimination.

HUBBLE TELESCOPE LAUNCHES
The Hubble Telescope is the first space telescope to be launched into the Earth's orbit.

CHANNEL TUNNELERS MEET
The two halves of the Channel Tunnel being constructed between Britain and France are connected, linking the UK with mainland Europe for the first time since the Ice Age.

"NC-17" INTRODUCED
The Motion Picture Association of America (MPAA) introduces the NC-17 (No children under 17 admitted) rating for films.

CARTOONS FOR ADULTS
Following the success of The Simpsons, animated cartoons aimed at adult audiences become popular. Later programs include South Park, King of the Hill, Family Guy, and Futurama. Highly satirical, the shows parody American life and society.

AND AT THE MOVIES...
Edward Scissorhands, social outcast Edward Scissorhands is adopted into society through his hedging and hairdressing skills in Tim Burton's updated Frankenstein fairytale; Goodfellas, Martin Scorsese's frantic account of the rise and fall of a real-life mobster; Pretty Woman, high-grossing 1940s-style romantic comedy starring Julia Roberts and Richard Gere, given the modern Cinderella treatment.

> HAVE NO FEAR... I WILL DO WHAT MUST BE DONE.

1991
FLASH VERSUS SUBSTANCE

By 1991, story was becoming secondary. Variant covers and sealed issues were on the upswing, inspiring some to not even read the comics they purchased and store them away as investments. In an era where flashy splash pages and characters wielding large weapons were selling comics, the few gems of storytelling were almost overlooked. Among them was writer and artist Frank Miller's *Elektra Lives Again*, a graphic novel as innovative as it was retrospective, while storyteller Barry Windsor-Smith created what some consider the ultimate Wolverine story in the otherwise quiet anthology *Marvel Comics Presents*.

THE NEW FANTASTIC FOUR GO INTO ACTION
• *Fantastic Four* #348
January saw the formation of a new Fantastic Four. When the alien Skrull rebel De'Lila incapacitated the current FF in their own headquarters, Spider-Man, the Hulk, Wolverine, and Ghost Rider were tricked into forming a new Fantastic Four and helping her in her quest to slay the Skrull emperor. Written by Walter Simonson with art by Arthur Adams, this new FF found themselves locked in battle with the Mole Man before bringing De'Lila to justice.

> IT ISN'T *POSSIBLE!*

> ARE THEY--?

> ALL DEAD, HULK. AND THEIR *KILLERS* STILL *LIVE!*

> MY SPIDER-SENSE WAS TINGLING LIKE CRAZY, BUT I NEVER THOUGHT IT WOULD BE SOMETHING LIKE THIS!

DEADPOOL, DOMINO, AND GIDEON
• *The New Mutants* #98
Continuing to hook readers and gather steam, artist Rob Liefeld, along with writer Fabian Nicieza, introduced Deadpool, the slightly unbalanced assassin dispatched to kill the mutant Cable. Though unsuccessful at the task, Deadpool never lost his sense of humor, despite being quite literally stabbed in the back by another character to debut in this issue, the femme fatale Domino. This comic also featured the debut of a future thorn in the New Mutants' side, the mysterious Gideon.

WEAPON X
"Everybody's got one. Or two, maybe. Secrets, I mean. I got a doozie. It's a serious motherload. Hard hidin' it, sometimes. But I get by."

• *Marvel Comics Presents* #72
A successful anthology title, *Marvel Comics Presents* had been headlining an X-Men related story since its conception, with Wolverine receiving more than his fair share of the spotlight. But it was not until Barry Windsor-Smith wrote and illustrated the thirteen-chapter *Weapon X* serial, that fans really sat up and paid attention. The serial displayed a mature approach to comic book storytelling complimented by equally sophisticated artwork. In it,

Windsor-Smith set out to tell one of the most anticipated X-Men stories ever told: the secret of Wolverine's adamantium skeleton.

Weapon X, a secret Canadian government program run by Professor Thorton, took Wolverine captive and placed him into a special tank. Here, he became the victim of experiments that took advantage of his mutant healing factor in an attempt to create the ultimate human weapon. Coating his bones with adamantium, an unbreakable metal alloy, the technical experts of the Weapon X program monitored Logan's thoughts and watched as he reverted to his primitive, violent instincts. Using technology to control his functions, Thorton and his crew pit Wolverine against wild wolves and bears, before Logan managed to escape in a fit of rage. However, in a twist, Wolverine's escape was actually a computer-generated fantasy of his mind's eye, and the real Wolverine was still under the control of Weapon X personnel. Now with a taste of freedom, Wolverine acted out his fantasy, freeing himself and escaping into the wild, and was left to wonder if he was still more man than animal.

DARKHAWK MAKES HIS DEBUT

• *Darkhawk #1*
Darkhawk was created by editor Tom DeFalco and artist Mike Manley with scripts by Danny Fingeroth. It was the latest creation in the movement toward darker vigilantes, waging a hard war on crime, but was seen through the mind set of Darkhawk's alter ego, high school student Chris Powell.

Powell had followed his brothers into an amusement park fun house after closing, and saw his police officer father taking a bribe from some gangsters. As the deal went sour, Chris stumbled upon an odd amulet that transformed him into the adult Darkhawk, letting him fight the noble battle his father could not.

OUT WITH THE OLD, IN WITH THE NEW

• *The New Mutants #99*
Solar-powered Sunspot may have quit the New Mutants, but it was not long before he was replaced. Feral, a female mutant, found her way to the New Mutant's bunker hideout, courtesy of writer Fabian Nicieza, with art and plot by Rob Liefeld. This issue also saw the first cameo of future member Shatterstar.

Feral and Shatterstar more than made up for Sunspot's hasty departure.

ELEKTRA LIVES AGAIN

"The fire—even across the street it's blistering. But she's cold. She's someplace cold."

Frank Miller made a triumphant return to Elektra, the character he breathed life into and then subsequently snuffed out, with the graphic novel *Elektra Lives Again*. Miller both wrote and drew this deluxe oversized hardcover, with breathtaking painted coloring from his wife, Lynn Varley. The pair had already perfected their craft on the highly acclaimed miniseries for DC Comics, *Batman: The Dark Knight Returns*.

The story featured an obsessed Matt Murdock (Daredevil's alter ego), who was questioning his own reality, as Elektra, his former lover, returned from the dead. Elektra was being pursued by dozens of reanimated corpses created by the ninja clan, the Hand. To make matters worse, the newly deceased body of Daredevil's arch foe Bullseye went missing from a morgue. Catching up with the ninja clan, Murdock realized he was too late, as Bullseye had already been resurrected and had succeeded in killing Elektra for the second time. However, with her dying breath, Elektra managed to decapitate the villain, and say farewell to Daredevil, dying again in his arms.

Elektra Lives Again was removed from cannon Marvel continuity due to the death of Bullseye and this version of Elektra's resurrection. Nonetheless, the graphic novel was a critical success. Published under the Epic Comics label, *Elektra Lives Again* featured mature ultra-violence and nudity, a rarity for stories featuring mainstream Marvel Super Heroes.

AGAMEMNON APPEARS

• *The Incredible Hulk #381*
The Hulk first met Agamemnon, the leader of the Pantheon team, in a story written by Peter David with art by Dale Keown. After describing his team's daring method of operations to help mankind, Agamemnon successfully recruited the Hulk to his cause.

The Pantheon initially held the angry Hulk captive to try to reason with him.

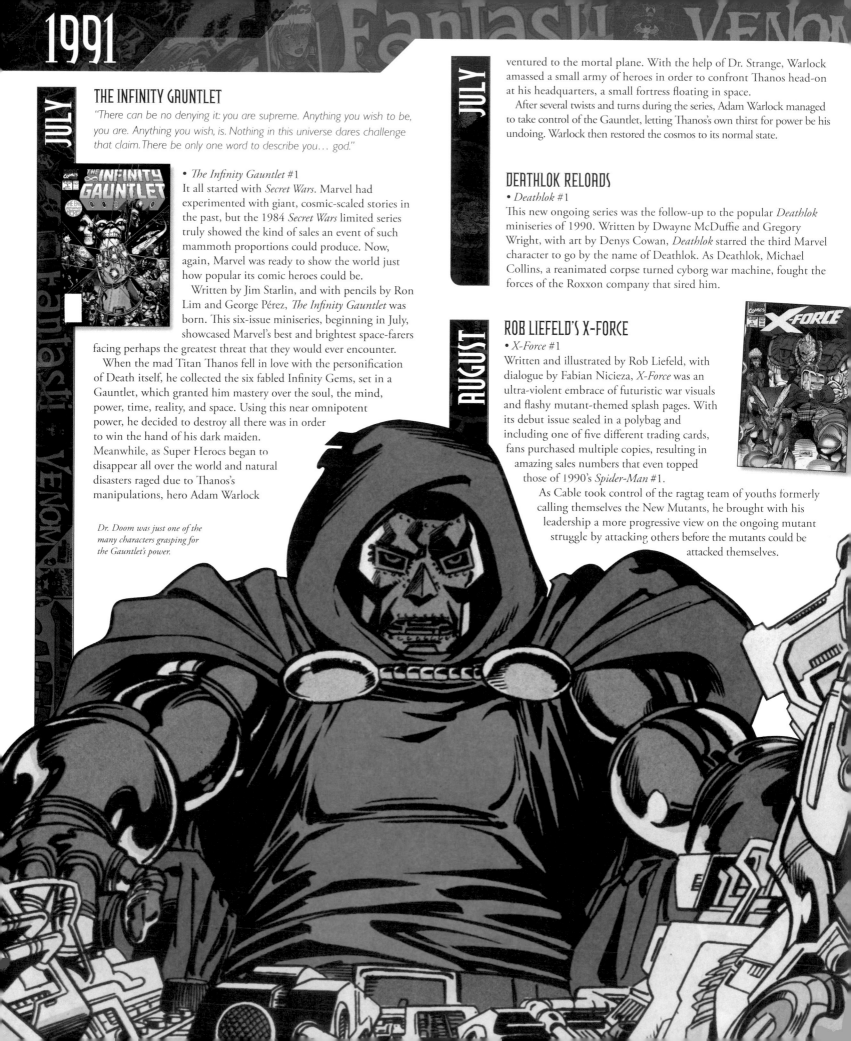

JULY

THE INFINITY GAUNTLET

"There can be no denying it: you are supreme. Anything you wish to be, you are. Anything you wish, is. Nothing in this universe dares challenge that claim. There be only one word to describe you… god."

• *The Infinity Gauntlet* #1
It all started with *Secret Wars*. Marvel had experimented with giant, cosmic-scaled stories in the past, but the 1984 *Secret Wars* limited series truly showed the kind of sales an event of such mammoth proportions could produce. Now, again, Marvel was ready to show the world just how popular its comic heroes could be.

Written by Jim Starlin, and with pencils by Ron Lim and George Pérez, *The Infinity Gauntlet* was born. This six-issue miniseries, beginning in July, showcased Marvel's best and brightest space-farers facing perhaps the greatest threat that they would ever encounter.

When the mad Titan Thanos fell in love with the personification of Death itself, he collected the six fabled Infinity Gems, set in a Gauntlet, which granted him mastery over the soul, the mind, power, time, reality, and space. Using this near omnipotent power, he decided to destroy all there was in order to win the hand of his dark maiden. Meanwhile, as Super Heroes began to disappear all over the world and natural disasters raged due to Thanos's manipulations, hero Adam Warlock

Dr. Doom was just one of the many characters grasping for the Gauntlet's power.

JULY

ventured to the mortal plane. With the help of Dr. Strange, Warlock amassed a small army of heroes in order to confront Thanos head-on at his headquarters, a small fortress floating in space.

After several twists and turns during the series, Adam Warlock managed to take control of the Gauntlet, letting Thanos's own thirst for power be his undoing. Warlock then restored the cosmos to its normal state.

DEATHLOK RELORDS

• *Deathlok* #1
This new ongoing series was the follow-up to the popular *Deathlok* miniseries of 1990. Written by Dwayne McDuffie and Gregory Wright, with art by Denys Cowan, *Deathlok* starred the third Marvel character to go by the name of Deathlok. As Deathlok, Michael Collins, a reanimated corpse turned cyborg war machine, fought the forces of the Roxxon company that sired him.

AUGUST

ROB LIEFELD'S X-FORCE

• *X-Force* #1
Written and illustrated by Rob Liefeld, with dialogue by Fabian Nicieza, *X-Force* was an ultra-violent embrace of futuristic war visuals and flashy mutant-themed splash pages. With its debut issue sealed in a polybag and including one of five different trading cards, fans purchased multiple copies, resulting in amazing sales numbers that even topped those of 1990's *Spider-Man* #1.

As Cable took control of the ragtag team of youths formerly calling themselves the New Mutants, he brought with his leadership a more progressive view on the ongoing mutant struggle by attacking others before the mutants could be attacked themselves.

CLAREMONT AND LEE'S RECORD-BREAKING X-MEN

"Gotta say this for the man—he knows how to make an exit."

• *X-Men #1*

It was a simple matter of addition. Take Chris Claremont, the writer who had made *The Uncanny X-Men* the continual hit that it was, and add Jim Lee, the artist who had reinvigorated the title's popularity in recent months. Add the original founding members of Cyclops, Jean Grey, Beast, Iceman, and Archangel to newer fan favorites Wolverine, Storm, Gambit, Colossus, Forge, Banshee, Psylocke, and Rogue. Increase that impressive roster with the ultimate X-villain Magneto, and add in a new ongoing comic title with five variant covers for its first issue. The sum of all these parts was *X-Men #1*, the best selling comic book in the history of the medium, selling well over eight million copies.

When Magneto set up camp on Asteroid M, a floating fortress in Earth's orbit, the X-Men were called into duty by SHIELD Director Nick Fury. They soon confronted Magneto's acolytes in Genosha, where they were wreaking havoc on the country due to its unjust treatment of mutants. Finally gathering their forces, the X-Men headed into space and confronted Magneto in a violent battle of mutant abilities. In the end, when one of Magneto's supposedly loyal supporters fired a plasma cannon at Asteroid M from a shuttle located a safe distance away, Magneto chose redemption. He opted to save the life of his good friend Charles Xavier, sacrificing himself in the process.

This story, concluding in issue #3 of the series, also served as the end of Chris Claremont's association with the X-Men titles for nearly ten years. Claremont cited creative differences with the editorial staff as his reason for departing the X-Universe.

HIS GOAL WAS NOBLE, OR SO HE THOUGHT, TO REMOVE FOREVER FROM *ALL* PEOPLE-- MUTANTS AND BASELINE HUMANS-- THE THREAT OF NUCLEAR ANNIHILATION.

THE GOVERNMENTS HE CHALLENGED DIDN'T SEE IT THAT WAY.

Magneto considered himself the savior of mutantkind, but the X-Men didn't agree.

Four of the five X-Men #1 *covers combined to reveal this large panoramic image, containing probably the most impressive roster of X-Men ever assembled.*

BISHOP BURSTS ONTO THE SCENE

• *The Uncanny X-Men #282*

Created by writer John Byrne and artist Whilce Portacio, Bishop found himself traveling back in time to the 20th century, and coming face to face with the X-Men, as the team faced off against Trevor Fitzroy, a mutant able to open portals to the past. Bishop discovered that there was a traitor within the X-Men's ranks and joined their roster, using his energy-absorbing powers to aid the mutant cause until he could deduce the turncoat in their midst.

MEANWHILE IN 1991...

OPERATION DESERT STORM
The six-week Gulf War begins with air strikes against Iraq after the UN deadline for Iraq to withdraw from Kuwait expires.

AN END TO THE SOVIET UNION
The USSR officially ceases to exist. Throughout 1990 and 1991 Lithuania, Latvia, Belarus, Georgia, Estonia, Ukraine, Moldova, Azerbaijan, Kyrgyzstan, Uzbekistan, Tajikistan, and Armenia declare their independence. Boris Yeltsin is elected President of Russia.

PRESIDENT TAYLOR EXHUMED
Zachary Taylor, 12th President of the US, is exhumed to determine whether he died from arsenic poisoning, but no arsenic is found.

SONIC THE HEDGEHOG
The first computer game starring the blue hedgehog is released by Sega to rival Nintendo's Mario. The early 1990s see an explosion of home video-gaming.

FREDDIE MERCURY DIES
The solo musician and lead singer of Queen dies of bronchopneumonia resulting from AIDS.

THE RISE OF 24-HOUR MEDIA
Constant coverage of the Gulf War leads to 24/7 news reporting and increased awareness of world events.

THE GRUNGE ERA
Nirvana releases Smells Like Teen Spirit, *part of the grunge movement, famous for distorted electric guitars and angst-ridden vocals.*

MILES DAVIS DIES
Jazz trumpeter Miles Davis dies at the age of sixty-five. Famed for his development of the "cool" jazz style, Davis received the Grammy Lifetime Achievement Award the previous year.

GENERATION X
Douglas Coupland's book Generation X: Tales for an Accelerated Culture, *publishes, referring to the generation born in the late 1960s and early 1970s, which is now adult age.*

ROYAL SPLIT
It is announced that the Prince and Princess of Wales have decided to separate. They have no intention to divorce and will both continue to have an active role in their boys' lives.

AND AT THE MOVIES...
The Silence of the Lambs, Jonathan Demme's disturbing horror introduces a new kind of psychopathic but cultured anti-hero in Anthony Hopkins' cannibalistic Hannibal Lecter; Thelma & Louise, *Ridley Scott's groundbreaking feminist road movie follows two women outlaws on the run across America's southwest after shooting a would-be rapist;* JFK, *Kevin Costner's New Orleans DA discovers there is more to the Kennedy assassination than the official story in Oliver Stone's political tale.*

REST AND RELAXATION

Artist Jim Lee, master of the dynamic splash page, created this pin-up image of the X-Men taking a little well-earned "R and R" time as an extra bonus for the *X-Men*'s debut issue, a double-sized forty-eight-page giant, in October, 1991. These kinds of swimsuit scenes proved popular with the readers, resulting in the series *Marvel Swimsuit Special*, an annual publication that lasted for five consecutive years. Other gallery splashes in this issue of *X-Men* included a parade of X-Men villains, a shot of the X-Men's training facility known as the Danger Room, and a preview of "Things to Come," featuring the ominous villain Omega Red.

Wish you were here!

1992
THE UNIVERSE DARKENS

Sales never again saw the spike that they had in 1991, and many of the biggest names in the comic world began to depart for a bigger slice of the proverbial pie. Despite all this, 1992 saw a continued effort on Marvel's part to launch new titles, most with an emphasis on the dark and the violent. During this era, the antihero became the new hero, perhaps following in the footsteps of the popular *Punisher* and *X-Force* series. These series had caught such favor in the eyes of an audience that was clamoring to the theaters to see the next *Terminator* or *Robocop* film.

Though the hero himself was not getting darker, his world surely was. Villains were growing more bloodthirsty and were no longer content to merely plunder and scheme. The future certainly seemed grim, as showcased in its newest line of *2099* books set in a bleak, corporate-run vision of tomorrow.

JANUARY

THE NEW SWORDSMAN
• *Avengers* #343
Written by Bob Harras with pencils by Steve Epting, the Avengers faced the menace of a mysterious man calling himself the Swordsman, the second one to do so. Later, the Swordsman and his partner Magdalene became honorary Avengers, once the smoke of battle had cleared.

JANUARY

THE FALL OF THE KINGPIN
• *Daredevil* #300
Culminating in the anniversary 300th issue, Daredevil would finally gain the upper hand against longtime foe Wilson Fisk (the Kingpin) in this moody tale by writer D.G. Chichester and penciller Lee Weeks. Serving as an almost sequel to Frank Miller's classic Born Again story line, The Fall of the Kingpin story line began as Daredevil took away Fisk's prized possession, Typhoid Mary. Matthew Murdock, Daredevil's alter ego, then set Kingpin against his former allies, the terrorist organization HYDRA, resulting in the Kingpin losing his home. Finally, Daredevil bested Fisk, leaving the Kingpin a homeless vagrant.

FEBRUARY

MAVERICK MAKES HIS MOVE
• *X-Men* #5
Jim Lee continued to plot and draw the *X-Men* series and was joined by scripter John Byrne. In the fifth issue, the pair introduced Maverick, an old ally of Wolverine's who had fought alongside him as a fellow CIA operative.

MAVERICK TO CENTRAL.

THIS IS GOING *SOUR* FAST, MAJOR. LOGAN DOESN'T KNOW WHAT THE @#%'S HAPPENING TO HIM!

I'M GONNA *REMIX* THIS LITTLE PARTY A BIT!

MARCH

PUNISHER ENTERS THE WAR ZONE
• *The Punisher: War Zone* #1
The third ongoing series to star vigilante Frank Castle was *The Punisher: War Zone*, written by Chuck Dixon and with art by John Romita Jr. and Klaus Janson. Though focusing on the Punisher's tough form of vigilante justice, the comic relied on solid storytelling and craft to give the series more appeal to fans than other ultra-violent titles. The comic put a fast-paced spin on the Punisher's usual war on drug runners, and sprouted some memorable moments, including one involving the Punisher interrogating a thug with a popsicle. This scene found its way into the first Punisher movie.

OPERATION: GALACTIC STORM
• *Captain America* #398
The major Avengers crossover story line, Operation: Galactic Storm, began in *Captain America*. It told the story of the Avengers intervening in a battle between the Kree and the Shi'ar. This first episode was written by Mark Gruenwald, with pencils by Rik Levins.

FIRST APPEARANCE OF CARNAGE

"Why am I killin' you…? That's easy. I'm killin' you… 'cause I can."

• *The Amazing Spider-Man #361*
In a genre that was slowly watching its heroes walk a darker path, it simply stood to reason that the villains would have to trump them in that respect. Enter Carnage, the brainchild of writer David Michelinie and penciller Mark Bagley. Carnage was a crueler, more terrible form of the already dark Venom, a symbiote whose fantastic powers were only surpassed by his fanatical blood lust.

After a dozen brutal murders had taken place over the course of a week in Manhattan, Spider-Man finally got a lead on the case when a good friend of his from Empire State University was slaughtered "like a pig on a spit." Peter Parker realized that the villain shared common traits with his old foe Venom and decided to research the prison records of Venom's alter ego, Eddie Brock. In doing so, Parker discovered that Brock had shared a prison cell with unrepentant mass murderer Cletus Kasady. Investigating Kasady's bizarre past history, Spider-Man eventually chanced upon him in an abandoned old orphanage, the only place Kasady ever truly called home. There, Spider-Man caught his first true glimpse of Carnage, the blood-red, souped-up version of Venom's alien symbiote.

Carnage was given life when Brock's symbiote had freed Brock from his jail cell, unwittingly leaving a spawn of itself behind in the chaos. That small slither of the alien symbiote formed so completely with cell mate Kasady that the two considered themselves to be a singular entity, a creature whose only desire was to kill and bring chaos to the world.

A geek at heart, Peter Parker was never above doing a little computer research.

Carnage often caught Spider-Man by surprise, as Peter's spider-sense could not detect the villain.

Ⓜ The Fantastic Four's favorite blue-eyed monster received his own four-issue miniseries, beginning in April. *The Adventures of the Thing* reprinted some of the Thing's most important stories.

ENTER THE EXTERNALS

• *X-Force #10*
The Externals, a secret group of immortal mutants, had been mentioned earlier in *X-Force* but were finally seen in issue #10 as frequent X-Force adversary, Gideon, ventured to their secret mountaintop retreat in the Swiss Alps. The series was plotted by Rob Liefeld, scripted by Fabian Nicieza, and penciled by Mark Pacella.

Carnage was a violent sociopath who was said to be loosely modeled after Batman's archenemy, the Joker, of DC Comics fame.

JUNE

SILVER SABLE'S SPOTLIGHT

Silver Sable & The Wild Pack #1

A frequent nemesis of Spider-Man, Silver Sable finally netted her own series thanks to writer Gregory Wright and penciller Steven Butler. Silver Sable teamed with reformed Spidey-foe Sandman and the rest of her cut-throat Wild Pack for a new set of adventures.

OCTOBER

THE X-MEN GET ANIMATED

The new *X-Men* cartoon debuted on October 31st as part of Fox Kids' Saturday morning programming. Featuring the voices of such actors as Tara Strong, Christopher Jay Potter, and Melissa Sue Anderson, and the scripts of known comic book writers like Len Wein and Elliot S. Maggin, the *X-Men* cartoon consisted of seventy-six episodes divided into five seasons. The series held the record for the longest lasting Marvel animated program.

CABLE'S FIRST ROUNDS

• *Cable: Blood & Metal* #1

Mutant Cable's first turn at a starring role was this two-issue limited series from writer Fabian Nicieza and artist John Romita Jr. Detailing Cable's time with his Six Pack mercenary group, the series included members Domino and Cable's later adversary, Garrison Kane.

NOVEMBER

SPIDEY TURNS 2099

"I have respect for the system.... Just none for you."

• *Spider-Man 2099* #1

Writer Peter David and artist Rick Leonardi's *Spider-Man 2099* character was first glimpsed in a sneak preview in the pages of *The Amazing Spider-Man* #365 in August 1992. The comic showed a dark vision of the future of the Marvel Universe, and would be the flagship title for a new line of comics set in this dystopian corporate nightmare.

Opening on a new Spider-Man on the run from the police, *Spider-Man 2099* chronicled the life of Miguel O'Hara. O'Hara had just quit his position as head of the genetics program at the large corporation Alchemax when an experiment was rushed without his permission, permanently mutating a willing test subject. Not taking his resignation lying down, the corrupt head of the company, Tyler Stone, infected Miguel with a designer drug known as Rapture. This forced O'Hara to subject himself to the genetic experimental process he had been working on, in order to release the toxic drug from his system. When a jealous coworker noticed Miguel's late night experiment and sabotaged it, Miguel was caught in an accidental explosion that he barely survived. Weakly emerging from the test chamber, O'Hara soon discovered that he now possessed spider-like powers, including fangs and spiked fingers that allowed him to adhere to surfaces. Like the Spider-Man of generations past, Miguel donned a blue and red costume, but this one bore an ominous "death's head" logo, and a web-like "light byte" cloth that allowed him to glide on wind currents. His one goal: to right the corporate wrongdoings that he was powerless to oppose in his civilian identity.

Just like his present day counterpart, the Spider-Man of the year 2099 often found himself at odds with the authorities.

NOVEMBER

Stryfe shook the X-Men to their core when he nearly assassinated their mentor and friend, Professor Charles Xavier.

X-CUTIONER'S SONG

• *The Uncanny X-Men #294*

The creators of the X-Men books had something to prove. Now that their big name artists had left the company, they needed to show a demanding fan base that they could still deliver the kind of giant comic blockbusters that had made the X-titles the current sensations that they were. So, writers Scott Lobdell, Peter David, and Fabian Nicieza, along with artists Brandon Peterson, Jae Lee, Andy Kubert, and Greg Capullo crafted the X-Cutioner's Song, an epic twelve-part crossover showcasing the various X-teams' battle with the Cable-clone Stryfe. The crossover also contained the stunning revelation that Cable was actually the long lost son of Cyclops and his former lover Madelyn Pryor.

DECEMBER

STAN LEE IS RAVAGED

• *Ravage 2099 #1*

Stan Lee returned to his rightful place behind the typewriter with this new series pencilled by Paul Ryan. *Ravage 2099* detailed the struggle of the betrayed head of Eco Central, who had to retire his corporate suit in favor of his primitive instincts as the vigilante Ravage.

Ravage was framed when a Mutroid was paid to burst into his office, claiming that Ravage had betrayed his own company.

1993
THE MORE THE MERRIER

The number of Marvel titles continued to expand in 1993, while Marvel talent continued to be spread thinner and thinner. But it wasn't just Marvel's library that was growing, it was also the number of characters in each story.

It seemed heroes couldn't be bothered to stick to their own titles anymore. Characters like Punisher and Venom were popping up in almost every comic on the shelves. And the larger the story, the more heroes were needed to team-up in it. This emphasis on the idea of the super-team combating a larger threat was illustrated in such stories as Spider-Man's Maximum Carnage and the Midnight Sons' Siege of Darkness epic that crossed through the magic corners of the Marvel Universe. This change of direction culminated in *The Secret Defenders*, where, as well as frequent guest appearances, a different roster of heroes were formed for each new adventure.

JANUARY
THE FUTURE IS DOOMED
• *Doom 2099* #1

Writer John Francis Moore and artist Pat Broderick transported Dr. Doom home to Latveria in this new series. To Doom's surprise, the year was now 2099, and his castle was in ruins. As he donned a new costume, the readers were left wondering if this was the Doom they knew, or a disturbed newcomer.

FEBRUARY
VENOM VEERS WEST
• *Venom: Lethal Protector* #1

This six-issue miniseries was created by Venom veterans writer David Michelinie and artist Mark Bagley, and was the first comic in which Venom was the main character. Setting up camp in his new home base of San Francisco, Venom dealt out his fatal form of justice.

THE PUNISHER OF TOMORROW
• *The Punisher 2099* #1

The 2099 alternate reality saw a world where the innocent were only guarded if they had paid up on their police protection plan, and organ harvesting street gangs ran wild through the back alleys of Manhattan, untouched by authority. It was clear that a Punisher was needed more than ever. After seeing his family gunned down while on a trip to the zoo, Jake Gallows donned a uniform similar to that of the original Punisher, Frank Castle, and set out on a bloody quest.

Punisher 2099 was written by Pat Mills and Tony Skinner, with pencils by Tom Morgan.

MARCH
DR. STRANGE'S SECRET DEFENDERS
• *The Secret Defenders* #1

Writer Roy Thomas and penciller Andre Coates created this new series that ran until 1995. Using a set of magic and tarot cards, Dr. Strange picked teammates appropriate to the crisis at hand. The first team included Wolverine, Spider-Woman, Nighthawk, and Nomad.

MAY
CABLE CUTS LOOSE
• *Cable* #1

Due to the popularity of *Cable: Blood & Metal*, Cable received his own ongoing series courtesy of writer Fabian Nicieza and artist Art Thibert. The saga opened on Cable's grim future as Garrison Kane, stuck in a time not his own, researched the mysterious Cable to discover that he had a wife and son. On the run due to his snooping into public history files, Kane's life was spared by the arrival of Cable.

MAXIMUM CARNAGE

"Here comes the bride! All dressed in white! I wish it was red! Then you'd all be dead!"

• *Spider-Man Unlimited* #1

Spider-Man's Maximum Carnage story line was an attempt to explore the darkest side of evil. The mammoth fourteen-part story began in the new title *Spider-Man Unlimited*, and continued throughout the Spider-Man line of books, crossing into *The Amazing Spider-Man, Spider-Man, The Spectacular Spider-Man,* and *Web Of Spider-Man*. Writers J.M. DeMatteis, Tom DeFalco, Terry Kavanagh, and David Michelinie and artists Mark Bagley, Sal Buscema, Ron Lim, Tom Lyle, and Alex Saviuk all brought their talents to this key story line.

The story began as Cletus Kasady, the deranged killer also known as Carnage, summoned his alien symbiote while being transferred from the Ravencroft maximum security institution for the criminally insane. Slaughtering the guards, Carnage escaped from captivity after meeting Shriek, a psychotic prisoner who shared his appetite for death. The two began to carve a swath of terror through Manhattan, accepting others to join their cause of chaos, including the evil Spidey duplicate Spider-Doppelganger, demonic Demogoblin, and clone Carrion. Meanwhile, Spider-Man formed an army to confront these villains, including Venom, Cloak and Dagger, the Black Cat, Morbius, Deathlok, Iron Fist, and Captain America himself.

The story line ended when Spider-Man confronted Carnage in Central Park, after Spidey's team took down Kasady's various partners. With help from the unlikely source of Venom, Spider-Man chased Carnage to a graveyard, where Venom knocked Carnage into a generator, causing an explosion that seemingly destroyed the disturbed killer once and for all.

THE DEATH OF HARRY OSBORN

• *The Spectacular Spider-Man* #200

The 200th issue of *The Spectacular Spider-Man,* written by J.M. DeMatteis and with art by Sal Buscema, featured the shocking death of Spider-Man's close friend Harry Osborn. Peter Parker had been dealing with Harry's insanity since Harry's father's death as the original Green Goblin. But their relationship came to a head when Harry kidnapped Peter's wife, Mary Jane. As Spidey faced off against Harry, the tormented Osborn began to have second thoughts, and rescued his son Normie, Mary Jane, and Peter from bombs he had set earlier as the Green Goblin. However, in one last twist, Harry died, poisoned by the goblin formula he had finally willingly rejected.

DEADPOOL MINISERIES BEGINS

• *Deadpool* #1

The mentally unstable Wade Wilson scored his own four-issue miniseries written by Fabian Nicieza with art by Joe Madureira in August. Throughout the series, Deadpool faced some serious opposition in the forms of Garrison Kane as Weapon X, mutant Black Tom Cassidy, and the unstoppable Juggernaut.

Deadpool, with his carefree attitude, can be his own worst enemy.

FALL FROM GRACE

• *Daredevil* #319

The seven-part Fall From Grace epic story line began in issue #319 of *Daredevil*. When a powerful chemical weapon was lost in the New York City subways, Daredevil found himself in the fight of his life versus the Hand, Silver Sable, Venom, Morbius, SHIELD cyborg John Garrett, the living killing spirit of Elektra, and a literal demon Hellspawn. Daredevil donned a new black costume made of experimental biomimetic material and paired up with Elektra, who was back from the grave. The pair managed to destroy the chemical agent and Hellspawn. However, the resultant battle merged Elektra with the murderous side of her personality that she'd worked so hard to escape from.

Fall From Grace was written by D.G. Chichester, with art by Scott McDaniel.

Filmmaker Clive Barker's dark vision found its way into comic shops with *Razorline: First Cut*, a special preview edition of his new line of ongoing Super Hero comics for Marvel.

THE NEXT GENERATION OF X-MEN
• *X-Men 2099* #1
Writer John Francis Moore and artist Ron Lim birthed a new team of mutants adopting Charles Xavier's dream in this uncertain future. The team included leader Xi'an Chi Xan, superspeedster Meanstreak, the self-explanatory Junkpile, and the mineral-condensing Krystalin.

Bloodhawk, Krystalin, Xi'an Chi Xan, Skullfire, Metalhead, Cerebra, and Meanstreak race to the rescue!

DAREDEVIL'S ORIGIN RETOLD
"The costume is probably a good idea. Sewed it myself. God only knows what it looks like."

• *Daredevil: The Man Without Fear* #1
Comic legends Frank Miller and John Romita Jr. united to tell a new version of Daredevil's origin in this carefully crafted five-issue

miniseries. Though considered mostly out of the canon of continuity due to a few minor conflicting details with past and future stories, *Daredevil: The Man Without Fear* detailed the tragedy of the life of Matt Murdock and the obstacles he had to overcome to become the just vigilante of the present.

Young Matt's father was a boxer and an unwilling enforcer for local mobsters, so Matt grew up being told to solve his problems with his head, not his fists. He was forced to adopt this attitude when he was blinded by chemicals splashed into his eyes as he saved the life of an elderly man in the path of a runaway truck carrying hazardous materials. Trained by the mysterious martial artist Stick, Matt grew adept at triumphing over his handicap, only to discover further hardships when his father was murdered after refusing to take a dive in one of his fights. Young Matt donned a ski mask and utilized his training to beat his revenge into the men responsible for his father's death. He continued in this manner until a stray fist accidentally knocked an innocent woman out of a window, killing her, and further torturing Matt Murdock's already troubled mind.

Considered a failure by Stick, Murdock later attended college at Columbia University, where he met best friend Foggy Nelson and femme fatale Elektra. Parting ways with Elektra after her father was murdered, Murdock returned to New York, where a kidnapping led to his first costumed caper as Daredevil, and a lifetime of animosity towards Manhattan's king of crime, the Kingpin.

Distancing himself from his former identity as Thor, Eric Masterson earned his own ongoing series by Tom DeFalco and Ron Frenz in *Thunderstrike* #1.

Battlin' Jack Murdock's death set the direction of Matthew's life.

OCTOBER

"I CANNOT LEAVE THIS *MORTAL COIL* WITHOUT BRINGING OUR BITTER *RIVALRY* TO ITS DESTINED CONCLUSION..."

...BY DESTROYING YOU!!

THE DEATH OF MR. FANTASTIC

• *Fantastic Four* #381

The Fantastic Four battled a mysterious demon-like creature in this issue penned by Tom DeFalco and pencilled by Paul Ryan. Dr. Doom had to step in to protect his native country, and nearly died before teleporting the monster away. Doom then managed to lure Reed Richards to him and seemingly ended both of their lives.

In a final deadly act of betrayal, Doom tricked Reed Richards into taking his hand.

NOVEMBER

THE DEATH OF MOCKINGBIRD

• *Avengers West Coast* #100

In a story by writer Roy Thomas and artist David Ross, marksman Hawkeye and his teammates faced off against the demons Satannish and Mephisto in hell. They finally escaped just as a stray fireball struck Hawkeye's wife, Mockingbird, killing her in Hawkeye's arms.

FATAL ATTRACTIONS

• *Wolverine* #75

Beginning with *X-Factor* #92 in July 1993, the Fatal Attractions story line was meant to celebrate the 30th anniversary of the X-Men and crossed over into all the X-titles. The X-Men once again faced off against Magneto, but this time with disastrous results. After Magneto literally ripped the adamantium out of Wolverine's body in the pages of *X-Men* #25, Charles Xavier did the unthinkable and took away Magneto's mind. In *Wolverine* #75, Wolverine was left a shell of his former self, barely surviving Magneto's attack, and now brandishing claws made of solid bone, thanks to writer Larry Hama and penciller Adam Kubert.

DECEMBER

GAMBIT PLAYS SOLITAIRE

• *Gambit* #1

Everyone's favorite smooth-talking Cajun, Gambit, made his way into his first miniseries by writer Howard Mackie and artist Lee Weeks. The miniseries' story revolved around Gambit's ex-wife, Bella Donna, his old clan of thieves, his partnership with Rogue, and a mysterious figure known as the Tithe Collector.

ALSO PUBLISHED

CAPTAIN MARVEL'S LEGACY

• *The Silver Surfer Annual* #6

Writer Ron Marz and penciller Joe Phillips created Genis-Vell, whose cosmic abilities kicked in during the sixth *Silver Surfer Annual*. Originally going under the code name Legacy, Genis-Vell was the son of Mar-Vell of the Kree Empire and helped the Silver Surfer in a battle against Ronan the Accuser. He was later known as Captain Marvel, like his father, and, even later, as Photon. Genis-Vell also became a member of the Thunderbolts.

MEANWHILE IN 1993...

CLINTON IS PRESIDENT
Bill Clinton succeeds George H.W. Bush and is sworn in as the 42nd President of the United States.

WORLD TRADE CENTER BOMBING
A car bomb explodes in the underground car park of Tower One of the World Trade Center in New York, injuring 1,042 people and killing six.

WACO MASSACRE
Agents raid the compound of the Branch Davidians at Mount Carmel near Waco, Texas. After a fifty-one-day standoff, a fire kills over seventy people, including the Branch Davidian leader David Koresh.

CZECHOSLOVAKIA SPLITS
Czechoslovakia is officially dissolved and becomes two countries: the Czech Republic and Slovakia.

THE BEGINNING OF THE INTERNET
A text-based World Wide Web browser is put in the public domain, revolutionizing the way information is used and shared.

BEAVIS AND BUTT-HEAD AIRS
The animation Beavis and Butt-Head debuts and becomes a classic of 1990s youth culture and the MTV generation, with its lewd humor and social criticism.

MAASTRICHT TREATY
The Maastricht Treaty takes effect, creating the European Union. It covers both the political and monetary union of many European countries.

ESCOBAR KILLED
In the war on drugs, Colombian drug baron Pablo Escobar is finally tracked down and is killed by police.

FIRST BIONIC ARM
A team of Scottish scientists create the first bionic arm, which uses microchips and sensors to interpret electrical pulses from the brain and move the artificial arm accordingly.

MIDWEST FLOODS
The Mississippi and Missouri Rivers flood the American midwest and cause $15 billion worth of damage.

AND AT THE MOVIES...
Jurassic Park, CGI predators on the loose in a remote theme park provide plenty of thrills in this monster movie; Groundhog Day, Bill Murray's grumpy weatherman finds himself doomed to replay the same day for the rest of his life in this charming comedy; Schindler's List, Steven Spielberg's biographical film of Oskar Schindler, a German businessman who saved the lives of more than 1,000 Polish Jews during the Holocaust.

MAXIMUM CARNAGE

When writer J.M. DeMatteis was first offered the job to write for the Maximum Carnage story line of 1993 by group editor Danny Fingeroth, he was at first adverse to the idea. Not a fan of Spider-Man foes Venom and Carnage, or the trend of mass murdering Super Villains, DeMatteis did not accept the job until he realized that the series would be his chance to air these opinions on a grand scale, pitting the relatively innocent Peter Parker against the darkest corners of the human psyche in the form of these twisted adversaries. While Spider-Man was tempted to sink to his foes' level in the pages of this crossover, he nevertheless managed to cling to a more heroic path.

1994
CLONES AND MARVELS

The year 1994 was one that sparked conversation, acclaim, and debate. Marvel continued to introduce new titles that drew on what had connected with their readers in years past, influenced by the success of the heavily armored heroes of the beginning of the decade. *War Machine* birthed a more gun-friendly version of Iron Man; *Fantastic Force* saw a tech-garbed version of Marvel's first family; and *Force Works* let its title speak for itself.

However, it was a very different kind of clone story that would spark controversy in the eyes of the fans for years to come when Marvel decided to spice up the life of their resident icon, Spider-Man. They reintroduced Spider-Man's clone that was last glimpsed in the 1970s, and created the Clone Saga. This giant event crossover seemed to almost spin out of the control of those that orchestrated it, making Peter Parker, and an increasingly discontented fan base, wonder exactly which Spider-Man was the original, and which was the clone.

Through it all shined *Marvels*, written by Kurt Busiek and painted by Alex Ross. This limited series reinvigorated painted comics as a genre, went on to become an acclaimed masterpiece, and spawned more than its own fair share of imitators.

JANUARY

MARVELS

"It was life or death—it was grand opera—it was the greatest show on Earth—and we—every single one of us —we had the best seat in the house."

• *Marvels #1*

Marvels was a four-issue prestige-format graphic novel, written by Kurt Busiek, illustriously painted by then relative newcomer Alex Ross, and printed on high-quality paper. The limited series utilized a realistic style in narrative as well as in artwork, a style seldom seen before in mainstream comic books, and was both a critical and financial success. *Marvels* also took the unusual viewpoint of an outsider, of a civilian witnessing firsthand the greatest events in human history.

The series chronicled the life of photojournalist Phil Sheldon from a young man at the dawn of World War II, to his retirement in the 1970s. From the public unveiling of the original android Human Torch, to the flooding of Manhattan by the Sub-Mariner, from the anti-mutant hysteria that evolved with the X-Men, to the coming of the world-eater Galactus, and on to the death of a lone innocent girl named Gwen Stacy, Phil Sheldon saw it all, and recorded it for the rest of his world to see. He called these super-powered figures Marvels, and his affection for these amazing men and women would drive his very existence. But what the world didn't see, the picture Sheldon's photos couldn't paint, was of the death of his optimism, the story behind the scenes of a man mad at the world for not lauding its fantastic protectors, and then furious at that same world for not noticing the little people that were there all along.

Alongside other struggling journalists like J. Jonah Jameson, Phil Sheldon attended the press conference of scientist Phineas Thomas Horton as he unveiled his creation.

HUSK'S HERALDING

• *X-Force #32*

Husk, the skin-shedding future Generation X member and little sister of X-Force's Cannonball, had appeared in comics as early as 1986 but never as a mutant. Her character and mutant abilities, which enabled her to change into various substances, emerged in issue 32 of *X-Force*, thanks to writer Fabian Nicieza and penciller Tony Daniel.

THE WEDDING OF PHOENIX AND CYCLOPS

• *X-Men #30*

X-Men founders Scott Summers and Jean Grey finally got hitched thanks to writer Fabian Nicieza and artist Andy Kubert, amidst all their friends and loved ones. Even Wolverine attended, although he watched from a distance, ever the loner.

The story revealed some benefits to a mutant marriage: The bride could tell if her guests were having a good time just by being near them; some of the attendees could dance on air; and the maid of honor could literally guarantee that there would be no rain.

WAR MACHINE FLIES SOLO

• *War Machine #1*

Jim Rhodes, Iron Man's friend turned ex-employee, piloted his War Machine silver armor into his own ongoing series. Written by Scott Benson and Len Kaminski, with pencils by Gabriel Gecko, the series saw a battle with fellow heavily-armed Cable and Deathlok.

THE RESURRECTION OF GHOST RIDER

• *Ghost Rider 2099 #1*

Under the Marvel 2099 imprint, this story was written by Len Kaminski, with art by Chris Bachalo and Mark Buckingham. In it, Kenshiro Cochrane traveled to another dimension to become a superstrong, robotic Ghost Rider.

FORCE WORKS PREMIERS

• *Force Works #1*

When the West Coast Avengers disbanded, some of its members, led by Iron Man, went on to form a new team, Force Works, which took a more aggressive stance toward superheroics. Writers Dan Abnett and Andy Lanning, alongside penciller Tom Tenney, showcased the team with a unique pop-up, folding cover in its debut issue.

THE BLACK CAT CROSSES PATHS

• *Felicia Hardy: The Black Cat #1*

Anti-hero the Black Cat was given her first miniseries in July. Written by Terry Kavanagh and Joey Cavalieri, with art by penciller Andrew Wildman, the series lasted for four issues. The series saw the Black Cat fight Cardiac and Spider-Man and undergo a search for a mysterious resource referred to as the Chimera.

Black Cat was hired by the Morelle company to steal the Chimera.

THE CLONE SAGA BEGINS

• *Web Of Spider-Man* #117

The 117th issue of *Web Of Spider-Man* was considered the start of the mammoth crossover known as the Clone Saga, although the story had roots stemming back to the 1970s, when Peter Parker and Gwen Stacy were both cloned by the villainous Jackal.

The beginning of the saga saw Spider-Man come face to face with Peter Parker. Written by Terry Kavanagh and pencilled by Steven Butler, this issue was available in flip book format.

Besides chronicling the return of Spider-Man's original clone, Web Of Spider-Man #117 *also marked the first appearance of Dr. Judas Traveller, a new Spidey foe obsessed with studying the criminal mind.*

TALES TO ASTONISH MAKES A RETURN

• *Tales To Astonish*

Fan-favorite Hulk writer Peter David teamed with painter John Estes for this one-shot that began a series of retro-titled prestige-format specials, including *Strange Tales* and *Tales Of Suspense*. The *Tales To Astonish* special continued the trend, popularized in *Marvels*, of painted comics wrapped in an acetate cover.

When a madman named Knut Caine shot a police officer in broad daylight, Janet Van Dyne (the Wasp) and Hank Pym's peaceful visit to Norway suddenly transformed into a team-up battle with the Hulk versus the forces of the trickster god, Loki. Luckily the heroic trio triumphed, but only after Hulk resisted the temptation for power.

GENERATION X MAKES ITS MARK

• *Generation X* #1

Writer Scott Lobdell and artist Chris Bachalo introduced Generation X, the new team of mutants first glimpsed in this month's *The Uncanny X-Men* #318, to their own ongoing series with this deluxe first issue.

Taking place at Xavier's School For Gifted Youngsters, *Generation X* focused on a group of fresh-faced, untrained mutants just as the original *X-Men* series of the 1960s, and *The New Mutants* series of the 1980s, did before it. Brimming with teen angst and the cynical attitude of teenagers of the 1990s, *Generation X* starred Jubilee, Husk, M, Skin, and Synch, under the tutelage of Banshee and the White Queen, and debuted new members Chamber, Mondo, and Penance.

Ben Reilly's costume was composed of a pair of red tights, some old web-shooters, and an altered blue Spider-Man sweatshirt he had noticed in a store window.

THE SCARLET SPIDER

"He goes by the name of Ben Reilly, in honor of lost family… but not his family. Not his world, not his memories. Not his life."

• *Web Of Spider-Man* #118

After a supposed death at the hands of the demented geneticist the Jackal in Gerry Conway's classic original clone saga of the 1970s, Peter Parker's clone had recently reemerged in Spider-Man's life, calling himself Ben Reilly. Not wanting to step on the true Spider-Man's toes, but unable to shake his sense of power and responsibility, Ben Reilly could no longer deny his role when he heard that the symbiotic Venom was loose in New York City and causing havoc and mayhem. So, he donned a costume and was dubbed the Scarlet Spider by the press—and by writer Terry Kavanagh and penciller Steven Butler.

This Clone Saga story line continued through the Spider-Man range of books for the next two years. Meanwhile, Ben Reilly learned from the Jackal that he was actually the true Spider-Man, and not the clone as he had always suspected. He even ended up taking over for Peter Parker as Spider-Man, when Peter briefly retired in order to raise the child that he and his wife, Mary Jane, had been expecting.

FORGING THE FANTASTIC FORCE

• *Fantastic Force* #1

Created by writers Tom Brevoort and Mike Kanterovich, the Fantastic Force was a spin-off of the Fantastic Four. The team comprised members Vibraxas, a Wakanda native; Devlor, a boy turned beast; the savage Huntara; and Psi-Lord, the son of Mr. Fantastic and the Invisible Woman.

Ⓜ Following the continued success of the *X-Men* cartoon, Fox Kids debuted Peter Parker's newly animated adventures, beginning a series that lasted five seasons with sixty-five episodes to its credit.

1995

APOCALYPSE NOW

There was no question about it. The X-Men books were back in the spotlight, and were the first line of defense in Marvel's ongoing battle for sales.

As Spider-Man's Clone Saga story line continued, some fans and critics grew tired of the multiple shifts in the story's direction. However, the unified feel created in the Age of Apocalypse X-Men event would attract some of those same disgruntled fans. This story line dominated the many miniseries that appeared in 1995, including *The Astonishing X-Men, Generation Next, X-Calibre, The Amazing X-Men, Weapon X,* and *Gambit And The X-Ternals.* The event was also significant for the roster of writers and artists that it showcased. Creatives working on this story line included Warren Ellis, Jeph Loeb, Mark Waid, Joe Madureira, Chris Bachalo, and Andy and Adam Kubert, who were destined to be some of the biggest names in comics.

FEBRUARY

THE AGE OF APOCALYPSE

"His name is Erik Lehnsherr, called Magneto by some... and how he continues to stand is anyone's guess."

• *X-Men: Alpha* (Age Of Apocalypse) The Age Of Apocalypse was a major crossover event that drastically changed the landscape of the universe that the X-Men existed in. The story began in this *X-Men: Alpha* special by writers Scott Lobdell and Mark Waid and pencillers Roger Cruz and Steve Epting.

Charles Xavier had died and Magneto now headed Xavier's freedom force of mutants, still struggling for Xavier's dream of a peaceful human/mutant coexistence. As the regular line of X-Men books suspended publication for four months in order to make way for a group of various new miniseries, fans were introduced to a world now ruled by the mutant overlord Apocalypse. Under his rule, humans were slaughtered en mass in routine "cullings" and the X-Men were considered traitors to their own species. It was a world where Wolverine, called only Weapon X, had lost a hand in a battle with Cyclops, and where Angel ran a swanky nightclub, more interested in saving his own skin than fighting the good fight.

Fueled by their introduction to the time-traveling Bishop, who remembered how things were before this shift in reality, the X-Men organized a strike to overthrow Apocalypse's rule. At the same time, the humans attacked America from their safe base of resistance in Europe to try to ruin Apocalypse. Magneto and his X-Men triumphed by the end of the story line. They destroyed Apocalypse and sent Bishop back in time to save Xavier's life and change history, just as the humans' bombs began to fall across North America.

Some of the X-Men in this alternate reality included Morph, Rogue, Magneto, Quicksilver, Storm, Iceman, and Nightcrawler.

JANUARY

ROGUE'S RECKONING

• *Rogue* #1

X-Men member Rogue finally starred in her own four-issue miniseries, beginning in January. Written by Howard Mackie with art by Mike Wieringo, *Rogue* told a tale of the Assassin's Guild, which rivaled the guild of thieves that mutant Gambit had belonged to; Gambit's dedication to his "chere" (as he referred to Rogue); and Rogue's first love, Cody, who fell into a coma after a kiss with Rogue sapped him of his energy.

MARCH

ASTONISHING ASSAULT

• *The Astonishing X-Men* #1 (Age of Apocalypse)

In this four-issue miniseries by writers Scott Lobdell and Jeph Loeb, and artist Joe Madureira, Magneto divided his troops in order to organize a severe strike against mutant overlord Apocalypse. The miniseries chronicled the adventures of the X-Men as they shut down Apocalypse's Infinites processing plant, a facility used to manufacture soldiers to serve the overlord.

X-MAN ESCAPES

• *X-Man* #1 (Age Of Apocalypse)
Created by writer Jeph Loeb and artist Steve Skroce, X-Man was perhaps the most popular character to emerge out of the Age of Apocalypse event. Nate Grey, X-Man's alter ego, was grown in a lab by evil genius Mr. Sinister. Sinister was planning a revolution against his master, Apocalypse, by combining the DNA of mutant prelate Scott Summers and rebel Jean Grey to create a mutant strong enough to overthrow Apocalypse. Nate fled from Sinister's lab and joined a traveling band of actors, led by the rebel Forge. As his telepathic powers matured, Nate used them to shut down the experiments of the Dark Beast, and to battle the evil Holocaust.

X-Man's troupe of traveling "actors" included familiar faces Toad, Soaron, Brute, Mastermind, and Forge.

COLOSSUS' GENERATION

• *Generation Next* #1 (Age Of Apocalypse)
Artist Chris Bachalo and writer Scott Lobdell crafted this four-issue miniseries, beginning in March, detailing the first appearance of super-strong Colossus's team of young mutants and their attack on a slave-run energy factory owned by Apocalypse.

NAVIGATING NIGHTCRAWLER

• *X-Calibre* #1 (Age Of Apocalypse)
With his X-Calibre team, Nightcrawler traveled to Avalon in order to find the clairvoyant Destiny to help prove Bishop's theories about an alternate reality, in this four-issue miniseries by writer Warren Ellis and artists Roger Cruz, Ken Lashley, and Renato Arlem.

AMAZING AGENDA

• *The Amazing X-Men* #1 (Age Of Apocalypse)
Written by Fabian Nicieza with art by Andy Kubert, this four-issue miniseries focused on Quicksilver, Banshee, Iceman, Storm, Dazzler, and Exodus as they tried to aid humans escape from America to a safer Europe.

SECRET WEAPON

• *Weapon X* #1 (Age Of Apocalypse)
Mutant rebels Logan and Jean Grey helped the human attack on America before parting ways when Jean became concerned about the amount of casualties in this four-issue tale by writer Larry Hama, with art by Adam Kubert.

THE CYCLOPS FACTOR

• *Factor X* #1 (Age Of Apocalypse)
One-eyed prelate Scott Summers rebelled against his master Apocalypse and his jealous brother Havok, siding with Jean Grey's cause in this four-issue miniseries by writer John Francis Moore and artists Steve Epting and Terry Dodson.

X-TERNAL QUEST

• *Gambit And The X-Ternals* #1 (Age Of Apocalypse)
X-Men member Gambit, alongside a team of familiar mutants including Sunspot, Jubilee, Strong Guy, and Lila Cheney, set off on a space-faring adventure in search of the legendary M'Kraan Crystal, which could glimpse into the different realities, including the one that Bishop claimed was the X-Men's true universe.

THE DEATH OF AUNT MAY

• *The Amazing Spider-Man* #400
Amidst the chaos of the ongoing Clone Saga, Peter Parker's aunt May had suffered a stroke. However, in the opening of the 400th anniversary issue of *The Amazing Spider-Man*, written by J.M. DeMatteis and penciled by Mark Bagley, she seemed to be completely recovered as she checked herself out of hospital. A week later, May revealed that she had known about Peter's dual life for years, before she collapsed weakly into his arms. Peter took May home, and she passed away after saying her final goodbyes to her treasured nephew.

Though Aunt May's death would later be revealed as an elaborate hoax perpetrated by Norman Osborn, her death seemed very real to Peter Parker.

MAY

DR. DRUID GETS SURGERY

• *Druid #1*

Writer Warren Ellis had developed his distinctly dark and morbid vision in the pages of *Hellstorm*. Beginning in May, he took supernatural monster-hunter Dr. Druid to new depths in this dark series. With art by Leonardo Manco, the series saw the good doctor truly earn the sinister title of Druid.

JULY

THE X-MEN REOPEN FOR BUSINESS

• *X-Men: Prime*

With their world restored to normal after the Age of Apocalypse, the X-Men returned to business as usual in this extra-sized special by writers Scott Lobdell and Fabian Nicieza and artists Bryan Hitch, Jeff Matsuda, Gary Frank, Mike McKone, Terry Dodson, Ben Herrera, and Paul Pelletier.

AUGUST

MARVELS GETS RUINED

• *Ruins #1*

Labeled a Marvel Alterniverse story, this two-issue prestige-format limited series was written by Warren Ellis and painted by Cliff and Terese Nielsen and Chris Moeller. It showed a morbid vision of the Marvel Universe, a "what if" tale that was an antithesis to Kurt Busiek and Alex Ross's *Marvels*. *Ruins* examined the life of photojournalist Phil Sheldon, as did *Marvels*, but this miniseries saw Sheldon witness an Avengers Quinjet exploding and later die from radiation spread to him by Peter Parker.

DEATH OF THE JACKAL

• *Spider-Man Maximum Clonage: Omega*

Continuing the epic Clone Saga, the team of artists Tom Lyle, Robert Brown, Roy Burdine, and Mark Bagley revealed the supposed final fate of the genius Jackal. Facing Spider-Man and the Scarlet Spider on the rooftop of the *Daily Bugle*, the Jackal was intent on setting off a deadly virus bomb. However, after plaguing Spider-Men with his machinations and other clones, the Jackal fell to his death while trying to rescue the clone of Gwen Stacy.

SEPTEMBER

SECRETS OF SPIDEY'S PAST

• *Untold Tales Of Spider-Man #1*

With all the confusion going on in Peter Parker's life in his other books, writer Kurt Busiek and artist Pat Olliffe stepped in to fill the void for the kind of classic Spider-Man stories that Stan Lee and Steve Ditko had imagined at the character's inception.

Telling stories set in Peter's high school days, *Untold Tales Of Spider-Man* still managed to create a host of new characters, including the flame-wielding Scorcher and the misunderstood monster Batwing. And to further contrast with the other Spider-Man titles of its day, this series also strived to tell easily accessible one-part stories, much like the original comics that inspired it.

Each issue of Untold Tales Of Spider-Man *was priced at only ninety-nine cents to try to gain a new and wider readership.*

MEANWHILE IN 1995...

OKLAHOMA CITY BOMBING
In Oklahoma, 168 people are killed and over 800 are injured in a terrorist attack on an office complex by Timothy McVeigh and Terry Nichols.

MILLIONS WATCH THE LIVE O.J. SIMPSON TRIAL
More than half of the US population watches the verdict of the actor and American football player O.J. Simpson trial as he is declared not guilty. The "trial of the century" is one of the most watched moments in the history of American television.

SARIN ATTACK ON THE TOKYO SUBWAY
Members of the Aum Shinrikyo religious movement release sarin gas on five trains, killing twelve, seriously harming fifty-four, and affecting hundreds more.

WINDOWS 95 RELEASED
This new operating system goes on sale with a revolutionary graphical user interface that is highly consumer-orientated.

AMAZON.COM GOES LIVE
The commercial website amazon.com starts trading and grows steadily over the next few years, rather than at the fast—but unstable—rate at which many of the internet companies appear to grow.

NEW EUROPEAN UNION MEMBERS
Sweden, Austria, and Finland join the European Union.

FIRST SOLO PACIFIC BALLOON FLIGHT
Steve Fossett becomes the first person to cross the Pacific in a solo hot air balloon flight.

RABIN ASSASSINATED
Israeli Prime Minister Yitzhak Rabin is assassinated at a Tel-Aviv peace rally, two years after shaking hands with PLO leader Yasser Arafat in Washington DC.

EXTREME SPORTS ARE BIG
Thanks to an explosion in their popularity, extreme sports are given their own tournament on EXPN's The X-Games.

AND AT THE MOVIES...
Toy Story, Pixar's groundbreaking CGI "buddy" movie about toys coming to life is the first CGI animation feature; The Usual Suspects, Bryan Singer's purposefully confusing con-trick film is full of misdirection, convoluted plotting, and macho repartee; Heat, Michael Mann's gripping account of a symbiotic relationship between a cop and a criminal and the dangers of bonding with other people; Apollo 13, Ron Howard's dramatization of the ill-fated Apollo 13 mission to the moon in 1970.

Tales To Astonish *(Dec., 1994)*
John Estes, an artist also known for his work on the Fleer Ultra X-Men trading card series from 1994 and the Marvel Masterpiece trading cards from 1993, painted this one-shot. The script was by Peter David, who also was no stranger to the Hulk, having scripted the brute's adventures for several years.

1996

CROSSOVERS TAKE OVER

The crossover had gone from being a clever way to attract new readers to a particular title to a necessary industry standard. With the Onslaught and Heroes Reborn events starting in this year, and the Clone Saga finally dragging itself to a halt, Marvel set out for the ultimate crossover—one with DC Comics.

Having produced joint ventures in the forms of stand alone specials dating back to *MGM's Marvelous Wizard Of Oz* comic adaptation of 1975, Marvel and DC set out to accomplish something on a larger scale, and the result was *Marvel Versus DC* (or *DC Versus Marvel*, depending on which issue of the series you were reading), a miniseries that would spin off into not just two sequels, but also the creation of a third fictional comic company, Amalgam. Under the Amalgam label, Marvel and DC produced two waves of twelve specials that featured combined versions of their characters, creating the illusion of a long-standing merged company, and going so far as to include fake letters columns and footnotes within the issues, referring to other comics that never actually existed.

But despite the popularity of all the events of 1996, at the end of the year Marvel made the most drastic crossover of its publishing history—into bankruptcy.

JANUARY

THE FUTURE OF THE FF

• *Fantastic Four 2099 #1*
After an accident in the Negative Zone landed the Fantastic Four in the dystopian 2099 future, they finally saw what life was like without constant accolades and admiration. This eight-issue series was written by Karl Kesel with art by *2099* veteran penciller Rick Leonardi.

FEBRUARY

MARVEL TAKES ON THE COMPETITION

"The showdown of the century! Who will win? You decide!"

Marvel Comics Versus DC *pitted each company's iconic characters against each other. It also introduced the first character to be shared by both comic companies—Axel Asher. Also known as Access, Axel Asher was the guardian of the gateway between worlds.*

• *Marvel Comics Versus DC #1*
Marvel and DC heroes had faced each other before. Some had even teamed up on that rare, special occasion. But finally, in this deluxe four-issue miniseries by writers Ron Marz and Peter David and pencillers Dan Jurgens and Claudio Castellini, with two issues published by Marvel and two by DC, comic fans got to see their favorite heroes from both Marvel and DC Comics battle it out in fights with actual definitive outcomes. And better yet, the fans got to vote for the victor of each bout.

Using ballots sent in advance to their local comic store, fans were able to vote for who they wanted to win in five different battles. Along with their ballot, readers received a free preview of the miniseries itself, along with a promotional trading card, advertising the upcoming 100-card set from SkyBox International, also a joint venture between the two comic book publishing houses.

In the series, two cosmic entities became aware of the other's existence, and decided to have a duel for supremacy, each choosing powerful representatives from his world to wage his private war for him. After a few preliminary fights, Wolverine defeated the alien powerhouse Lobo in a barroom brawl; Storm bested Wonder Woman using the power of the elements; Spider-Man used his years of experience to take down the Superman-clone Superboy; Superman showed Hulk who truly was the strongest one; and Batman KOed Captain America with a batarang to the head. After the fights, the cosmic entities merged their worlds into one whole, creating the new and unique universe, and thereby spinning the story off into a series of joint one-shots published under the label Amalgam Comics.

JUSTICE HAS A NEW NAME

- *JLX* #1

Combining DC's Justice League and Marvel's X-Men, this Amalgam special was written by Gerard Jones and Mark Waid, with pencils by Howard Porter. The one-off featured combined characters like Mariner (Namor and Aquaman) and Night-Creeper (Nightcrawler and the Creeper).

JLX also included J'onn J'onzz, the last survivor of the Martian race known as the Skrulls.

THE DARK CLAW DETECTIVE

- *Legends Of The Dark Claw* #1

Dark Claw, a combination of Wolverine and Batman, cut his way into his own Amalgam special, thanks to writer Larry Hama and penciller Jim Balent. Also featured in the issue was Dark Claw's sidekick, Sparrow, a mix of Jubilee and Robin.

AMERICA'S MAN OF STEEL

- *Super-Soldier* #1

Amalgam's Super-Soldier emerged in the days of World War II and was a cross between classic patriots Captain America and Superman. Super-Soldier fought such foes as Amalgam's Ultra-Metallo and the green skulled Lex Luthor, as chronicled by writer Mark Waid and artist Dave Gibbons.

A NEW CLONE

- *Spider-Boy* #1

Written by Karl Kesel with pencils by Mike Wieringo, the "awesome arach-kid" Amalgam hero Spider-Boy faced the likes of Bizarnage (Carnage and Bizarro), with the help of the Challengers of Fantastic (the Fantastic Four and the Challengers of the Unknown).

THE STORMING OF THE AMAZONS

- *Amazon* #1

In her own Amalgam special by writer/artist John Byrne, Princess Ororo of the hidden island Themyscira, a combination of Wonder Woman and Storm, fought the very gods themselves and reminisced about her childhood among the Amazons and her old friend Diana.

THE ONSLAUGHT EPIC

- *X-Men* #53

Jean Grey was the first to encounter the mysterious entity calling himself Onslaught, as he tried to recruit her for his war. After a tour through the psyche of her mentor, Professor X, Jean rejected the ominous being's offer, scarred by witnessing the dark side of her teacher's mind. First appearing in this issue by writer Mark Waid with pencils by Andy Kubert, Onslaught's emergence would spell doom for many of the Marvel heroes.

Onslaught left Jean Grey with a warning: his name literally written across her forehead.

ONSLAUGHT EPIC ENDS

"It was an age unlike any other. And this is the story of its end…"

• *Onslaught: Marvel Universe*
Labeled "Marvel's latest rage" in its house ads, the Onslaught epic story line had been crossing over through many of the publisher's various titles since power-mad villain Onslaught's formal debut in the pages of *X-Men* #53 in June of this year. Tying into all of the X-Men titles, as well as comics starring the Avengers, Ghost Rider, Daredevil, Spider-Man, the Fantastic Four, and the Hulk, this gigantic story filled six volumes when it was originally reprinted in trade paperback form.

A manifestation of the dark halves of Charles Xavier's and Magneto's psyche, Onslaught truly rose to power in the *Onslaught: X-Men* special (August) by writers Mark Waid and Scott Lobdell and artist Adam Kubert. Quickly besting the X-Men after failing to recruit them to his cause, Onslaught began to battle other heroes as the Avengers and Fantastic Four were alerted to his presence.

Although there were many artists and writers who contributed to Onslaught's attack on mankind, it was again the three main masterminds behind the event, Waid, Lobdell, and Kubert, who would craft the *Onslaught: Marvel Universe* special, the final chapter in this dramatic tale that saw a plethora of heroes engaged in one final battle with Onslaught, now evolved into a state of pure psionic energy. The heroes realized that if enough of them threw themselves into this energy void, making the ultimate sacrifice, Onslaught was affected, and would be defeated. Therefore the Avengers and the Fantastic Four leaped into the unknown as the X-Men attacked one last time, finally destroying the psychic beast.

ELEKTRA CARVES HER NICHE

• *Elektra* #1
Finally given her own ongoing series by writer Peter Milligan and artist Mike Deodato Jr., Elektra found a new use for her grace and skill after defeating a group of ninjas robbing a theater company. Taking a job as a dancer to help fund the martial arts training center she'd invested herself into, Elektra soon realized she was being stalked by psychopathic assassin Bullseye. The two later had a vicious battle in a back alley but Elektra managed to avenge her earlier death at Bullseye's hands by besting him.

JIM LEE'S IRON MAN

Iron Man #1
Part of the Heroes Reborn event, Iron Man was relaunched into a new universe courtesy of writers Scott Lobdell and Jim Lee, with pencils by Whilce Portacio. In this new world birthed through Onslaught's death, Tony Stark squared off against the Hulk.

JIM LEE'S FANTASTIC FOUR

• *Fantastic Four* #1
Jim Lee both wrote and drew this Heroes Reborn relaunch title with the help of fellow scripter Brandon Choi. This issue retold the origin of the Fantastic Four and their fateful space mission that granted them superpowers. It also saw the introduction of the Mole Man.

ROB LIEFELD'S CAPTAIN AMERICA

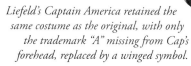

• *Captain America* #1
Steve Rogers earned a fresh start in the Heroes Reborn universe by writer Jeph Loeb and artist Rob Liefeld. This creative team portrayed Rogers as a regular suburban family man who slowly began to remember his previous life as war hero Captain America.

Liefeld's Captain America retained the same costume as the original, with only the trademark "A" missing from Cap's forehead, replaced by a winged symbol.

ROB LIEFELD'S AVENGERS

• *The Avengers* #1
Another Heroes Reborn title, *The Avengers* was plotted and drawn by Rob Liefeld with a script by Jim Valentino and additional pencils by Chap Yaep. This issue saw Thor, Scarlet Witch, Swordsman, Captain America, the Vision, and Hellcat face off against the villain Loki. Along with the three other Heroes Reborn titles, this new series marked the return to Marvel for several of Image Comics' hottest creators, including Liefeld and Valentino, giving them free reign in this new universe.

MARVEL AND DC GRANT FANS ACCESS

• *DC/Marvel: All Access #1*

In this sequel to the hit *Marvel Versus DC* miniseries, Access, the hero shared by both comic companies, began to notice characters appearing in the wrong universes. In this four-issue miniseries, writer Ron Marz and artists Jackson Guice and Josef Rubinstein featured interesting pairings, such as Venom battling Superman, the Scorpion being bested by Batman, and the X-Men fighting the JLA. The series also saw a return of several of the fan-favorite Amalgam heroes, including the powerful Dr. Strangefate and mutant Dark Claw.

THE DEATH OF BEN REILLY

• *Spider-Man #75*

The Clone Saga finally came to a dramatic close thanks to the team of writer Howard Mackie and artist John Romita Jr. The original Green Goblin, Norman Osborn, was revealed to be alive and the ultimate mastermind behind all of Spidey's clone troubles. Peter Parker also discovered that he was not a clone, and that Ben Reilly was, forcing Peter back into action as Spider-Man after Osborn caused the death of Spidey's unborn daughter, and then that of Ben Reilly himself.

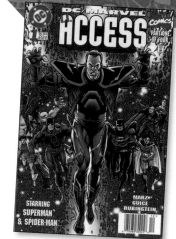

Ben Reilly died the same way that Norman Osborn had seemingly perished all those years ago, speared by the Green Goblin's glider.

After Spider-Man defeated the Goblin, he watched Ben Reilly's body turn to dust, proving Peter Parker to be the genuine article.

MARVEL FILES FOR BANKRUPTCY

After businessman Ron Perelman purchased Marvel Entertainment Group, the parent company of Marvel Comics, he attempted to expand the business by purchasing ToyBiz, Fleer/Skybox, and Malibu Comics. This culminated in a debt Marvel could not pay off, forcing the company to file for bankruptcy.

MEANWHILE IN 1996...

UNABOMBER ARRESTED
Theodore Kaczynski is arrested on suspicion of being the "Unabomber" terrorist, who caused a series of bombings across the US during the 1970s, 1980s, and 1990s.

DOLLY THE SHEEP IS BORN
In a landmark step for genetic cloning, the first mammal to be cloned from an adult.cell is born in Scotland. This breakthrough establishes that a cell from a particular body part can be used to create an entire individual.

CENTENNIAL OLYMPIC PARK BOMBING
Two are killed when a bomb explodes during a rock concert in a park developed by the Atlanta Olympic Committee.

A ROYAL DIVORCE
The Prince and Princess of Wales are officially divorced after marrying in 1981.

THE TALIBAN TAKE KABUL
The Taliban take control of Afghanistan's capital, Kabul, and overthrow the existing regime of President Burhanuddin Rabbani.

FIRST US WOMAN SECRETARY OF STATE
Madeleine Albright becomes the first women to be the US Secretary of State. She is nominated by President Clinton and then confirmed by the US Senate 99-0.

THE MYSTERY OF JONBENET RAMSEY
The six-year-old beauty-pageant contestant is found dead in the basement of her parents' home in Boulder, Colorado, drawing immense media coverage and national interest.

"POSSIBLE LIFE ON MARS"
Scientists who have been studying an ancient Martian meteorite announce that a primitive type of microscopic life may have been present on Mars around four billion years ago.

POKÉMON CRAZE BEGINS
The first Pokémon video games are released in Japan. The characters become a worldwide phenomenon, popularized in video games, a television cartoon series, trading cards, and other merchandise.

NINTENDO 64 RELEASED
The Nintendo 64 is released. Gamers rejoice.

AND AT THE MOVIES...
Fargo, this tragic-comic murder investigation is a flamboyant confection of genres given a modern twist by the quirky Coen brothers; Mission: Impossible, Brian De Palma's glossy, fast-paced, high-octane version of the TV series has Tom Cruise racing against time to save his name; Scream, a psychopathic serial killer is stalking a group of teens in Wes Craven's postmodern horror movie.

> BUT I AM SANE ENOUGH TO KNOW THIS... IN A WAR BETWEEN MAN AND MUTANTKIND... NO ONE WINS.

1997
MANY HAPPY RETURNS

Despite the ongoing legal battles for control of the company, and the uncertain fate of the Marvel Universe in the real world, the fictional world was following a definitive course. Although the flashy excitement of the Heroes Reborn event had given fans a nostalgic visit to the early part of the decade, by the end of the year, Marvel had set the stage for a return to its time-honored classic lineup, not wanting to lose readers who were put off by the change.

Also returning was Marvel's crystallized working relationship with DC Comics. Another wave of Amalgam specials debuted in the summer, and a third and final sequel to the popular *Marvel Comics Versus DC* miniseries hit the stands before the end of 1997.

As the X-Men comics returned to their tried and true method of netting sales—the crossover event—writer Kurt Busiek returned to what he did best, creating innovative story concepts. This was evidenced in his new series, *Thunderbolts*. Marvel's marketing division prevented advance information from being leaked, returning comic book fandom to the unsuspecting audience they were in days gone by.

DEADPOOL GETS A LIFE

• *Deadpool* #1
Marvel's Merc with a Mouth landed his own title in the form of this monthly series by writer Joe Kelly and artist Ed McGuinness. In this debut issue, Deadpool took an assignment to disrupt gamma testing in Antarctica, a mission that brought him face to face with Alpha Flight's Sasquatch, who was performing experiments under his alter ego of Walter Langkowski. After being told about the damage he would do to the southern hemisphere if the testing plant were to reach critical mass, Deadpool saved the plant from a meltdown of his own design.

DOMINO BRANCHES OUT

• *Domino* #1
Writer Ben Raab and penciller David Perrin gave X-Force member Domino her own three-issue miniseries. Domino's Carnaval vacation was interrupted when she ran into Alpha Flight's Puck, and discovered Lady Deathstrike had kidnapped one of Domino's old flames.

THE THUNDERBOLTS DEBUT

• *The Incredible Hulk* #449
Writer Peter David and artist Mike Deodato Jr. debuted Marvel's newest superteam, the Thunderbolts, in issue 449 of *The Incredible Hulk*. This was an attempt to make the public aware of this fledgling group before they got their own comic. When the Hulk was literally shot out of the sky by a missile, he found himself locked in battle with these mysterious heroes, who were intent on bringing him to justice.

THE THUNDERBOLTS' BIG CON

"The world will discover what a viper it has clasped to its breast, but by then it will be too late—far too late!"

• *Thunderbolts* #1
Onslaught had taken the heroes and America was left with quite a void to fill. So when the Thunderbolts first appeared on the scene and stopped a group of thieves from looting the rubble from what was once a pleasant New York neighborhood, the public was quick to embrace them as the next generation of Super Heroes. But what the world didn't know was that the Thunderbolts were secretly the old Avengers foes, the Masters of Evil, masquerading as heroes. Baron Zemo was posing as Citizen V, the Beetle was disguised as Mach-I, Moonstone had dubbed herself Meteorite, Screaming Mimi had transformed herself into Songbird, Fixer had become Techno, and Goliath was calling himself Atlas.

Writer Kurt Busiek had pitched his idea just before the Onslaught crossover had rocked the Marvel landscape. Realizing that the only heroes left to fight crime in their universe were shadowy figures like Spider-Man and Daredevil, Busiek thought that some of the villains might use this to their advantage, gaining the public's trust in order to slowly take over the world. So, along with penciller Mark Bagley, Busiek set out to create the Thunderbolts, realizing that the tricky part would be to keep this secret from the readers.

Busiek and company ignored the pleas from Marvel's marketing division who thought that sales would be affected by not revealing the comics' twist. They managed to conceal their comic's confidential ending until the release of the first issue, and indeed shocked their entire fan base with their dramatic reveal.

OPERATION: ZERO TOLERANCE

"I wanted you to see this, Charles. But more than that… I wanted you to understand. Your goal? Your crusade? Your sacred dream? It's over."

• *X-Men* #65
The Operation: Zero Tolerance event was the brainchild of writer Scott Lobdell. This massive X-Men crossover had been foreshadowed for some time, its roots planted in the pages of various comics even before the Onslaught event. In an attempt to give the anti-mutant cause a face as iconic and recognizable as Magneto, Lobdell created Bastion, a super-powered individual whose secrets were embedded in the history of the X-Men themselves. Bastion had been worming his way through the government machine, and was now in

a position of power to unleash his desire to destroy all mutants on an unsuspecting public.

Operation: Zero Tolerance truly began in the prologue within *X-Men* #65 as the government blasted the X-Men's blackbird plane out of the sky. Written by Scott Lobdell and drawn by Carlos Pacheco, the story sprang from there into all the other X-titles of the time, and featured the work of writers James Robinson, John Francis Moore, Larry Hama, Steve Seagle, and Joe Kelly, and artists Randy Green, Chris Bachalo, Adam Pollina, Leinil Francis Yu, Pop Mahn, Pascual Ferry, Rob Haynes, and Salvador Larroca.

As the story line continued, Bastion took the most powerful X-Men hostage, backed by a US government that had given up on mutantkind after the Onslaught disaster and the Legacy virus. Meanwhile, Iceman amassed a team of unlikely heroes to oppose Bastion and his army of Prime Sentinels, humans turned powerful cybernetic killing machines. He succeeded with a little help from SHIELD, and the ever shifting opinion of the fickle public.

When activated, the human carrier of the Prime Sentinel ceased to be, taken over by the Prime Sentinel's computerized programming.

Bat-Thing was actually scientist Kurt Sallis who experimented on himself with gene splicing in order to stage off a terminal illness.

BAT-THING FLIES HIGH
• *Bat-Thing* #1
In this Amalgam special written by Larry Hama with pencils by Rodolfo Damaggio, Gotham City was patrolled by Bat-Thing. A combination of Marvel's Man-Thing and DC's Man-Bat, Bat-Thing subdued criminals with his acid touch and bestial nature.

LANTERN LIGHTS UP

• *Iron Lantern* #1
Writer Kurt Busiek and artist Paul Smith created Iron Lantern, the Amalgam of Marvel's Iron Man and DC's Green Lantern, for this special. By day, Iron Lantern was the millionaire Hal Stark, and by night he was a hero who fought Madame Sapphire and Great White.

THE MAIN DUCK

• *Lobo The Duck* #1
A combination of Howard the Duck and ultra-violent alien Lobo, this Amalgam special was written by Alan Grant with pencils by Val Semeiks. The special centered around a foul-mouthed fowl as he explored a New York City that lay in ruins.

MARVEL'S METAL MEN

• *The Magnetic Men Featuring Magneto* #1
Magneto (a combination of Magneto and Will Magnus) returned in his second Amalgam special, care of writer Tom Peyer and artist Barry Kitson. This special featured Magneto's Magnetic Men (an amalgam of Brotherhood of Evil Mutants and Metal Men).

THE DOOM OF X-FORCE

• *The Exciting X-Patrol* #1
Writer Barbara Kesel, along with penciller Bryan Hitch, created this second Amalgam special to feature the X-Patrol. A combination of X-Force and Doom Patrol, the team included members Shatterstarfire (Shatterstar and Starfire) and Beastling (Beast and Changeling).

SPIDER-MAN TURNS JAPANESE

• *Spider-Man: The Manga* #1
The black and white Japanese Spider-Man comics of the late 1970s were published for an American audience that now embraced the style of Manga storytelling. Written and drawn by Ryoichi Ikegami, with English translation by Mutsumi Masuda and C.B. Cebulski, the series ran until April 1999.

BORN AGAIN HEROES

"And with the explosive force of air rushing to fill a vacuum, the travelers are drawn back into their homeworld, leaping into existence all over the world… or… to put it simply… the heroes… return."

• *Heroes Reborn: The Return* #1
Sales were high for the four different 1996 *Heroes Reborn* series that were born out of the ashes of the Onslaught event. However, the drastic changes to the origins and continuity of the main characters proved quite controversial with the fans, many of whom had invested years of their lives reading about the personal history of these heroes. While the change to these reimagined versions of the Marvel icons was never intended to be permanent, the return of their old favorites could not come soon enough for many readers. That was where legendary scribe Peter David and artist Salvador Larroca came in.

Creating a four-issue miniseries that tied up the loose threads left hanging in the *Heroes Reborn* universe, David and Larroca cast Franklin Richards, son of the FF's Mr. Fantastic and Invisible Woman, in a starring role, as he became aware of his parents living in this newly imagined universe. With the help of Man-Thing, and the coldly distant Celestial Ashema, Franklin was able to help lead his heroes home, despite losing Thor and Dr. Doom in the tumultuous journey.

To attract new readers to this series, each extra-sized issue featured four pages of summary text, giving the audience an update on the recent history of the major players in the saga. The readers also got sneak peaks into the four new ongoing titles, including *The Avengers*, that Marvel was launching to coincide with the return of their icons to the mainstream Marvel Universe.

ACCESS THROUGH THE AGES

• *Marvel/DC: Unlimited Access* #1
Unlimited Access was the third and final major intercompany four-issue miniseries of the late 1990s. The series continued the adventures of Access, the "cosmic hall monitor" who policed the DC and Marvel Universe to prevent another Amalgam event from happening. This series, by writer Karl Kesel and artist Pat Olliffe, featured such momentous bouts as the Hulk versus Green Lantern, the Sentinels hunting the Legion of Super-Heroes, and the classic Avengers battling the original JLA.

SUPER-SOLDIER LEADS THE FIGHT

In 1996, writer Mark Waid and artist Dave Gibbons
collaborated on *Super-Soldier* (April), an Amalgam
one-shot that featured the combination of Marvel's
Captain America with DC's Superman. When Marvel
and DC released a second wave of Amalgam specials,
super-strong Super-Soldier was one of the few characters,
along with Dark Claw and the Magnetic Men, to garner
a second special, this time entitled *Super-Soldier: Man Of
War* (June, 1997). In this second one-shot, Dave Gibbons
took a more active role, and not only drew the issue, but
also co-plotted the story with Mark Waid.

1998

NEW DAYS AND NEW KNIGHTS

By 1998, Marvel's bankruptcy issues had been settled in court, and ToyBiz, a large toy manufacturer and former subsidiary of Marvel Comics, was now running the show. And with a secure rock to stand on, Editor-in-Chief Bob Harras, along with publisher Bill Jemas, set out to bring Marvel's stable of well-known characters back out of the shadows and into the black.

Attracting new readers was at the forefront of the company's game plan. With the Heroes Return event, many classic characters saw their comic restarted and brandishing a new first issue, including Captain America and Iron Man. Making the most of these revamps, Marvel began to add a gatefold cover to many of their comics, a trend which had started at the end of the previous year. These fold-out covers were packed with information that would bring new readers up-to-speed instantly with the recent happenings and history of each comic's title character, making each issue that much more accessible to Marvel's audience.

It was this kind of thinking that led to the creation of the Marvel Knights imprint, a line of comics exploring the darker side of the Marvel Universe by the hottest name talents of the day, including writer/director Kevin Smith and artist and editor Joe Quesada.

JANUARY

FANTASTIC FOUR'S FRESH START

• *Fantastic Four #1*
Writer Scott Lobdell rearranged his X-schedule to try his hand at writing a different team of Marvel heroes in this new *Heroes Return* series. It was drawn by Alan Davis, and featured the debut of a new team of villains called the Ruined.

CAPTAIN AMERICA FIGHTS BACK

• *Captain America #1*
Writer Mark Waid began what many fans still consider to be the ultimate run on the *Captain America* title with this new series penciled by Ron Garney. This issue featured a disoriented Cap returning from the *Heroes Reborn* universe, and finding himself mysteriously in Japan. At the back of the comic was an interview with Garney, discussing the creation of his dynamic cover. Besides showcasing Cap's battle with Lady Deathstrike, this issue also saw the return of Kang the Conqueror.

Cap was floored to discover that a blockbuster movie had been made about him during his absence.

THAT ...TERTAINMENT ...MAGINE GAVE ME THE ...ION, BUT THIS ...INCHES IT.

DID A *BIG-BUDGET* ...OUT *MY LIFE* GET MADE ...MY *KNOWING* ABOUT IT? ...BEEN GONE LESS THAN A DAY.

The Avengers reunited to battle Mordred and his powerful aunt Morgan Le Fay.

George Pérez was known for his attention to detail and often drew large team spreads.

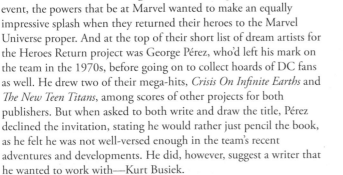

BUSIEK'S AVENGERS ASSEMBLE

"And the crowd goes wild --!"

• *The Avengers* #1

After the sales boost *The Avengers* received during the Heroes Reborn event, the powers that be at Marvel wanted to make an equally impressive splash when they returned their heroes to the Marvel Universe proper. And at the top of their short list of dream artists for the Heroes Return project was George Pérez, who'd left his mark on the team in the 1970s, before going on to collect hoards of DC fans as well. He drew two of their mega-hits, *Crisis On Infinite Earths* and *The New Teen Titans*, among scores of other projects for both publishers. But when asked to both write and draw the title, Pérez declined the invitation, stating he would rather just pencil the book, as he felt he was not well-versed enough in the team's recent adventures and developments. He did, however, suggest a writer that he wanted to work with—Kurt Busiek.

Making small waves with *Thunderbolts* and *The Untold Tales Of Spider-Man*, Busiek had recently made a successful play to scribe the newly relaunched *Iron Man* series, but he was blown away when offered the seat at the helm of *The Avengers*. He quickly jumped at the opportunity to work on his dream project with his dream collaborator. With the debut issue, he reintroduced the classic team, now consisting of members Captain America, Iron Man, Hawkeye, Scarlet Witch, Thor, Vision, Iron Man, Warbird with new members, the former New Warriors Justice and Firestar, alongside cameo appearances by nearly every single former Avenger in the team's long and varied history.

SPIDER-GIRL

What If...? #105

What if the daughter of Peter Parker and Mary Jane Watson had survived the Clone Saga? That was the question that writer Tom DeFalco and artist Ron Frenz posed in this stand-alone issue that starred the teenager May Parker. It focused on her coming to terms with the spider-powers she inherited from her father, who had now retired from a life of fighting crime to become a police scientist. Proving popular, Spider-Girl not only spun off into her own long-lasting title, but helped establish this new possible future of the Marvel Universe, referred to as the MC2 Universe.

IRON MAN REINVENTS HIMSELF

• *The Invincible Iron Man* #1

Tony Stark returned in style, opening a new branch of his company called Stark Solutions, in this new ongoing series by writer Kurt Busiek and artist Sean Chen.

X-MEN HIT THE ORIENT

• *X-Men: The Manga* #1

Under the Marvel Imports label, writer/artist Hiroshi Higuchi chronicled the black-and-white newsprint tales of the X-Men as translated by Mutsumi Masuda. This title showed the X-Men struggling against familiar foes in stories similar to that of the X-Men animated cartoon.

THOR GETS IN TOUCH WITH HIS HUMANITY

• *The Mighty Thor* #1

Thor thundered into his new ongoing series by writer Dan Jurgens and artist John Romita Jr. Thor returned to the fabled Asgard to find this once majestic home of the Norse Gods now lying in ruins. He headed back to the mortal plane only to meet Jake Olson, a human paramedic whose life would be forever intertwined with that of the thunder god.

Blade was released on August 21 and starred Wesley Snipes as Marvel's resident half-vampire/half-human, as well as actors Kris Kristofferson and Stephen Dorff. The film was directed by Stephen Norrington and written by David S. Goyer.

SPIDER-GIRL WEBS HER OWN SERIES

• *Spider-Girl* #1
Spider-Man's daughter May Parker swung to new heights in her own ongoing series. Written by Tom DeFalco and drawn by artist Pat Olliffe, she faced such threats as Crazy Eight and Mr. Nobody. The series followed a zero issue, also in October, that reprinted her origin from *What If…?* #105.

MAKING MUTANT X

Mutant X #1
Written by Howard Mackie and artist Tom Raney. Alex Summers, the mutant known as Havok, awoke in a world not his own after narrowly surviving a jet explosion. He joined ranks with strange new mutants including Marvel Woman, Bloodstorm, and the Brute.

THE INHUMAN STRUGGLE

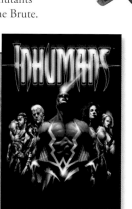

• *Inhumans* #1
In this twelve-issue Marvel Knights limited series, writer Paul Jenkins and artist Jae Lee put a realistic face on the denizens of the mystical city Attilan. It detailed the Inhumans' conflicts with the easily threatened human population and showcased the tragic lives of King Black Bolt, his Queen Medusa, and their royal court. This new title earned much critical acclaim, including the prestigious Eisner award for Best New Series.

BLACK PANTHER HITS THE STREETS

• *Black Panther* #1
Writer Christopher Priest, and artists Mark Texeira and Joe Quesada put a new spin on the life of Wakanda Warrior King, Black Panther as he ventured to the concrete jungle of New York City. This quirky Marvel Knights title was known for its innovative storytelling, including its use of titles before each scene.

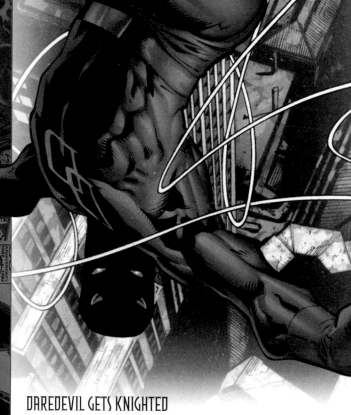

DAREDEVIL GETS KNIGHTED

"When it rains, it pours."

• *Daredevil* #1
It was a dream come true for many comic fans. Kevin Smith, the writer/director of such cult films as *Clerks, Mallrats,* and *Chasing Amy,* which had taken the comic book world by storm mostly due to their Super Hero in-jokes and *Star Wars* debates, had been hired by Marvel to write for *Daredevil,* a character whose title many thought could use a major facelift. To top it all off, fan-favorite artist Joe Quesada was not only going to draw the comic, but would also be at the helm of its creative direction as the editor.

Viewed as the flagship title for the new Marvel Knights imprint, *Daredevil,* along with fellow titles *Inhumans, Black Panther,* and *The Punisher,* was the result of Marvel outsourcing these darker titles to Joe Quesada and Jimmy Palmiotti's company, Event Comics, in an effort to create a line of books that dealt with more sophisticated and mature themes. And with Kevin Smith writing the first eight issues of this series, *Daredevil,* was an instant hit, and helped start the trend of comic companies recruiting writers from other media besides merely the close-knit world of comic books.

In this epic story, Matt Murdock saw his life turned upside down as he found himself the unwilling caretaker of a baby supposedly born by immaculate conception. He also discovered that his former love Karen Page had been diagnosed with HIV and then saw her die at the hands of Bullseye. He finally deduced it was all a ploy of a revenge-seeking Mysterio whom Daredevil had bested in a previous battle.

Matthew Murdock became a "guardian devil" when a young girl showed up at his offices and handed him her baby, telling him an angel had commanded her to do so.

At 5:26 p.m., the savior was left in the devil's care.

HEY! WAIT A SECOND!

End of Issue One

REWRITING SPIDER-MAN'S HISTORY

• *Spider-Man: Chapter One* #1
John Byrne tried his hand at writing and drawing this thirteen-part retelling of Peter Parker's past, which sparked much controversy with the fans, and is now generally considered outside the realm of canon Spider-Man continuity.

Kurt Busiek and Carlos Pacheco teamed together to tell a time-spanning adventure in the twelve-issue limited series *Avengers Forever*. They pitted various teams of heroes against Kang the Conqueror, Immortus, and the Kree Supreme Intelligence.

THE SLINGERS SURFACE

• *Slingers* #0
The young Slingers team consisted of Prodigy, Hornet, Ricochet, and Dusk. They debuted in a preview zero issue available only through *Wizard Magazine*, written by Joseph Harris with art by Adam Pollina.

MEANWHILE IN 1998...

MONICA LEWINSKY SCANDAL
After allegations of an affair with a 24-year-old White House intern, President Clinton states that he "did not have sexual relations with that woman."

US EMBASSY BOMBINGS
Simultaneous attacks hit US embassies in Dar es Salaam, Tanzania and Nairobi, Kenya. The explosions kill hundreds and are linked to terrorist group al-Qaeda.

SMOKING BAN IN CALIFORNIA
Smoking is outlawed in all Californian bars and restaurants.

GOOD FRIDAY AGREEMENT
The British and Irish Governments sign a landmark agreement, endorsed by most Northern Ireland political parties. It is a major political development in the peace process in which all parties agree to use "extensively peaceful and democratic means."

THE iMAC IS UNVEILED
Apple launches its first "all-in-one" desktop computer. The brightly colored translucent computers, inspired by gumdrops, become a design classic of all time.

GOOGLE IS BORN
Google, Inc. is founded in California by Larry Page and Sergey Brin, who are Ph.D. students at Stanford University.

MATTHEW SHEPARD KILLED IN "GAY-BASHING" ATTACK
The 21-year-old student's death brought national attention to the issue of hate crime legislation at both the state and federal levels and sparked public reflection on homophobia.

CLINTON IMPEACHED
Impeachment hearings against President Clinton for perjury and obstruction of justice, begin over claims he lied about his sexual relationship with White House intern Monica Lewinsky.

INDIA GOES NUCLEAR
India resumes nuclear testing on May 12, violating a worldwide ban on nuclear testing.

ARKANSAS SCHOOL MASSACRE
Two young boys kill five people at an Arkansas middle school after a hoax fire alarm.

AND AT THE MOVIES...
Saving Private Ryan, from the opening visceral scenes of the D-Day landings, Steven Spielberg brings an intensity missing from earlier war films; A Bug's Life, Pixar's inspired recreation of The Seven Samurai with a misfit ant recruiting a gang of insect mercenaries to defend his colony from marauding grasshoppers; Ring, Japanese horror, reliant on sound and atmosphere, about a cursed videotape that kills anyone who watches it.

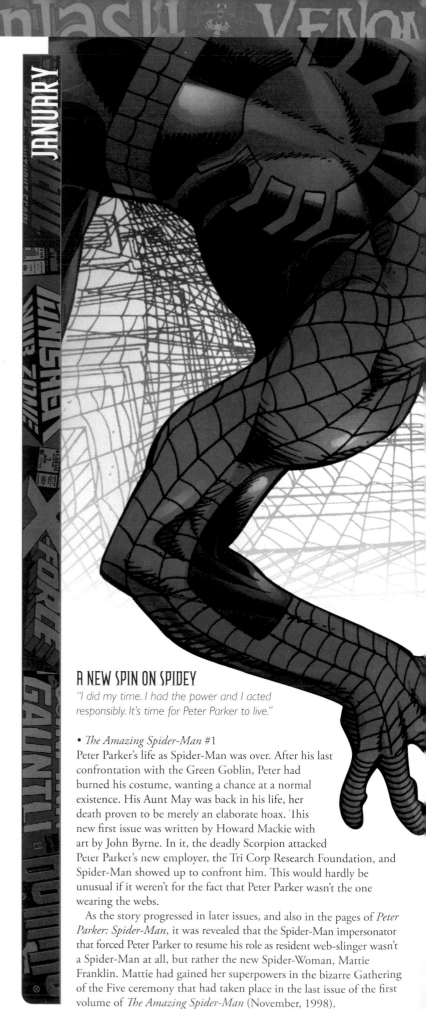

1999

SEEING WHAT WOULD STICK

Marvel was throwing everything against the wall. After the successful revamps of most of their major iconic characters, Marvel had still been unable to find a stable foothold for Spider-Man, as most fans were still put off a bit from the elaborate continuity originating in the Clone Saga. As the maxi-series *Spider-Man: Chapter One* continued to instigate much debate with the fans, while still becoming a modest success, Marvel decided to try their hand at restarting Spider-Man's monthly comics, weeding the many books down to a manageable two main titles— *The Amazing Spider-Man* and *Peter Parker: Spider-Man*. All in all, despite John Byrne and company's best efforts, Spider-Man still wouldn't find his footing until the arrival of J. Michael Staczynski in 2001.

The year 1999 also saw other concepts being tossed up for the fans to judge. A new Black Widow debuted in the pages of *Inhumans*, The New Warriors were granted another chance at a monthly comic, and the untold past of the X-Men was explored in *X-Men: The Hidden Years*, but none of these ideas really took a hold of the readers. However, things were changing, and an editorial shuffle was about to take place, one that would see a familiar face be promoted to Editor-In-Chief the following year.

A NEW SPIN ON SPIDEY

"I did my time. I had the power and I acted responsibly. It's time for Peter Parker to live."

• *The Amazing Spider-Man* #1
Peter Parker's life as Spider-Man was over. After his last confrontation with the Green Goblin, Peter had burned his costume, wanting a chance at a normal existence. His Aunt May was back in his life, her death proven to be merely an elaborate hoax. This new first issue was written by Howard Mackie with art by John Byrne. In it, the deadly Scorpion attacked Peter Parker's new employer, the Tri Corp Research Foundation, and Spider-Man showed up to confront him. This would hardly be unusual if it weren't for the fact that Peter Parker wasn't the one wearing the webs.

As the story progressed in later issues, and also in the pages of *Peter Parker: Spider-Man*, it was revealed that the Spider-Man impersonator that forced Peter Parker to resume his role as resident web-slinger wasn't a Spider-Man at all, but rather the new Spider-Woman, Mattie Franklin. Mattie had gained her superpowers in the bizarre Gathering of the Five ceremony that had taken place in the last issue of the first volume of *The Amazing Spider-Man* (November, 1998).

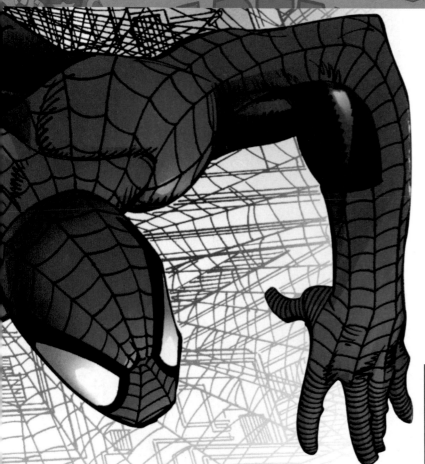

FEBRUARY

GAMBIT GOES MONTHLY

• *Gambit* #1

Scribe Fabian Nicieza, along with penciller Steve Skroce, chronicled Gambit's first ongoing series. They had him pilfering an ancient tomb guarded with the latest technology, battling the X-Cutioner, and charming a score of ladies, including his longtime flame, fellow X-Men member Rogue.

MARCH

THE NEW BLACK WIDOW

• *Inhumans* #5

As writer Paul Jenkins and artist Jae Lee continued their award-winning Marvel Knights limited series, they introduced Yelena Belova, the second Soviet super spy to go by the moniker Black Widow. The story followed Belova as she arranged to undermine the Inhumans' vaunted security system.

JANUARY

   Besides launching this new storyline, and featuring an impressive roster of guest stars, including the Fantastic Four, the Avengers and Daredevil, this introductory issue also featured a wrap-around, gatefold cover, a back-up story drawn by Rafael Kayanan, and an extra comic story written and drawn by Byrne that detailed Peter Parker's many powers, and harkened back to the Stan Lee and Steve Ditko bonus stories that appeared as early as the first Spider-Man annual of 1964.

PETER PARKER CAN'T LOSE

• *Peter Parker: Spider-Man* #1

Peter Parker tried to stay retired as his replacement tackled a new foe called the Ranger in this story written by Howard Mackie with art by John Romita Jr. This issue also featured a backup story from Peter's childhood, and Romita Jr. model sheets that artists could use as reference.

X MARKS THE SPOT

• *Earth X* #0

After his success detailing the future of the DC Universe in his epic painted miniseries *Kingdom Come*, Alex Ross took a turn playing fortune-teller for the Marvel stable of heroes. He wrote this fourteen-part saga alongside Jim Krueger, with pencils by John Paul Leon. Ross painted each lavish cover himself and told this epic tale through the eyes of Machine Man as he took the place of the Watcher, recording the future of the Marvel Universe. This was a world where everyone had superpowers, and an aged Captain America fought alongside his partner Redwing against the forces of the brainless parasites known as HYDRA.

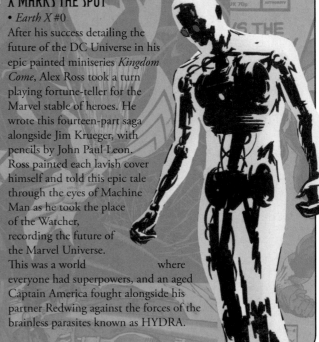

APRIL

THE HULK UNLEASHED

• *Hulk #1*
Bruce Banner took to the road in an attempt to escape his past in this new series by writer John Byrne and artist Ron Garney. This debut issue saw Banner arrive in the small town of Faulkner and rent a vacant room. Suffering from nightmares, Bruce awoke to discover that the town had almost destroyed as the Hulk refused to give Banner a moment's peace.

MAY

MARVEL SUPER HERO ISLAND

When the Universal Studios theme park in Orlando, Florida opened up a sister park called Universal's Islands of Adventure, Marvelites young and old got the chance to walk into the pages of their favorite comic books at Marvel Super Hero Island, one of the five new islands that made up the park. The Marvel Island included such rides as the Incredible Hulk Coaster, Doctor Doom's Fearfall, the scrambler-like Storm Force Accelatron, and perhaps the gem of the bunch, the Amazing Adventures of Spider-Man, a 3-D romp through the rooftops that began in the heart of the *Daily Bugle* itself.

In Hulk #1, *Bruce Banner spent his days trying to repair the damage that the Hulk caused at night.*

JUNE

BLACK WIDOW VS. BLACK WIDOW

• *Black Widow #1*
Devin Grayson, a writer who had demonstrated her ability to craft strong women a few years earlier at the helm of DC's *Catwoman*, made the switch to Marvel in order to orchestrate the first Black Widow miniseries alongside artist J.G. Jones. This new three-issue series pitted Yelena Belova, the new cutthroat heir to the Black Widow title who'd debuted a few months prior in the pages of *Inhumans*, against Natasha Romanov, the defender and originator of the Black Widow name. It saw the two femme fatales battling it out over an experimental military drug that reduced its users into frenzied, feral madmen.

THE NEWER WARRIORS

The New Warriors #1

In an attempt to garner the same warm reception they received at the decade's start, the New Warriors were given a new ongoing series by writer Jay Faerber and penciler Steve Scott, starring a few familiar faces, including Speedball, Nova, and Namorita.

The New Warriors only lasted eleven issues, perhaps due to the absence of popular members like Firestar and Night Thrasher.

ORIGINS OF THE X-MEN

• *X-Men: Children Of The Atom #1*

Feeling that the legacy of the X-Men lacked a true origin story, writer Joe Casey joined with pencillers Steve Rude, Paul Smith, Essad Ribic, and Michael Ryan to create this six-part miniseries in the same vein as the hit *Batman: Year One* saga, with which writer Frank Miller and artist David Mazzucchelli had taken the comic world by storm in the 1980s. The tragic events of the school shooting in Columbine, Colorado, that occurred while Casey was crafting the book's second issue affected the tone of the series, which was rife with race metaphors and coming-of-age drama.

Chronicling Professor X's initial recruitment of the X-Men, Children of the Atom *introduced Angel as a shadowy crime fighter.*

THE X-MEN'S LOST ADVENTURES

• *X-Men: The Hidden Years #1*

In 1970, with the arrival of the 67th issue of the original *X-Men* comic, the title began to reprint old material, and wouldn't be revitalized until the *Giant-Size X-Men* special of 1975 that launched the comic to new heights of popularity. This left fans to wonder what the originals were up to in all that time, a question that writer/artist John Byrne decided to answer in this new ongoing series. Set in those mysterious in-between years, decades-old loose ends were tied up as the X-Men faced teenaged infighting, journeys to the Savage Land, and even a rematch bout with Magneto.

"I DON'T UNDERSTAND WHY THEY ARE HATED FOR BEING GOOD."

"THEY ARE HATED BECAUSE THEY HAVE WHAT OTHERS DO NOT.

"POWER. DISTINCTION. PURPOSE.

BACK AND FORTH

Jim Krueger and Alex Ross, the writing team who later collaborated on DC's *Justice* miniseries, kicked off their epic fourteen-part *Earth X* saga with a special #0 issue in March, 1999, that explained just how robot Machine Man became the eyes and ears for the blind Uatu the Watcher. Just as each issue of the ensuing series revealed a bit of the future of the Marvel Universe, it also delved back into Marvel's rich history, as shown in this double-page splash image by interior artist John Paul Leon. Ross himself painted the series' covers, as well as those of its two sequel series, *Universe X* and *Paradise X*, after *Earth X* proved to be a hit with the readers.

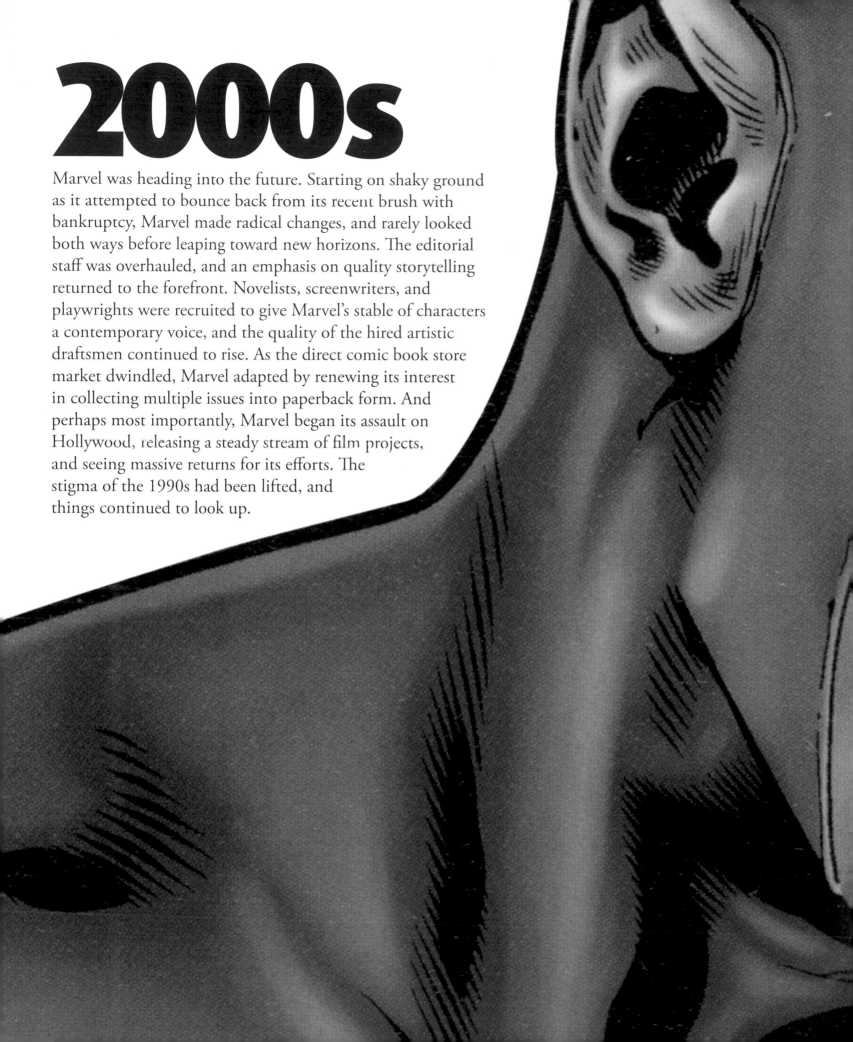

2000s

Marvel was heading into the future. Starting on shaky ground as it attempted to bounce back from its recent brush with bankruptcy, Marvel made radical changes, and rarely looked both ways before leaping toward new horizons. The editorial staff was overhauled, and an emphasis on quality storytelling returned to the forefront. Novelists, screenwriters, and playwrights were recruited to give Marvel's stable of characters a contemporary voice, and the quality of the hired artistic draftsmen continued to rise. As the direct comic book store market dwindled, Marvel adapted by renewing its interest in collecting multiple issues into paperback form. And perhaps most importantly, Marvel began its assault on Hollywood, releasing a steady stream of film projects, and seeing massive returns for its efforts. The stigma of the 1990s had been lifted, and things continued to look up.

WHAT'S HAPPENED TO YOU...? YOU SHOULDN'T HAVE STAYED THIS WAY—YOU SHOULD'VE EVOLVED BY NOW.

2000
NEW KIDS IN TOWN

Bill Jemas became the new President of Marvel Comics and he quickly promoted Joe Quesada—a superstar comic artist who had done wonders in recent years with his Marvel Knights imprint—into the position of Editor-in-Chief. They seemed to have the magic touch. Through a combination of brainstorming and butting heads, these two set out to recreate Marvel Comics into the thriving company that it is today.

And they didn't do it quietly. Among many of the changes Quesada and Jemas brought about was hiring new editors like Axel Alonso and Stuart Moore, both formerly of DC/Vertigo Comics, who applied their success and connections to their new Marvel assignments. Quesada also created a few editorial mandates, instructing his staff to stop bringing characters back to life in order to up the drama and consequence when they die in the first place, as well as to cease the constant nostalgia and self-referential elements that seemed to plague a majority of Marvel's books at the time.

The Marvel Knights line continued its success, Jemas and Quesada went one better, and created the Ultimate imprint—a long-lasting line of blockbuster comics that would remain at the top of the sales charts for years.

APRIL

Having witnessed his family die before his eyes as innocent bystanders caught in the crossfire of a mob dispute, Frank Castle set off down a lonely path as the Punisher. Writer Garth Ennis, no stranger to chronicling the adventures of cut-throat anti-heroes after writing the series Hitman for DC Comics, was drawn to Punisher due to the character's twisted nature as the only serial killer who was also a Super Hero.

WELCOMING THE PUNISHER BACK

"Gunfight in a morgue, rule one: don't hide behind the thin guy."

• The Punisher #1
The team of writer Garth Ennis and artist Steve Dillon, best known for their award-winning series *Preacher* for DC/Vertigo Comics, took a shot at the Punisher in this twelve-issue series that was then followed up by an ongoing volume. With the last Marvel Knights *Punisher* miniseries taking more of a supernatural approach to Frank Castle's obsessive war on crime, Ennis returned the Punisher to his roots, reinstating him as a near-emotionless killing machine in this bloody black comedy adventure that instantly won over the readers. In fact, the first issue of this new Punisher series debuted fifth in sales out of all the comics released that month, only bested by four X-Men titles.

As the Punisher waged a gory war on mob boss Ma Gnucci, reducing her to a quadriplegic before later killing her altogether, he was pursued by the hapless Detective Soap, a down-on-his-luck cop given the near-impossible task of taking the Punisher in for his crimes. Attempting to ignore a supporting cast of neighbors living in his rundown apartment building, including the obscenely obese Mr. Bumpo, and the overly excited Spacker Dave, the Punisher set up a life for himself under the transparent alias of John Smith.

As the series progressed, the Punisher took on the overly tough and aloof assassin the Russian, bested Daredevil, and became the inspiration for a league of killers called the Vigilante Squad, a murderous group that Frank Castle put an end to in true Punisher fashion.

After the initial twelve-issue series, Ennis and Dillon paired up again on Punisher's ongoing series, with Dillon leaving the title after seven issues. Ennis himself took a brief hiatus at the same time, before returning to the comic with issue thirteen and staying until its conclusion at issue #37.

JULY

THE X-MEN COME TO LIFE

• X-Men: The Movie
In July, the X-Men exploded into theaters. A comic-book adaptation was published to coincide with the movie release and carried a cover date of September. Featuring a script by Ralph Macchio, with pencils by Anthony Williams and inks by Andy Lanning, it told the story of Wolverine and Rogue's first meeting with Charles Xavier's X-Men. This first X-Men feature film was directed by Bryan Singer, with a screenplay by David Hayter and Tom DeSanto, and starred Patrick Stewart as Professor X, Halle Berry as Storm, Ian McKellen as Magneto, James Marsden as Cyclops, Famke Janssen as Jean Grey, Anna Paquin as Rogue, and Hugh Jackman as Wolverine.

BEFORE THE THING

• Before The Fantastic 4: Ben Grimm And Logan #1
Beginning in July, this three-issue miniseries, written by Larry Hama and with art by Kaare Andrews, detailed an early team-up of the Thing and Wolverine, before they each earned their respective monikers, as the two participated in a government mission together. It also featured Carol Danvers, the heroine who would later become Ms. Marvel, as well as an appearance by the future Black Widow.

MAY

GENERAL RYKER

• The Incredible Hulk #14
Hulk was once again plagued by the military thanks to writer Paul Jenkins and artist Ron Garney. As Bruce Banner mourned his wife, General Ryker, a military mastermind who wanted to recreate the Hulk, slowly unearthed his trail.

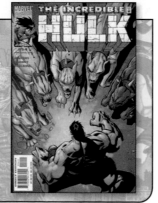

AUGUST

MARVEL BOY MAKES THE SCENE

• Marvel Boy #1
Writer Grant Morrison and artist J.G. Jones introduced a new Marvel Boy in this six-issue Marvel Knights miniseries, as the space-faring anti-establishment alien Kree adventurer crash-landed on Earth and found himself the captive of the villainous Dr. Midas.

THE SECRET OF THE SENTRY'S SUCCESS

"The other people on the train… you're making them nervous now… Maybe it's because you look like hell. Or maybe it's because now that you're beginning to remember… you're no longer casting a shadow."

• *The Sentry* #1

Some felt it was a big con, while others saw it as an inspired marketing strategy. The team of writer Paul Jenkins and artist Jae Lee had already proven themselves with their award-winning earlier collaboration on the *Inhumans* series for the Marvel Knights imprint. So, when they re-teamed on a new limited series entitled *The Sentry*, Editor-in-Chief Joe Quesada knew he was sitting on a winner. The only real question was how to get the public as excited about this brand new character as he was.

So Quesada called *Wizard* magazine. Long established as the go-to guide for comic teasers and inside scoops, *Wizard* was covering new and upcoming comic releases for an ever-increasing audience. But Quesada didn't want a simple plug, or even an in-depth article. He wanted to try something different.

Inspired by the Orson Welles *War of the Worlds* radio hoax from 1938, Quesada had *Wizard* run a fake obituary for a fictional comic book artist named Artie Rosen. Later, a follow-up article was printed, stating that a secret cache of Rosen's artwork had been discovered by his family, and included drawings of the hero the Sentry, a tormented character that Stan Lee and Rosen had created prior to *Fantastic Four* #1, the comic that was recognized as kicking off the Marvel era.

With this fictional groundwork properly laid, the Sentry's five-issue miniseries was released, along with five tie-in one-shot specials, to the now eagerly anticipatory masses, showcasing the hero's fight with the dark half of his personality, an entity known as the Void.

The Sentry battled the Void through the pages of his own title. He continued the fight through a series of specials, drawn by Phil Winslade, Mark Texeira, Rick Leonardi, and Bill Sienkiewicz, as the heroes of the Marvel Universe began to slowly remember him.

BEFORE MR. FANTASTIC

• *Before The Fantastic 4: Reed Richards* #1

Continuing the trilogy of pre-Fantastic Four adventures, the man who would become Mr. Fantastic starred in a three-issue miniseries. Courtesy of writer Peter David and artist Duncan Fergredo, it was an Indiana Jones-like adventure, opposite Victor Von Doom.

PATSY WALKER GOES TO HELLCAT

• *Hellcat* #1

Longtime Marvel mainstay Patsy Walker stole a brief moment in the sun in this three-issue miniseries by writer Steve Englehart and artist Norm Breyfogle. It delved into Pasty's past as a romance comics star, and her present, fighting the evil sorcerer Dormammu as Hellcat.

SPIDER-MAN REACHES THE ULTIMATE

"Great things are going to happen to you and your life, Peter. Great things. And with that will come great responsibility."

• *Ultimate Spider-Man #1*
It had been attempted before, and had failed miserably. There was just no re-imagining Spider-Man's origin story. The fans liked him the way he was, and projects that tweaked, revamped, or dramatically altered Peter Parker's past, like John Byrne's *Spider-Man: Chapter One* limited series, had fallen by the wayside and were forgotten almost as soon as they were created. So, everyone said it couldn't be done.

But Bill Jemas and Joe Quesada weren't about to believe that for a second. With Quesada ordering a new forward-looking policy, rather than falling back on what had been done in the past, Jemas decided to recreate a Spider-Man that would capture the energy and vitality of today's youth, and would speak to a contemporary audience, rather than one young in the 1960s. To reach that goal, he hired indy-comic rising star Brian Michael Bendis to co-write the series with him,

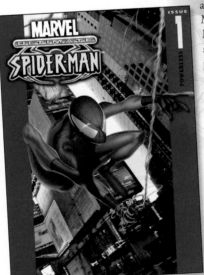

and popular Spider-Man veteran artist Mark Bagley to serve as the book's penciller. Soon, *Ultimate Spider-Man* was released, stunning the masses and sparking the red-hot fire that would launch an entire line of comics based in this newly formed Ultimate universe's reality.

After the initial origin arc, which saw Peter Parker first don his webs when inspired by the death of his uncle Ben, Bendis took the writing chores over completely. He slowly departed from the basic storyline that Stan Lee and Steve Ditko had crafted all those years ago, and headed in a brave new direction to create Marvel's newest consistent best-seller. In this new universe, Peter Parker was reborn as a troubled teenager, balancing his life as a website technician for the *Daily Bugle*, typical high school angst, and tumultuous friendships with Gwen Stacy, Harry Osborn (Hobgoblin), and even Eddie Brock (Venom).

The Peter Parker that starred in Ultimate Spider-Man *wasn't an adult, but a struggling high school student who quickly confided his secret identity to his girlfriend, Mary Jane Watson.*

Ⓜ *X-Men: Evolution*, an animated series, debuted on Kids WB on November 4th. It lasted four seasons, and amassed fifty-two episodes. Dealing with core X-Men members Professor X, Wolverine, Jean Grey, Cyclops, Storm, Nightcrawler, Rogue, and Shadowcat, *X-Men: Evolution* also debuted new member Spyke.

A STORM COMING

• *Before The Fantastic 4: The Storms #1*
Written by Terry Kavanagh and drawn by Charlie Adlard, this final three-issue installment of stories reaching into the Fantastic Four's past detailed an early adventure of siblings Johnny and Sue Storm as they uncovered the secret of an ancient amulet.

MEANWHILE IN 2000...

Y2K
The new millennium begins and the world braces itself for computer havoc when computers hit January 1, 2000, but the feared havoc does not materialize.

THE FIRST FIRST-LADY SENATOR
Hillary Clinton becomes the first First Lady to win office when she is elected to the US Senate.

GEORGE W. BUSH ELECTED PRESIDENT
The Florida presidential recount is halted and so victory goes to George W. Bush.

CIVIL UNION FOR SAME-SEX COUPLES
The state of Vermont legalizes civil union for same-sex couples.

REFORMISTS IN IRAN
Reformists win control of the Iranian parliament for the first time since the 1979 Islamic revolution.

ANTI-GLOBALIZATION PROTESTS TURN VIOLENT
The era of globalization is accompanied by regular anti-globalization demonstrations. Violence breaks out during protests at the IMF and World Bank summits in Prague.

WORLDWIDE COMPUTER DISRUPTION
The "I love you" virus wreaks havoc on computers.

DIGITAL MOVIE DISTRIBUTION
The short film 405 is the first movie to be distributed on the Internet.

THE HUMAN GENOME DECIPHERED
A working draft of the genome (DNA) is published as part of the Human Genome Project.

FIRST DOUBLE ARM OP
A team of international surgeons conduct the first double arm transplant in France in a seventeen-hour operation.

NEW GALLERY FOR MODERN ART
The Tate Modern gallery opens in London in a former power station on the River Thames.

AND AT THE MOVIES...
X-Men, when embittered mutant Magneto declares war on humanity, the X-Men are charged with saving the world in this story of Marvel's popular team; Gladiator, Hollywood's first classical epic for thirty years tells the story of Maximus, an exiled Roman General turned gladiator, played by Russell Crowe; Crouching Tiger, Hidden Dragon, Ang Lee's sweeping, romantic, gravity-defying take on the martial arts genre; Mission: Impossible II, Tom Cruise reprises his role as Ethan Hunt, trying to stop a virus being released by a former agent.

THIS BLADE I AM HOLDING.
I HAVE DIED AT THE END OF IT.

2001
THE HERO IS BACK

It was a whole new ballgame. Now firmly behind the wheel as Marvel's Editor-in-Chief, Joe Quesada brought to mainstream Marvel all he had learned in the Marvel Knights corner of the universe. Big-name creators and innovative storytelling were at the forefront of his new direction.
Several of the company's icons were about to get a facelift, and not through gimmicky, ad-driven events, but through solid writing and art, with the emphasis firmly on character development. Established pros like Grant Morrison and Peter Milligan mixed with relative newcomers like Brian Michael Bendis and Judd Winick. What's more, Quesada had learned from movie writer and director Kevin Smith's run on *Daredevil* that looking outside the comic book writer pool to other media had its rewards, so he recruited creator of TV's *Babylon 5*, J. Michael Straczynski, who had recently made a splash with Top Cow's *Rising Stars* comic series, to take over the writing on Spider-Man's flagship title. Marvel's characters were returning to their roots, and good stories were once again at the forefront.

BLACK WIDOW TIMES TWO
• *Black Widow* #1
Devin Grayson returned to scribe the adventures of Natasha Romanov and her would-be successor Yelena Belova, this time joined by co-writer Greg Rucka and painter Scott Hampton. This three-issue miniseries saw the two Black Widows switch identities.

THE ULTIMATE X-MEN EXPLODE
"No wonder we call ourselves Homo Superior. Any species this stupid deserves its little free-fall down the food chain."

• *Ultimate X-Men* #1
Looking to repeat the success of *Ultimate Spider-Man* in 2000, the second major title of this alternate universe was crafted by esteemed writer Mark Millar along with the famed Kubert brothers, Andy and Adam, taking turns at the drawing table. Starting in a fresh new universe with no back-story for new readers to sift through, Millar envisioned the X-Men as teenagers, fighting for a world that fears and hates them, much as writers Stan Lee and Chris Claremont had done before him.
The core team was made up of Marvel Girl, Cyclops, Beast, Storm, and Colossus, but by the second issue's end, new recruits Iceman and Wolverine had already been added to their ranks.
In a world where the US government had created giant Sentinel robots to rid the Earth of mutantkind, the Ultimate X-Men wore black leather uniforms that shielded their mutant physiology from the Sentinel's detection equipment, and rescued innocent mutants from annihilation at the robots' gigantic hands. Not content at mere survival, the mutant terrorist Magneto, along with his villainous Brotherhood, set out to conquer the nation altogether, reprogramming the Sentinels to attack humans instead of mutants. After a violent battle on the lawn of the White House, the X-Men prevailed, winning worldwide favor and seemingly killing Magneto.
As the series progressed further, the X-Men's roster and creative teams changed a few times, but the book remained a solid seller for Marvel, even spawning a crossover with the Ultimate Universe equivalent of the Avengers in a miniseries entitled *Ultimate War*.

Much like in the original X-Men comics of the 1960s, Henry McCoy, the X-Men's Beast, had a human look when he first debuted in the pages of Ultimate X-Men. *And much like his mainstream Marvel Universe counterpart, Beast soon developed a familiar blue hue.*

FEBRUARY

THE DEATH OF COLOSSUS
• *Uncanny X-Men #390*
Beast was elated to find a cure for the Legacy Virus that had been killing mutants for the last few years. However, in order to be released into the air where it could harmlessly cure all those infected, the antivirus had to be injected into a single carrier, causing that person's death. In a story by Scott Lobdell with art by Salvador Larroca, Colossus valiantly sacrificed himself so that mutantkind would survive.

MARCH

BLINKING IN
• *Blink #1*
Written by Scott Lobdell and Judd Winick with pencils by Trevor McCarthy, the four-issue *Blink* miniseries chronicled the teleporting mutant Blink's travels as she left the Age of Apocalypse, journeyed to the Negative Zone, and discovered the dimension-hopping Exiles.

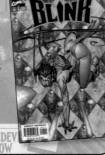

MAY

BENDIS' DAREDEVIL
• *Daredevil #16*
Writer Brian Michael Bendis began his impressive run on the *Daredevil* title with a small character-driven four-part story, teaming with his old friend David Mack. Mack had just written the previous story line, which debuted the character Echo, and his partnership with Bendis served as a great transition to Bendis' monumental fling with the Man Without Fear. Very early in his run, Bendis outed Daredevil's secret identity to the press, exposing Matt Murdock to a different kind of danger. Bendis would go on to have Daredevil declare himself Kingpin, get married, and, most shockingly of all, be sent to prison for his illegal vigilante acts.

MAY

MARVEL ABANDONS THE COMICS CODE
Fearing that the Comics Code Authority rating system misled the public into believing all comics were merely for children, Joe Quesada finally ended Marvel's longstanding relationship with the Code. Instead he implemented a new ratings system similar to that of the Motion Picture Association.

JUNE

STRACZYNSKI'S SPIDEY
• *The Amazing Spider-Man #30*
Peter Parker had always thought he had problems in the past, but as it turned out, the web-slinger hadn't seen anything yet. TV creator J. Michael Straczynski and comics legend John Romita Jr. not only exposed Spider-Man to a horde of mystical foes, they also introduced the idea that Parker's origin may not be as accidental as he had thought, but rather a predestined event brought on by totemistic animal forces—in Peter's case, the spirit and abilities of a spider. Peter was also introduced to Ezekiel, his advisor in this unknown realm, who greedily sought the kind of power that Peter had amassed naturally.

Just as there was a long line of animal-powered warriors like Spidey, so were there those who fed off them. Morlun was one such energy vampire who happened to have Spider-Man right in his glowing red sights.

87

X-MEN BECOMES NEW X-MEN

"Forget your dental practice. Your future lies in genocide.'"

• *New X-Men #114*
Despite the success and mainstream attention from the blockbuster *X-Men* movie of the previous summer, the mainstream *X-Men* comics themselves seemed to lack the innovation and creative direction that had given the team such staying power. That all changed when respected writer Grant Morrison and talented artist Frank Quitely took center stage. Morrison was no stranger to reinvigorating franchises, having relaunched the Justice League a few years prior for DC Comics in 1997's *JLA*. With that series, Morrison had stripped the title down to its bare essence and examined what made it popular and exciting in the first place. This, too, was his approach when brought on board for the X-Men.

Renaming the *X-Men* comic *New X-Men*, Morrison ignored the convoluted plot threads that had seemed to plague the X-family of books for years, and instead focused on the original idea of a mutant school run out of Charles Xavier's mansion. The roster was simplified to focus on the mainstay stars of the book: Cyclops, Beast, Jean Grey, Wolverine, and the classic former villain Emma Frost (aka the White Queen), who was thrown in for a touch of new blood and diversity. The characters all received a visual makeover as well, now wearing black leather uniforms, similar to the costumes seen in the feature film. This trend would be carried over to the other X titles of the time, including *X-Treme X-Men* and *Uncanny X-Men*. Morrison also introduced a new villain for the team, Cassandra Nova, a bodiless parasite and the evil twin of Xavier, who had a vendetta toward mutants and humans alike.

Used to battling traditional giant Sentinels, the X-Men were unprepared to face Cassandra Nova's army of Wild Sentinels. These self-replicating robots used spare parts to evolve into more effective forms, allowing Nova to destroy the mutant nation of Genosha.

X-FORCE OVERHAUL

• *X-Force #116*
X-Force, an X-Men spinoff, received a makeover in July thanks to writer Peter Milligan and artist Mike Allred. A mixture of dark comedy and underground heroics, *X-Force* received critical acclaim, but a mixed reaction from fans. This all-new X-Force roster included the teleporting U-Go Girl, the alienated Orphan, the easily angered Anarchist, the exhaustively trendy Phat, the brutal bookworm Vivisector, and Doop—an alien sidekick.

DAREDEVIL'S TRUE COLORS

• *Daredevil: Yellow #1*
The creative team of writer Jeph Loeb and artist Tim Sale, known for their best-selling DC Comics miniseries *Batman: The Long Halloween* and *Batman: Dark Victory*, examined the early life of some of Marvel's iconic characters. First they tackled Daredevil in this six-issue miniseries, beginning in August, which focused on Matthew Murdock's time in his original yellow costume, and his relationship with Karen Page.

ENTER EXILES

• *Exiles #1*
Writer Judd Winick and artist Mike McKone told the story of a familiar band of dimension-hopping mutant heroes, including Sabretooth and Morph, as they traveled to different timelines to mend ripples in the time stream.

ELEKTRA'S SECOND CHANCE

• *Elektra #1*
The favorite female assassin of the Marvel Universe returned for her second ongoing series in September thanks to writer Brian Michael Bendis and artist Chuck Austen. Elektra faced off against the organizations of HYDRA and SHIELD, among other takers, before the new creative team of writer Greg Rucka and artist Carlo Pagulayan eventually took over.

WOLVERINE'S PAST REVEALED

"What's the matter, Jamey-Boy… forget where you came from?"

• *Origin #1*
Ever since his debut in the 1970s, Wolverine had been a character whose past was shrouded in mystery. But after the success of the first X-Men feature film, Editor-in-Chief Joe Quesada realized that sooner or later, the film franchise was going to want to examine Wolverine's enigmatic past. Rather than adapting what Hollywood envisioned for Logan's beginnings, Quesada, along with writer Bill Jemas, scripter Paul Jenkins, and artist Andy Kubert, decided to beat them to it with *Origin*, a six-issue miniseries, beginning in October, which told the story of Wolverine's early years. And sure enough eight years after *Origin*, Hollywood will release its own version with *X-Men Origins: Wolverine*.

After a couple of red herrings were planted to keep the fans guessing, Wolverine's real identity was revealed as James Howlett, the son of a self-made millionaire and his depressed wife. The story chronicled James' early life. A sickly child, his mutant powers manifested themselves when he witnessed his father's death at the hands of their groundskeeper, Logan, and his son, a boy known only as Dog. Thrown out by his family, James traveled to a remote part of Canada with his childhood sweetheart, Rose. Adopting the name Logan, James grew to manhood, but with little recollection of what had passed. When Dog reentered their lives, James accidentally killed Rose during the resulting combat. James then retreated into the woods away from society, and Wolverine was truly born.

Rose and James shared a life of privilege, while Dog had to endure a hard existence with an abusive alcoholic father. This made the troubled boy bitter and vengeful.

INTRODUCING ALIAS

• *Alias #1*
The herald to the start of Marvel's adult imprint, MAX, *Alias* was the first of a new comic series that was targeted specifically for a mature audience. Written by Brian Michael Bendis and featuring the art of Michael Gaydos and covers by David Mack, *Alias* explored the life of cynical private investigator Jessica Jones, who just happened to be a former Super Hero named Jewel. Armed with a realistic approach to the fantastic, the series chronicled Jessica's adventures as she protected Captain America's secret identity, dated and fell in love with Luke Cage, and even faced her past demons in the form of the villainous Purple Man—who had brainwashed her when she was known as Jewel.

THE BLACK ISSUE

• *The Amazing Spider-Man #36*
Writer J. Michael Straczynski and penciller John Romita Jr. paid tribute to those who died during the real-life terror attacks on the World Trade Center on September 11. A full-page splash saw "real life" heroes standing in front of Marvel Super Heroes.

MEANWHILE IN 2001...

PRESIDENT BUSH SWORN IN
George W. Bush succeeds Bill Clinton and becomes 43rd President of the US.

9/11
Al-Qaeda terrorists hi-jack planes and destroy the World Trade Center, attack the Pentagon, and crash in Pennsylvania killing more than 3,000 people.

BUSH: "WAR ON TERROR"
President Bush declares that the US is at war against terror after the 9/11 attacks on the US.

ANTHRAX ATTACKS
Letters containing anthrax are posted to media offices and two US senators, killing five people.

2001 CINCINNATI RIOTS
African-American Timothy Thomas is shot dead by a police officer in Cincinnati. The event sparks three days of riots in the city.

OPERATION "ENDURING FREEDOM"
As part of the War on Terror, US and UK forces invade Afghanistan to overthrow the Taliban.

9/11 BENEFIT CONCERTS
The Concert for New York City *and the* United We Stand *concert in Washington take place to pay tribute to the victims and heroes of the 9/11 terrorist attacks.*

THE USA PATRIOT ACT
The USA PATRIOT—Uniting and Strengthening America by Providing the Appropriate Tools to Intercept and Obstruct Terrorism—Act becomes law to strengthen the US's armory in the War on Terror, but sparks debate on civil liberties.

FIRST "SPACE TOURIST"
Multimillionaire Dennis Tito is the first person to pay for his ticket to travel to outer space.

CONTROVERSY OVER STEM CELL RESEARCH
Embryos are created for the harvest of stem cells, sparking strong ethical debate.

A PATENT FOR GOOGLE
Google is awarded a patent for the search algorithm used by its search engine.

WIKIPEDIA.ORG
The free, online encyclopedia goes live, and transforms the way people share information.

AND AT THE MOVIES...
Spirited Away, Hayao Miyazaki's fantastical anime about a sullen girl lost in the spirit world who must find her way back to reality; Lord of the Rings: The Fellowship of the Ring, *director Peter Jackson's special effects-laden tale of Hobbit Frodo's epic quest, adapted from J.R.R. Tolkien's classic fantasy;* Shrek, *DreamWorks hits the big time in this irresistibly witty animation about a giant green monster and his donkey friend.*

New X-Men Annual *(2001)*
Writer Grant Morrison and artist Leinil Francis Yu helped launch a new approach to Super Hero storytelling, turning the comics world on end, literally. Dubbed "Marvelscope," by Editor-in-Chief Joe Quesada, this extra-sized issue had to be held on its side in order to be read, creating a widescreen, cinematic effect for its readers. This comic also marked the first appearance of Xorn, a new X-Men member. Xorn later went insane, and attacked the team who had treated him like family.

2002
HITTING THEIR STRIDE

Marvel seemed to have it figured out. The plan of attracting big name creators to big name projects had slipped into cruise control. As if a continuation of the last two years, 2002 stayed the course—and fans stuck around for the ride.

Continuing the success of the Ultimate titles, *The Ultimates* did not disappoint fans, or the Marvel sales division. Continuing the trend of modern, cinematic storytelling, writer Bruce Jones took over *The Incredible Hulk*, breathing new life into the title that it hadn't seen since Peter David's innovative rollercoaster scripts. Continuing the string of X-Men related revamps, *Cable, Deadpool,* and *X-Force* all underwent title changes in an attempt to attract the multitudes of readers who jumped onboard when *X-Men* began calling itself *New X-Men*. As *Spider-Man: Blue* continued the string of colorful hits by Jeph Loeb and Tim Sale, Captain America continued to fight for his country in the pages of his own new title. And continuing the idea of big-budget Marvel movie blockbusters, *Spider-Man* hit theaters, finally giving everyone's favorite wall-crawler a movie worthy of his iconic status. Even the toy company ToyBiz found success with their new action figure line called Marvel Legends.

JANUARY

JONES' HULK

"And what're you runnin' from… mister…?"
"Myself."

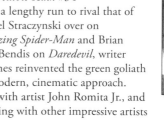

• *The Incredible Hulk* #34
Creating a lengthy run to rival that of J. Michael Straczynski over on *The Amazing Spider-Man* and Brian Michael Bendis on *Daredevil*, writer Bruce Jones reinvented the green goliath with a modern, cinematic approach. Starting with artist John Romita Jr., and later pairing with other impressive artists including Lee Weeks, Stuart Immonen, and Mike Deodato Jr., Bruce Jones told the simple human story of a man on the run, a man who just happened to be able to turn into a monster whenever he got angry.

When the Hulk was framed for the murder of a little boy by a secret organization calling itself Home Base, Bruce Banner found himself hunted by local law enforcement, as well as by the clandestine organization itself. Roaming from state to state and in constant contact with a mysterious Mr. Blue—later revealed to be the resuscitated Betty Ross Banner—the Hulk fought perverted clones of himself, undead double agents, the robotic blood-thirsty Krill, and his old foes the Abomination and the Absorbing Man, before getting to the bottom of the giant conspiracy. With the help of Doc Samson, Betty Ross Banner, and new love interest Nadia Dornova, the Hulk finally uncovered the man behind his recent troubles and Home Base itself. It was the the Leader—his old mind-manipulating enemy—now reduced to little more than a brain in a jar. Eventually Hulk defeated the Leader, but when shattering his foe's encasement, an unchecked shard of glass accidentally pierced Nadia's heart, killing her and sending the Hulk back into a life of isolation and loneliness.

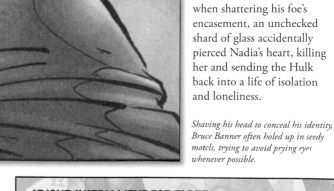

Shaving his head to conceal his identity, Bruce Banner often holed up in seedy motels, trying to avoid prying eyes whenever possible.

MARCH

SECOND INSTALLMENT FOR BLADE

• *Blade II: Bloodhunt—The Official Comic Adaptation*
The March 22nd movie release of the sequel to the original *Blade* film was accompanied by a comic-book adaptation, coverdated April. The comic was adapted by Steve Gerber and David S. Goyer and the pencils were by Alberto Ponticelli.

THE ULTIMATE TEAM

"At ease, boys. Go get yourselves a glass of champagne, huh? Ain't every day we save the world."

• *The Ultimates* #1

With *Ultimate Spider-Man* and *Ultimate X-Men* serving as two of Marvel's most consecutive best sellers, it was only a matter of time before the decision was made to reinvent one of the most popular teams of heroes, the Avengers, into this fresh new universe. And writer Mark Millar and artist Bryan Hitch were up to the challenge.

As this new thirteen-issue limited series began, Nick Fury, now a man of African descent, was shown as the driving force behind a new government-sponsored team of super soldiers, called, simply, the Ultimates. Reacting to a fight between the Hulk and Spider-Man, shown in *Ultimate Spider-Man*'s companion title *Ultimate Marvel Team-Up*, Fury recruited Iron Man, Giant Man, the Wasp, and Bruce Banner himself onto his new private army. But the team wouldn't gel until World War II hero Captain America was discovered in the Arctic Ocean, perfectly preserved in a block of ice.

Joined by Thor later in the series, the team found that its first major challenge was to stop the rampage of one of its own, when Bruce Banner had a heart attack and lost control of his faculties, changing into the Hulk in the middle of Manhattan. More infighting occurred later as Captain America discovered that the Wasp had fallen victim to the spousal abuse of her husband, Hank Pym, and Captain America took down Giant Man in a ruthless battle. Finally, as new members Hawkeye, Black Widow, Quicksilver, and Scarlet Witch joined the team, the Ultimates found their place among their world's national heroes as they managed to stave off a massive alien invasion.

Climbing Mount Everest purely for the inspiration, Tony Stark, the head of the third largest company in America, Stark International, found the resolve to start a new chapter in his life as Iron Man.

WHAT ARE YOU WAITING FOR, LADIES? CHRISTMAS?

The heart and soul of the team, the Ultimate version of Captain America possessed enough strength to rival that of the Hulk, but at his core he remained a loyal soldier to his country.

MAY

SPIDER-MAN CASTS HIS WEB FAR AND WIDE

• *Spider-Man: The Official Movie Adaptation*
Marvel released an official forty-eight-page adaptation of the *Spider-Man* movie that hit the screens on May 3. With a coverdate of June, the script was written by Stan Lee with art by Alan Davis, Mark Farmer, and Dave Kemp. A trade paperback was also released to tie in with the film release. Cult movie director Sam Raimi and screenwriter David Koepp's presented an interpretation Peter Parker's origin story in the movie and it starred Tobey Maguire as Peter Parker, Willem Dafoe as the Green Goblin, and Kirsten Dunst as Mary Jane Watson.

JUNE

CAPTAIN AMERICA SOLDIERS ON

• *Captain America #1*
The darker Marvel Knights line of books accepted Steve Rogers under their umbrella as writer John Ney Rieber and artist John Cassaday restarted the series with a new first issue, showing how Captain America would exist in the post-9/11 world.

CAPTAIN AMERICA
JOHN NEY RIEBER   JOHN CASSADAY

This new series began showing Steve Rogers working in the wreckage of the Twin Towers, angry at the world for the events of September 11, but never giving up his faith that humanity is also capable of good.

JULY

JEPH LOEB   TIM SALE
SPIDER-MAN: BLUE

SHADES OF SPIDER-MAN

• *Spider-Man: Blue #1*
Jeph Loeb and Tim Sale reunited for their second examination of the origins of Marvel's icons with this six-issue miniseries. The series was based around Peter Parker's tape-recorded message for Gwen Stacy, the former love of his life who died tragically at the hands of the Green Goblin. In the process, Peter also discussed some of his early encounters with his rogues gallery, including the Rhino, Lizard, and the Vulture.

As he recorded his message to Gwen, Peter came to the conclusion that although he missed her dearly, his wife Mary Jane would not have become the strong and loving woman that she was without Gwen's passing. Because when Gwen died, M J gave up her party girl lifestyle and finally grew up.

THE EVIL THAT MEN DO

• *Spider-Man And The Black Cat #1*

Movie writer and director Kevin Smith returned to play in the Marvel sandbox alongside artist Terry Dodson for a six-issue miniseries. It pitted Spider-Man and the Black Cat against a new villain named Mr. Brownstone, a criminal with the ability to teleport drugs into his clients' systems. With the help of Daredevil and Nightcrawler, the duo put an end to Brownstone, accidentally helping create a new Mysterio in the process, in the form of Brownstone's brother, Francis Klum.

EX-X-FORCE

• *X-Statix #1*

With a voice clearly its own, the further adventures of Peter Milligan's and Mike Allred's version of *X-Force*, now received a name—*X-Statix*. It featured a few roster changes here and there, including new members Dead Girl and Venus Dee Milo.

EX-CABLE

• *Soldier X #1*

Following the popular changes to the other X-titles, Cable received his own facelift courtesy of writer Darko Macan and artist Igor Kordey. The pair examined Cable's life after he had purged the Techno-Organic virus from his body.

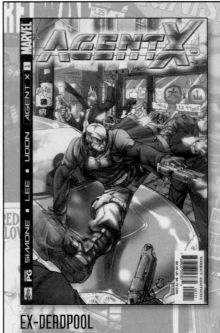

EX-DEADPOOL

• *Agent X #1*

Always in need of a makeover, Deadpool found something close in the pages of *Agent X*, thanks to writer Gail Simone and art team UDON Studios. This series kept fans guessing as to its protagonist's secret identity, finally revealing him to be Deadpool's enemy, Nijo Minamiyori.

IS THAT ALL YOU BOYS ARE INTERESTED IN, CELEBRITIES?

2003
MOVIES AND SHAKERS

Some people saw it as the next stage in the evolution of the medium: Marvel was hoping to bring its characters into the lives and homes of mainstream audiences. And the company was armed with two relatively new weapons in this ambitious battle—the Super Hero movie and the trade paperback.

Marvel had already reintroduced the Super Hero film for the next generation. From 2000 to 2002, moviegoers had enjoyed blockbuster movies featuring their favorite characters: *Blade*, *X-Men*, and *Spider-Man*. In 2003, three new Marvel movies burst onto the big screen, and the future would see at least one Marvel movie released every year.

Meanwhile, Marvel began to slowly discover the trade paperback market, an area that it had merely dabbled in before. More and more, comics became arc-based, telling five or six-part stories that transferred perfectly to trade form. The graphic novel section in bookstores had begun to grow, and it appeared that comics were no longer just for the "Wednesday crowd" anymore. Many of the diehard collectors had switched to the convenience of collected reprint editions, and the phrase "wait for the trade" became a permanent part of the average comic fan's vernacular.

THE TRUTH BEHIND CAPTAIN AMERICA

• *Truth: Red, White & Black* #1
This seven-issue miniseries from writer Robert Morales and illustrator Kyle Baker delved into the previously untold story of the original Captain America, Isaiah Bradley, a black serviceman of the US Army's Camp Cathcart. Bradley became an unwitting test subject of the government after the bombing of Pearl Harbor. As a result he gained super powers and donned a shield and uniform in service of his country.

DAREDEVIL ADAPTATION

• *Daredevil: The Official Adaptation Of The Hit Movie!*
With the movie release of *Daredevil* on February 14, Marvel produced a comic-book adaptation. The comic was adapted by Bruce Jones from the script by director Mark Steven Johnson, and featured a lone Daredevil on the cover, painted by Brian Stelfreeze. The movie starred Ben Affleck as Daredevil.

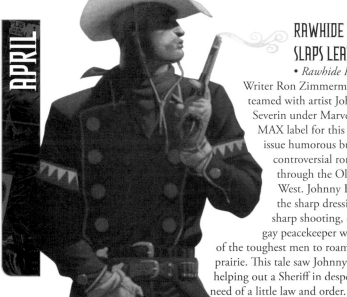

RAWHIDE KID SLAPS LEATHER

• *Rawhide Kid* #1
Writer Ron Zimmerman teamed with artist John Severin under Marvel's MAX label for this five-issue humorous but controversial romp through the Old West. Johnny Bart, the sharp dressing, sharp shooting, openly gay peacekeeper was one of the toughest men to roam the prairie. This tale saw Johnny helping out a Sheriff in desperate need of a little law and order.

X-MEN TRIUMPH AGAIN

• *X-Men 2*
In May, the second X-Men movie was released entitled *X2: X-Men United*. Marvel's comic-book adaptation of the movie carried a date of June and featured Lady Deathstrike, Storm, and Mystique on the cover. The screenplay's script, written by Bryan Singer, David Hayter, and Zak Penn, was adapted by Chuck Austen while Patrick Zircher, Larry Strucker, and Ian Hannin all worked on the art. As well as the characters featured in the original movie, this second installment also saw the inclusion of a few new X-characters, including Nightcrawler, portrayed in the movie by Alan Cumming.

HULK HITS HOLLYWOOD

- *Hulk: The Official Movie Adaptation*

In June, director Ang Lee brought Bruce Banner to the silver screen with the help of screenwriters John Turman, Michael France, and James Schamus. Marvel continued their trend of bringing out a comic-book adaptation of the movie, this time with pencils by Mark Bagley, inks by Scott Hanna, and a script by Bruce Jones. The cover art featured an angry Hulk reaching out to the reader and the story told how Bruce Banner transformed into the Incredible Hulk. Eric Bana starred in the film's title role alongside love interest Betty Ross, played by Jennifer Connelly. The movie also featured cameos from Stan Lee and Lou Ferrigno, the TV Hulk.

THE VENGERNCE OF VENOM

- *Venom* #1

Surprisingly Venom did not net his own ongoing series until over ten years after the height of his popularity. Even this thriller title by writer Daniel Way and artist Francisco Herrera actually starred a clone of the symbiote more than Eddie Brock himself!

PUNISHER: BORN

- *Born* #1

Garth Ennis and Darick Robertson teamed to tell the story of how Frank Castle came to possess the mindset of the unfeeling Punisher

in this four-issue miniseries for Marvel's mature MAX line. Set on the Cambodian border in the closing days of the Vietnam War, *Born* detailed Frank's merciless killing of not just enemy soldiers, but also of American men who crossed a moral line that Frank found unacceptable. The miniseries ended with Frank agreeing to wage a war with no end.

RUCKA'S WOLVERINE

- *Wolverine* #1

Novelist Greg Rucka restarted Wolverine's title and stayed on for a nineteen-issue run, pairing at first with artist Darick Robertson. During this time, Rucka set Logan out to avenge waitress Lucy Braddock, had him obsessed over by ATF agent Cassie Lathrop, forced him into a battle royal with Sabretooth, and introduced him to the Native, a female Weapon X survivor (and his forgotten former lover) before relinquishing the reins of the title over to writer Mark Millar.

MARVEL'S RUNAWAY HIT

"I've known our parents were evil since age five. This perverted little gathering just confirms it."

- *Runaways* #1

The kids thought it was all for charity. Once every year, teenager Alex Wilder's parents had a quiet little get-together in their suburban home with five other married couples. And every year, their children were forced to have awkward conversations as they attempted to hang out while their parents were conducting whatever kind of business it was they conducted. The problem with this scenario was, there were teenagers involved. And teenagers get bored.

Exploring a secret passageway Alex had discovered months earlier while hunting for Christmas presents, the seven kids decided to spy on their parents, and see what they were really like behind closed doors. Unfortunately, they weren't prepared for what they would see next. Their parents were actually members of a team of Super Villains known as the Pride, and their children watched in secret as the men and women that raised them killed an innocent girl in some sort of ritual sacrifice. So they did what any normal kids would do in their situation. They ran away from home.

Writer Brian K. Vaughan and artist Adrian Alphona crafted this ingenious premise, introducing this band of Runaways to the Marvel Universe and slowly, as each teammate gained powers or learned to harness their natural aptitudes, to the role of Super Heroes as well. Setting up camp in the "Hostel," the remains of an earthquake-destroyed home in California, the Runaways finally managed to halt their parents' plans for world domination, despite team member Alex showing his true colors as a traitor to their heroic cause.

The Runaways included teammates Arsenic and her telepathically linked dinosaur Old Lace, the sorceress Sister Grimm, the solar-powered Lucy in the Sky, heir to technological gadgets Talkback, and the aptly named Bruiser.

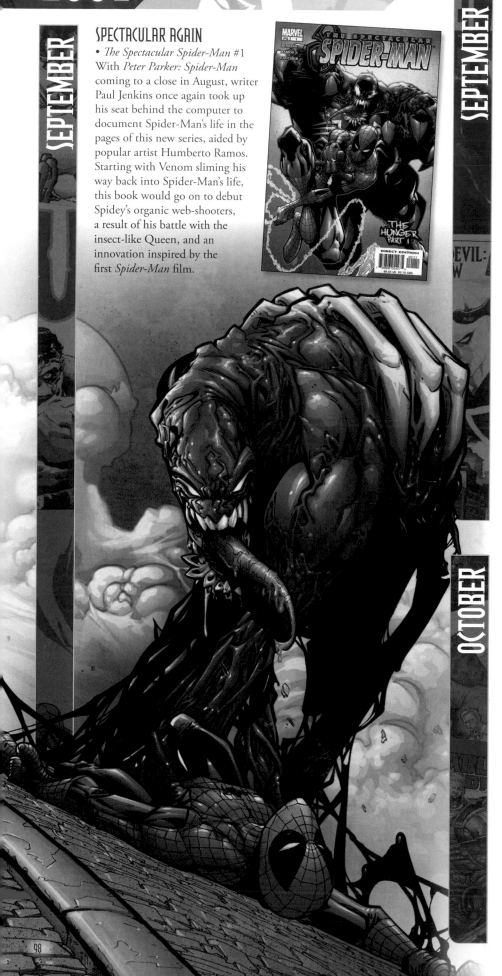

SEPTEMBER

SPECTACULAR AGAIN

• *The Spectacular Spider-Man* #1
With *Peter Parker: Spider-Man* coming to a close in August, writer Paul Jenkins once again took up his seat behind the computer to document Spider-Man's life in the pages of this new series, aided by popular artist Humberto Ramos. Starting with Venom sliming his way back into Spider-Man's life, this book would go on to debut Spidey's organic web-shooters, a result of his battle with the insect-like Queen, and an innovation inspired by the first *Spider-Man* film.

SEPTEMBER

JUSTICE FOR THE AVENGERS

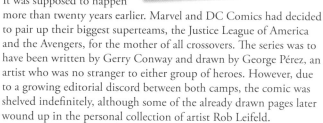

"In the nothingness of the trans-dimensional void, two worlds—two universes — convulse. And shudder. And begin to crumble."

• *JLA/Avengers* #1
It was supposed to happen more than twenty years earlier. Marvel and DC Comics had decided to pair up their biggest superteams, the Justice League of America and the Avengers, for the mother of all crossovers. The series was to have been written by Gerry Conway and drawn by George Pérez, an artist who was no stranger to either group of heroes. However, due to a growing editorial discord between both camps, the comic was shelved indefinitely, although some of the already drawn pages later wound up in the personal collection of artist Rob Leifeld.

Years passed and so did dozens of other collaborative comics between the two publishing houses, including the popular *Marvel Versus DC/DC Versus Marvel* miniseries. But while the Justice League and the Avengers did get a chance to square off a few times in these various specials and limited series, the fans always lamented the death of what would have been the ultimate in team-ups, pitting the iconic versions of each team versus the other.

But as 2003 rolled around, both Marvel and DC had spent years reestablishing their characters, and a classic feel was once again prevalent in the majority of their titles. The timing seemed perfect to give the fans what they wanted. So George Pérez returned, teaming with writer Kurt Busiek to create this four-issue prestige format limited series, to tell the story of the DC villain Krona breaching the barrier of the Marvel Universe, and Marvel's Grandmaster, pitting the unwitting Justice League against the Avengers in a contest meant to challenge this new threat.

OCTOBER

SUPREME POWER PREMIERS

• *Supreme Power* #1
Writer J. Michael Straczynski and artist Gary Frank took a surprisingly dark reassessment of the Squadron Supreme, Marvel's version of the most iconic DC heroes, in this new mature ongoing series under the MAX imprint. Telling the familiar story of an innocent married farm couple chancing upon a baby abandoned in the wreckage of a rocket ship from outer space, *Supreme Power* gave the story a cynical twist as the government then forcibly removed the child from the young couples' custody. The baby grew up to become Hyperion, the first of his new super-powered ilk, and one who was not quite content with the state of his world.

Hyperion had all the powers of DC's Superman, but a more rebellious attitude. He soon joined forces with other dark heroes including Dr. Spectrum, Nighthawk, and Blur.

MARVEL'S SWEET 1602

• *1602* #1

Neil Gaiman, the *New York Times* best-selling novelist and legendary writer of DC/Vertigo's acclaimed *Sandman* series, took his creative vision and penchant for times past to Marvel, crafting this eight-issue miniseries alongside fan-favorite artist Andy Kubert. Digitally painted by Richard Isanove, with woodcut-like covers by Scott McKowen, this series took an alternative look at what the classic Marvel pantheon would be like if they had existed in the 17th Century. Set in England as well as in the newly colonized America, *1602* featured the adventures of British intelligence agent Sir Nicholas Fury, his assistant Peter Parquagh, and the mysterious Virginia Dare.

Just as in modern times, in the alternate universe of 1602, mutants were hated and feared. At the story's start, original X-Men Angel was set to be executed by the ruling government of Spain.

X-23 AND THE NYX

• *NYX* #1

Taking a realistic approach to a group of New York City gutterpunks similar to the no-holds-barred film *Kids*, Joe Quesada wrote this seven-issue miniseries, teaming with artists Joshua Middleton and Robert Teranishi. *NYX* focused on the daily lives of a few teens with mutant powers, and in its third issue, debuted X-23 (left), a female clone of Wolverine whose origins dated back to the *X-Men: Evolution* animated series.

SPIDER-MAN HITS 500

• *The Amazing Spider-Man* #500

After issue # 58 of the second volume of *The Amazing Spider-Man*, writer J. Michael Straczynski and artist John Romita Jr. returned the title to its original numbering just in time for this landmark anniversary issue. In this third chapter of a story entitled "Happy Birthday," Spider-Man found himself witnessing his future and revisiting some of the most memorable moments in his career, as he and Dr. Strange fell victim to a magic spell while battling the evil Dormammu. Revisited memories included the death of Gwen Stacy and a ferocious bout with the Hulk.

Bruce Banner recounted his days as the gray Hulk to his old psychiatrist friend Dr. Samson, as he mourned the loss of Betty Ross.

HULK'S GRAY MATTERS

• *Hulk: Gray* #1

The team of writer Jeph Loeb and artist Tim Sale united once again for this six-issue mini series retelling the Hulk's origin and dealing with the relatively short period in his first adventures when his skin hadn't developed its green hue.

New X-Men #150 (Feb., 2004)

Scott Summers, the X-Man known as Cyclops, and his wife Jean Grey had always had a tumultuous relationship, even at the best of times. With the otherworldly Phoenix Force haunting Jean's life due to her mutant prowess as a telepath, Cyclops had seen Jean die in his arms before, only to have her rise from the ashes like her Phoenix namesake. And even though they'd grown apart in recent months due to his involvement with Emma Frost, Jean's death truly affected Scott.

THIS IS A NEW LOW.
AN UNDERWEAR MODEL
THINKS I NEED DEPTH.

2004
PLANTING THE SEEDS

Marvel watched the fruits of its labor grow and mature. Its new Ultimate and MAX lines had amassed fan and critical success, but Marvel refused to rest on its laurels and instead began to plant new ideas and concepts, hoping to harvest an equally successful crop in the future. It was this attitude and willingness to experiment that sprouted Icon, a new Marvel imprint that would publish creator-owned properties. With this new label, creators like Brian Michael Bendis and Michael Avon Oeming were able to move their popular *Powers* series from Image Comics to Marvel, gaining increased distribution. David Mack did likewise with his title *Kabuki*, and later, other major name talent would create original properties for the imprint, including writers like J. Michael Straczynski, Ed Brubaker and Mark Millar.

Simultaneously, Marvel was planting story seeds as well. Brian Michael Bendis ended the *Avengers* series, paving the way for a replacement title, as well as the upcoming *House of M* event. These new books, along with the *Secret War* miniseries that chronicled the fall of one of Marvel's oldest heroes and set the stage for an underground rebellion, helped form the roots of 2006's *Civil War*, and even 2008's *Secret Invasion*.

FEBRUARY

FANTASTIC FOUR GET THE ULTIMATE TREATMENT
• *Ultimate Fantastic Four* #1

Ultimate veterans Brian Michael Bendis, Mark Millar, and Adam Kubert reexamined Marvel's first family, creating this alternate version of the Fantastic Four. In it, genius Reed Richards developed a teleportation device as a young teen, which led to him getting drafted into a special school for gifted students run out of the Baxter Building in Manhattan. There Reed met Sue and Johnny Storm, and developed a larger scale version of his device. This was tampered with by fellow student Victor Van Damme, causing an accident that granted the four super powers, along with Reed's visiting boyhood friend, Ben Grimm.

Fighting such villains as their former friend Dr. Doom and their former teacher the Mole Man, this new FF even found time to travel to the Negative Zone.

THE DEATH OF JEAN GREY
• *New X-Men* #150

KILL THEM ALL.

Writer Grant Morrison and artist Phil Jimenez combined to put an end to Jean Grey. Xorn, a mutant posing as the villain Magneto, trapped Jean and Wolverine on Asteroid M and hurled it toward the sun. With no chance of escape, and with Jean dying before his eyes, Logan ran her through with his claws in order to spare her further suffering. This act released the Phoenix Force insider her, which she ultimately used to save both their lives and return them to Earth.

Thought defeated by Jean's Phoenix powers, Xorn had enough strength left to give Jean a lethal electromagnetic pulse, killing her before he in turn was beheaded by a feral Wolverine.

MARCH

PUNISHER GOES TO THE MAX
• *The Punisher* #1

When *The Punisher* was restarted to fall under the mature reader MAX label, longtime *Punisher* scribe Garth Ennis, alongside artist Lewis Larosa, was finally able to cut loose with all the trademark ultra-violence and adult-oriented black comedy that made his legendary *Preacher* run for DC/Vertigo such a smash hit. As the Punisher continued his war on the gangs of New York, he was kidnapped by his old sidekick Microchip in an attempt to get the Punisher to kill enemies of America on the government's dime. Castle rejected the offer in true Punisher fashion, and even killed his old ally for selling him down the river.

Artist Tim Bradstreet continued his long streak of Punisher covers into this new series. His realistic figures and dramatic lighting were a hit with the fans.

A NEW 4

• *Marvel Knights 4 #1*

Playwright Roberto Aguirre-Sacasa and artist Steve McNiven focused on the family dynamic that holds the Fantastic Four together in this new ongoing series. As the Four discovered that their money manager had stolen their fortune, the family was forced to grow closer together as they each entered the work force. The Invisible Woman became a teacher, the Thing became a construction worker, the Human Torch a fireman, and Mr. Fantastic took a job at a law firm.

FURY'S PRIVATE WAR

• *Secret War #1*

The top secret world of espionage and intrigue behind Marvel's super spy organization SHIELD met the world of spandex and Super Heroes in this five-issue painted miniseries by writer Brian Michael Bendis and artist Gabriele Dell'Otto. When it was discovered that

Super Villains were being bankrolled by foreign Prime Minister Lucia Von Bardas, Nick Fury organized a covert strike force in order to do what America's government was unwilling to do—invade Latveria. The result was a retaliatory battle in the streets of Manhattan, and Nick Fury being removed from his position as Director of SHIELD and given the new title of wanted war criminal.

🎬 On April 16, The Punisher hit theaters. Directed by Jonathan Hensleigh, the film starred Thomas Jane as Frank Castle opposite mob boss Howard Saint, portrayed by John Travolta.

MARVEL'S MERCENARIES TEAM UP

• *Cable & Deadpool #1*

Writer Fabian Nicieza returned to pair up two of his favorite creations. With artist Mark Brooks plus a few covers by *X-Force* alum Rob Liefeld, this ongoing series began with Cable and Deadpool on the hunt for the same dangerous biotoxin.

WHO'S YOUR DADDY NOW, HUH?

SHE-HULK GOES TO WORK

• *She-Hulk #1*

Fired from her law firm and kicked out of the Avengers Mansion for her rowdy behavior, She-Hulk (aka Jennifer Walters) started a new chapter in her life as chronicled by writer Dan Slott and artist Juan Bobillo. Finding employment with the most prestigious law firm in Manhattan, Goodman, Lieber, Kurtzberg, and Holliway, She-Hulk realized that her dream job might not be all that she had originally hoped for, as she found herself reduced to working on the firm's Superhuman Law division.

One of the stipulations of She-Hulk's new job was that she had to work as the shy Jennifer Walters, not the boisterous and confident She-Hulk.

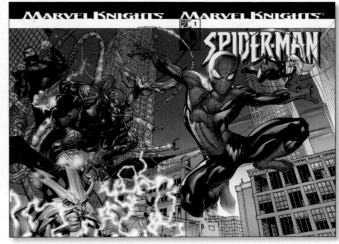

Viewed together, the front and back covers of this first issue made a complete action-packed image. Penciller Terry Dodson's wife, Rachel Dodson, inked this Spider-Man series.

MARVEL KNIGHTS SPIDER-MAN

• *Spider-Man #1*

Now secured in his superstar status due to the success of his mega-hit *The Ultimates*, Mark Millar decided to try his hand at writing the life of Peter Parker in this all-new ongoing series drawn by fan favorite penciller Terry Dodson. Together, the pair crafted a large-scale twelve-part story that saw Spider-Man's life being plagued yet again by the Green Goblin, as Osborn funded an elaborate plan against the web-slinger, financing power enhancements for Peter's old foes, kidnapping his aunt May, and even forming a Sinister Twelve. The series also saw the villainous Scorpion take up Eddie Brock's old mantle as the new Venom.

With a little help from some of the other heroes of the Marvel Universe, Spider-Man finally managed to defeat the Green Goblin and rescue his aunt.

🎬 The sequel to the 2002 movie, *Spider-Man 2* was released on June 30. The film saw the introduction of classic Spider-Man foe Dr. Octopus, portrayed by Alfred Molina, as well as the return of many of the supporting players from the previous film.

X-MEN ASTONISHES FANS

"Sorry, Logan. Super Heroes wear costumes. And quite frankly, all the black leather is making people nervous."

• *Astonishing X-Men* #1
Joss Whedon had already built himself quite an audience. Due to his creation of the popular *Buffy the Vampire Slayer* television series, as well as the sci-fi cult favorite *Firefly*, Whedon was given his own X-Men title, which quickly became a smash hit. Drawn by popular artist John Cassaday, whose realistic rendering had previously helped *Captain America* climb sales charts, *Astonishing X-Men* premiered, officially marking the end of the era of the *New X-Men* by doing away with the leather uniforms that had been the trademark of that period in the super heroes' lives.

Returning Kitty Pryde—a mutant with a hip and sarcastic nature—to Xavier's School, Whedon also resurrected her old flame, Colossus, revealing that the hero had been somehow revived after his death from the Legacy Virus. Whedon also continued to examine the friendship as well as the animosity between Cyclops and Wolverine, who were both still mourning the loss of fellow X-Men member Jean Grey.

As Whedon and Cassaday's run continued, they introduced a sub-division of SHIELD called SWORD (Sentient Worlds Observation and Response Department), as well as a new villain named Danger, the living personification of the X-Men's high-tech danger room training facility. The team also orchestrated an invasion of Xavier's School by a band of heavy-hitting villains and a treacherous Emma Frost. However, in actuality this was all the result of the mind manipulations of the imprisoned Cassandra Nova, the disembodied twin sister of Professor Charles Xavier.

When Wolverine returned from one of his extended absences, he found Cyclops in bed with the White Queen. Wolverine didn't approve of Cyclop's choice, and the two battled on the front lawn of the school.

ARAÑA AUDITIONS

• *Amazing Fantasy* #1
Thanks to writer Fiona Avery and artist Mark Brooks, average Brooklyn high schooler Anya Corazon began developing super powers and was recruited by the mystical secret Spider Society to fight against the Sisterhood of the Wasp. Named Araña, her story helped kick off the new *Amazing Fantasy* series, which focused on new characters by rotating creative teams.

SINS PAST

• *The Amazing Spider-Man* #509
In this storyline by writer J. Michael Straczynski and artist Mike Deodato Jr., Peter Parker was shocked when he encountered a woman who was the spitting image of Gwen Stacy. Spider-Man soon discovered that this Gwen look-alike was one of a pair of siblings who were the result of an affair that Gwen had had with Norman Osborn years ago. The two children had been aged by their father and given super powers in a plan to destroy Peter Parker for good.

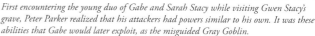

First encountering the young duo of Gabe and Sarah Stacy while visiting Gwen Stacy's grave, Peter Parker realized that his attackers had powers similar to his own. It was these abilities that Gabe would later exploit, as the misguided Gray Goblin.

CARNAGE'S KID

• *Venom VS. Carnage* #1
Writer Peter Milligan joined artist Clayton Crain in this four-issue miniseries which told the story of Carnage giving birth to a new symbiote. Police officer Patrick Mulligan became the creature's reluctant host, calling himself Toxin, as the creature's base instincts wrestled with his own good judgment.

SEPTEMBER

AVENGERS DISASSEMBLED

"If I told you a story like this, you'd say to yourself, this sounds like a person who has lost control of themselves on a deep psychological level. You'd say this sounds like a disturbed person."

- *The Avengers* #500

It started with a bang. Literally. Jack of Hearts, a former Avenger who had died in space on an earlier mission, returned to the Avenger's Mansion, a walking corpse. As Ant-Man Scott Lang rushed outside to greet his friend, Jack exploded, killing Scott and taking most of the mansion with him. And that was just the beginning.

Writer Brian Michael Bendis would turn the Avengers' world on its end with this shocking new crossover event drawn by artist David Finch. Originating in the pages of *The Avengers*, and crossing into *Captain America*, *The Invincible Iron Man*, *The Mighty Thor*, *Fantastic Four*, and *The Spectacular Spider-Man*, this mammoth story was constructed so that each title's adventure could be enjoyed separately, or the reader could choose to read all the various comics and get a thorough account of exactly how this storyline affected the entire Marvel Universe.

The Scarlet Witch warped reality so it appeared as if five Ultron androids were attacking the Avengers. She-Hulk lost control under Wanda's influence and literally ripped the Vision in two. Shortly after, Hawkeye died fighting a Kree battleship that Wanda had also conjured up.

As the tale continued, the Avengers lost Thor, the Vision, and Hawkeye to various, seemingly random battles. After uniting the remaining Avengers past and present, the team discovered that the cause of all their recent problems was in reality their teammate the Scarlet Witch. Having relied on her mutant ability to access what she called "chaos magic" to fight alongside the Avengers for years, the Scarlet Witch, aka Wanda Maximoff, had been slowly slipping into insanity, eventually losing her struggle with reality. Only with the help of Dr. Strange did the Avengers finally triumph over Wanda, delivering the disturbed shell of a woman into her father Magneto's custody.

OCTOBER

ULTIMATE GALACTUS

- *Ultimate Nightmare* #1
Beginning the *Ultimate Galactus Trilogy*, a trio of miniseries that introduced the Ultimate Universe to the world-killing Gah Lak Tus, *Ultimate Nightmare* was a five-issue limited series by writer Warren Ellis and artists Trevor Hairsine and Steve Epting, which teamed the Ultimates with the X-Men.

Ultimate Secret, the four-issue sequel, debuted Captain Marvel and the five-issue Ultimate Extinction *showed what happened as Gah Lak Tus finally made his way to Earth.*

NOVEMBER

STRANGE ORIGINS

- *Strange* #1
Scribes J. Michael Straczynski and Samm Barnes, with artist Brandon Peterson, retold Dr. Stephen Strange's mystical origin for a new generation of fans in this six-issue limited series. Given a new costume by artist Joe Quesada, this modernized version of Strange's beginnings

showed him involved in a skiing accident that mangled his surgical fingers, discovering magic in an elaborate mansion hidden in a back alley, and fighting Dormammu for the first time.

DECEMBER

Written and directed by David Goyer, *Blade: Trinity*, the third installment of the Blade films, once again starred Wesley Snipes as the Daywalker vampire hunter, alongside Kris Kristofferson as Blade's mentor, Abraham Whistler.

2005

THE RETURN OF THE EVENT

By 2005, Marvel had reestablished its properties by returning many characters to their roots with cutting-edge storytelling from hot creators. Now, Marvel was ready to reestablish another of its honored traditions—the crossover. With hints of major universe-spanning events in 2004's *Avengers Disassembled* and *Secret War* story lines, and with their main competitor DC Comics finding success in their major event crossovers like *Identity Crisis* and *Infinite Crisis*, Marvel and the marketplace seemed primed for larger, multi-part stories.

Having established himself as a major player in the world of comics with his fan-favorite titles *Ultimate Spider-Man* and *Daredevil*, writer Brian Michael Bendis made the *House of M* miniseries branch out past its own pages. Much like the X-Men story arc Age Of Apocalypse before it, *House of M* birthed a new reality with miniseries spin-offs starring the characters from the flagship title. Spider-Man, Iron Man, and the Fantastic Four were among those characters whose alternate realities were explored in this fashion.

At the end of the year, another crossover event began, though it was limited to the pages of Spider-Man's core titles. The Other storyline altered Peter Parker's life forever, and paved the way for the changes that Spider-Man was to endure in the future.

AVENGERS ASSEMBLE AGAIN

"We'll find out who our enemies are. We'll find out who did this. And then we'll avenge it."

The cover for The New Avengers *#1 was available in this standard version, as well as in three variant cover editions.*

• *The New Avengers* #1
In the aftermath of the *Avengers Disassembled* storyline, the Marvel Universe was purposely left without its mightiest team of heroes. This would all change as superstars writer Brian Michael Bendis and artist David Finch relaunched the title under the name *The New Avengers*. The comic focused more on Marvel's arguably most popular Super Heroes, including Spider-Man, Captain America, Iron Man, Wolverine, Spider-Woman, and Luke Cage.

Much like the original team of the 1960s, the New Avengers' origin was born by circumstance. The members were drawn together by a massive breakout attempt at the Raft, New York City's maximum-security installation. Meeting on the scene, the unofficial team managed to curb the riots, and together set out to discover the mastermind behind the escape attempt. Following a trail that led to the Savage Land, a time-lost island inhabited by dinosaurs and other primitive forms of life, the fledging group of heroes eventually discovered that the prison breakout was actually just part of a cover-up for a deeply rooted government conspiracy involving a rogue faction of SHIELD and an illegal slave-labor vibranium mine run by the second Black Widow.

As the series progressed, the mentally tormented powerhouse known as the Sentry and a mysterious ninja named Ronin (formerly Daredevil's ally Echo) both joined the team. The New Avengers announced themselves to the world, and based themselves in their new headquarters located atop Manhattan's Stark Tower.

Merely a hired gun, Spider-Man's old foe Electro used his electric powers to cause a blackout in the Raft prison, causing a riot that freed forty-two super-powered villains.

ELEKTRA MAKES IT BIG

• *Elektra: The Official Movie Adaptation*
To tie in with the January movie release of *Elektra*, Marvel brought out a comic-book adaptation, coverdated February. The movie was a spin-off from 2003's *Daredevil* and Jennifer Garner reprised her role as the assassin antihero.

IRON MAN'S NEW ARMOR

• *The Invincible Iron Man* #1

Writer Warren Ellis teamed up with illustrator Adi Granov to create a new spin on Iron Man that would have long-lasting effects. When a face from Tony Stark's past, Maya Hansen, injected an experimental electronic super-soldier serum known as the Extremis solution into a test subject, Iron Man was forced to undergo a drastic transformation in order to stop the resulting violent renegade. Critically injured, Iron Man injected himself with the same solution in order to interface with his armor on a biological level. Now able to control his armor with a mere thought, Iron Man became the ultimate blend of man and machine.

Stark also soared to new professional heights as Director of SHIELD.

CAP'S BACK

• *Captain America* #1

When acclaimed writer Ed Brubaker made the switch from DC to Marvel, he brought with him yet another relaunch for Steve Rogers. A critical and financial hit, this new *Captain America* series featured the art of realistic draftsman Steve Epting, and saw the supposed death of Cap's main adversary, the Red Skull. Later on in the series, Cap's former sidekick Bucky Barnes made his shocking return, his death apparently just as exaggerated as Cap's was at the end of World War II.

THE ULTIMATE SEQUEL

• *Ultimates 2* #1

Following the success of the original *Ultimates* maxiseries, Mark Millar and Bryan Hitch teamed up again for the thirteen-issue sequel. The series saw the creation of a multi-national Super Hero force, the redemption of the Hulk, and an attack by Thor's brother Loki on a level never before witnessed in the Ultimate universe. The series ended with Captain America proved innocent, but his team deciding to sever all government ties.

When Loki made the world believe that Captain America was a murderer, Cap went on the run from his own government.

RUNAWAYS RENEWED

• *Runaways* #1

Picking up where the first series left off, writer Brian K. Vaughan's *Runaways* was granted a new first issue, a rare move for Marvel. As the young band of misfit heroes were joined by new teammate Victor Mancha, they found themselves pursued by a team of former child Super Heroes and battling for their lives against the robot Ultron. Later on in the series, another fan favorite, Joss Whedon, replaced Vaughan.

YOUNG AVENGERS COME OF AGE

"They're not going to approve … but since when has that ever stopped us?"

• *Young Avengers* #1

In 2005, television writer and producer Allan Heinberg (*Grey's Anatomy*, *The OC*, *Sex and the City*) and penciller Jim Cheung teamed together to create a comic title that focused on younger counterparts to the Earth's Mightiest Heroes. Originally consisting of junior versions of Captain America, Iron Man, Hulk, and Thor (Patriot, Iron Lad, Hulkling, and Wiccan respectively), the Young Avengers instantly collected a sizable following of fans, all eagerly anticipating discovering the origins of the enigmatic young team.

Patriot, the Young Avengers' leader, was actually the grandson of the original Captain America born in the miniseries Truth: Red, White and Black *(Jan., 2003).*

As the the series progressed, Iron Lad was revealed to be in actuality a young version of the time-traveling Avengers foe, Kang the Conqueror. Rallying other young heroes to aid him in his fight against his future self, the young version of Kang formed the Young Avengers, despite the disapproval of the teams' older namesakes. Soon joined by Cassie Lang, daughter of the second Ant-Man calling herself Stature, and a new female Hawkeye, the team fought and defeated Kang's adult form, before Kang's younger self was forced to return back to his normal era of the future, to keep the time stream safe.

Shown his fate by his evil future self, Iron Lad traveled back in time to enlist some 21st Century help.

With a little funding from Hawkeye's father, the rest of the Young Avengers decided to stay together as a team. They reemerged with a new hideout and costumes more fitting to their individuality, which allowed them to step out of the Avengers' shadow.

PUMPING ULTIMATE IRON

• *Ultimate Iron Man* #1

Acclaimed sci-fi novelist Orson Scott Card, with Marvel artists Andy Kubert and Mark Bagley, delved into Tony Stark's past in the five-issue miniseries *Ultimate Iron Man*, inventing a bizarre skin condition for the young hero.

Ultimate Iron Man's body was mostly neural tissue, giving him superhuman intelligence but causing him constant pain.

THE FANTASTIC FOUR IN ACTION

• *Fantastic Four: The Movie*

In 2005, Marvel published an official comic adaptation of the *Fantastic Four* movie, which hit theaters on July 8. Adapted by Mike Carey, with art by Dan Jurgens and Sandu Florea, the trade paperback included a selection of classic Fantastic Four stories that inspired the movie as well as the movie adaptation itself. The movie was directed by Tim Story, written by Mark Frost and Michael France, and starred Jessica Alba as the Invisible Woman, Ioan Gruffudd as Mr. Fantastic, Chris Evans as the Human Torch, Michael Chiklis as the Thing, and Julian McMahon as Dr. Doom.

now they were the vast majority. Humans were now the outcasts, a dwindling few on the verge of extinction. The planet was ruled by Magneto and his royal family—the House of Magnus. They governed a brave new world. It was a world where Spider-Man was adored by the public and married to Gwen Stacy. A world where the Hulk ruled over all of Australia, and Wolverine served dutifully as an agent of SHIELD. And it would have stayed that way, if not for a little girl named Layla Miller, a mutant with the ability to restore people's minds to the way they were before the Scarlet Witch's tampering. Soon, a ragtag team of enlightened heroes took their fight to Magneto, showing him the way the world was supposed to be. Enraged by his son's presumptuous ambition, Magneto viciously attacked Quicksilver, until the Scarlet Witch was forced to return the world to normal. Or so the heroes thought.

The X-Men were among the heroes who gathered to discuss what punishment was to be given to the Scarlet Witch after she disassembled the Avengers.

WORLD OF M

"No more mutants."

• *House Of M #1*

After successfully disassembling the Avengers, the tormented Scarlet Witch still wasn't finished tampering with the lives of the men and women she'd fought beside for so many years. And writer Brian Michael Bendis certainly wasn't finished with her, either. Teaming with artist Olivier Coipel, Bendis created *The House of M*, a major Marvel crossover event centered around an eight-issue miniseries, beginning in August, that would have lasting repercussions to the entire universe the heroes populated.

At the insistence of her brother Quicksilver, the Scarlet Witch literally rewrote history, unleashing the full extent of her magic abilities to change the world in her own image. Where once mutants were a minority on Earth,

The House Of M miniseries featured painted covers by artist Esad Ribic.

DAREDEVIL'S PUNISHMENT

• *Daredevil Vs Punisher #1*

Crime writer David Lapham, who made a name for himself writing and drawing the independent hit *Stray Bullets*, set his sights on the Marvel Universe and crafted the six-issue miniseries *Daredevil Vs Punisher*, pitting the two vigilantes against each other.

Daredevil Vs Punisher marked the return of the classic Spider-Man foe, the Jackal, who ran his criminal organization from a jail cell.

SPIDER-MAN: THE OTHER

"You're a good man who's led a good life. Prepare to die."

• *Friendly Neighborhood Spider-Man* #1

Beginning in the pages of the new title, *Friendly Neighborhood Spider-Man*, the Other storyline crossed over with all the current Spider-Man books, chronicling the supernatural tale of Peter Parker's death and evolution. From a story orchestrated by writer J. Michael Straczynski, writers Peter David and Reginald Hudlin teamed with artists Mike Wieringo, Pat Lee, and Mike Deodato Jr. to tell this epic tale that altered Spider-Man's powers and proved quite controversial with the fans. Serving as a prelude to Spider-Man's future wardrobe change, each issue in the series was also available in a variant edition that showcased a different costume that Spidey had worn in the course of his long career.

The story began as Spider-Man was diagnosed with an unknown terminal illness while simultaneously being stalked by his mystical adversary, Morlun. After a furious battle with his hunter, Spider-Man was defeated and hospitalized, his face swollen past recognition. But as Morlun crept into the hospital to feed off Peter's powers, Spider-Man managed one last burst of animalistic energy, viciously beating Morlun, and magically devouring him. Returning to normal, Peter Parker managed a soft farewell to his loving wife before dying in her arms. But days later, Spider-Man would return, his body somehow regenerated anew after spending time in a giant cocoon. Now with new powers, including enhanced sensitivity and spike-like stingers that protruded from his forearms in times of danger, Spider-Man cautiously renewed his fight against crime, knowing he would never survive another such brush with death.

An energy vampire who wanted to feast on Parker's spider-based energies, Morlun had the ability to track Spider-Man wherever he went.

The main artist of Friendly Neighborhood Spider-Man, Mike Wieringo, had earned a strong following working with writer Mark Waid on their noted Flash *run for DC Comics, as well as their historic stint on Marvel's own* Fantastic Four *in the late 2000s.*

MEANWHILE IN 2005...

HURRICANE KATRINA
One of the five deadliest hurricanes in US history hits Louisiana and Mississippi, killing nearly 2,000 and creating economic disaster.

7/7 HORROR ATTACK
In the first suicide attack in Britain, four "homegrown" suicide bombers detonate themselves on the London Underground and bus system, killing fifty-six and injuring over 700.

"DEEP THROAT" REVEALED
Thirty years on from Watergate, the Washington Post reveals that the mystery source "Deep Throat" was deputy head of the FBI, Mark Felt.

PROTESTS AGAINST WAR IN IRAQ
Demonstrations against the war in Iraq take place around the world, with over 150,000 protestors gathering in Washington.

ISRAEL LEAVES GAZA STRIP
After thirty-eight years of occupation, Israel withdraws settlers and military forces from the Gaza Strip, leaving the territory under the control of the Palestinian Authority.

"ORANGE REVOLUTION"
Victor Yushchenko is sworn in as President of the Ukraine, bringing an end to the "Orange Revolution"—the upheaval that followed the corruption of the 2004 election.

A ROYAL WEDDING
His Royal Highness Prince Charles marries Camilla Parker Bowles at Windsor Castle.

LIVE 8
Twenty years after Live Aid, the Live 8 benefit concerts take place in nine countries as part of the "Make Poverty History" campaign, which coincides with the G8 Conference and Summit.

KYOTO PROTOCOL TAKES EFFECT
The Kyoto Protocol on climate change becomes law. Signatories are legally bound to lower worldwide greenhouse gas emissions, but the US and Australia are not included.

DEMOCRACY IN HONG KONG?
A quarter of a million people gather in Hong Kong to protest for democracy.

MISSION TO MARS
NASA launches the Mars Reconnaissance Orbiter to research the planet from its orbit.

AND AT THE MOVIES...
Batman Begins, Christopher Nolan's prequel looks behind the shadows to show how orphaned Bruce Wayne became a masked Super Hero; Sin City, Robert Rodriguez's distinctive monochrome vision of Frank Miller's popular graphic novel about the sleazy goings-on in Basin City; Corpse Bride, Tim Burton's sweetly macabre stop-motion masterpiece features the voice talent of Johnny Depp and Helena Bonham Carter.

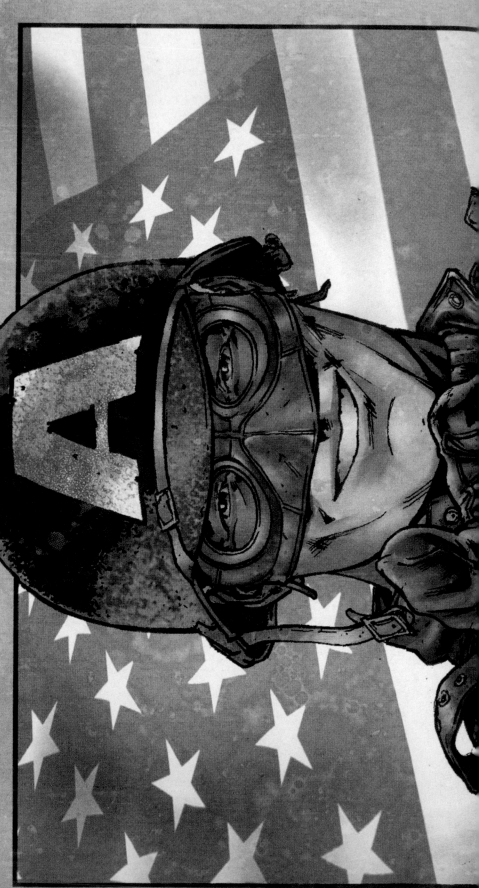

WANTS YOU TO SERVE YOUR COUNTRY

The Ultimates: Super-Human (2005)
Writer Mark Millar and artist Bryan Hitch were at the top of their respective games when they crafted the first Ultimates maxiseries. Both had attracted much attention on the Wildstorm title The Authority and with related JLA projects for DC Comics. With both men's past works rooted in books of blockbuster proportion, Millar and Hitch were the obvious team to recruit when Marvel decided it was time to revamp the Avengers and birth them into an Ultimate, more mature universe. And one of the pair's boldest reimaginings was Captain America, who traded in his mask's trademark wings for a painted Army helmet.

I DO THIS FOR FUN. MY MOM SAID IT WAS THIS OR A NEWSPAPER ROUTE...

2006
MARVEL GOES TO WAR

The entire universe had been drafted. As Tony Stark went to speak about the Super Hero Registration Act before a terrified congress, the hero community found itself split down the middle. Some heroes were siding with Iron Man, in favor of registering their powers with the government, and others were in Captain America's camp, choosing to help form an underground rebellion. But despite the split in their fictional universe, the editorial direction of Marvel Comics had rarely been more unified.

And that unity led to the *Civil War*, an epic miniseries event that garnered much media attention from various major newspapers, even prompting a visit by Editor-in-Chief Joe Quesada to Comedy Central's *Colbert Report*. Each comic that tied into the main storyline of the ongoing war sported a split-screen cover image, allowing the titles to be easily recognizable to a hungry fan base that was desperately seeking out every battle-hardened adventure.

And while the war at home racked up casualty after casualty, Marvel's space-faring heroes entered their own private war in the pages of *Annihilation*, a crossover event spotlighting lesser-used cosmic heroes like the Silver Surfer and Drax the Destroyer. War was everywhere, and Marvel was truly reaping the benefits.

X-FACTOR INVESTIGATIONS
• *X-Factor* #1
Writer Peter David returned to the team he popularized in the early 1990s, this time with artist Ryan Sook. Taking a noir approach, Jamie Madrox opened X-Factor Investigations, a private detective agency employing other mutants including Siryn, M, and Strong Guy.

VULCAN'S VENGEANCE
• *X-Men: Deadly Genesis* #1
A modern-day story revealing dark secrets of a supergroup's past, this six-issue miniseries by acclaimed writer Ed Brubaker and artist Trevor Hairsine delved into the hidden story behind the famous *Giant-Size X-Men* #1 of the mid 1970s. It told the story of another team of X-Men that Professor X had organized to invade the island of Krakoa, a team that had seemingly perished in battle.

As the X-Men began to experience strange visions, Cyclops and Marvel Girl were kidnapped, and Banshee was killed. Later, their enemy was revealed to be a mutant named Vulcan, a survivor of the first storm on Krakoa, and the brother of Scott and Alex Summers.

X-MEN FACE DECIMATION
• *House Of M: The Day After*
In this Decimation story line tie-in one-shot by Chris Claremont, Randy Green, and Aaron Lopresti, most of the mutant population awoke to discover that their abilities were gone thanks to the Scarlet Witch, with only an estimated 198 individuals unaffected.

SPIDER-WOMAN'S SECRETS
• *Spider-Woman: Origin* #1
With her popularity increased due to her inclusion on the roster of the New Avengers, Jessica Drew, the original Spider-Woman, had her origin updated in this five-issue limited series by writers Brian Michael Bendis and Brian Reed, and artists Jonathan and Joshua Luna. After a lab experiment on Wundagore Mountain altered her DNA in her mother's womb, Jessica Drew was born, developing superpowers at a very young age. Kept in a coma for years by HYDRA forces, Jessica was trained to be an agent of the evil spy organization, before later seeing the error of her ways and joining forces with SHIELD.

QUICKSILVER'S QUEST

• *Son Of M #1*

Tying into the Decimation fall-out from the *House Of M* miniseries, a de-powered Quicksilver traveled to Attilan and stole a portion of the Terrigen Mists (the source of the Inhumans' powers) in this six-issue limited series by writer David Hine and artist Roy Allan Martinez. Now with new time-leaping abilities, Quicksilver's heroic nature slowly began to fade away.

THE IRON SPIDER

"Not to put too fine a point on it… I need your help. And your word, that you'll stick with me through what's coming, no matter what."

• *The Amazing Spider-Man #529*

They were on the road to a civil war, but they just didn't know it yet. With a new lease on life after the Other story line, Peter Parker had become Iron Man's right-hand man, the two growing close as members of the New Avengers team. Tony Stark designed a new uniform for Spider-Man, with an array of new gadgets to help him in his crusade against crime. He also seemed to be trying to buy Peter's favor by creating a home for the Parker family in the illustrious Stark Tower, after their old home burned to the ground, But all these favors would come back to bite Parker harder than a radioactive spider, when Stark later asked Spider-Man to side with him over the controversial Super Hero Registration Act that the government was considering passing.

Written by J. Michael Straczynski with pencils by Ron Garney and a cover by Bryan Hitch, plus a variant cover by Mike Wieringo, *The Amazing Spider-Man #529* was the issue that debuted Spidey's new look. Spider-Man's new costume could allow him to glide for short distances, deflect small caliber bullets, listen to police and emergency bands, view the infrared and ultra-violet spectrums, and even breathe under water for a brief amount of time. The costume also included three arm-like waldoes at the back, and could camouflage itself at will so as to appear invisible to the naked eye or resemble Spider-Man's traditional blue and red uniform.

After the events of the Civil War, Peter Parker would abandon his new iron spider look in favor of his old duds. This costume was then used to arm Stark's Scarlet Spiders.

PLANET HULK

• *The Incredible Hulk #92*

Writer Greg Pak, along with artist Carlo Pagulayan, sent the Hulk into space where he crash-landed on the primitive planet of Sakaar, a world of gladiators and cruel kings. His powers severely reduced during the journey, Hulk was taken captive and sold as a slave. He met an army of alien allies in the gladiatorial arenas, and soon joined in the brotherhood pact of Warbound with them, before instigating a revolution against Sakaar's Red King. Called the Green Scar by a doting populace, the Hulk finally became emperor and even took a warrior queen Caiera, who soon became pregnant with his child.

The Hulk had seemed to find peace at last on Sakaar, until his spaceship, one crafted by the elite of Earth's heroes, exploded and tragically killed his wife and unborn child.

BRUBAKER'S DAREDEVIL

• *Daredevil #82*

Writer Ed Brubaker and artist Michael Lark had quite a challenge ahead of them when they took over the reins of *Daredevil* from the popular team of writer Brian Michael Bendis and artist Alex Maleev. Already forming a strong working relationship in the pages of DC Comics' *Gotham Central*, Brubaker and Lark began their run with Matthew Murdock in jail, as a Daredevil impersonator ran free around the rooftops of New York City. As their dark and moody tale progressed in later issues, Daredevil saw his best friend fake his death and then enroll in the witness protection plan, before he himself escaped prison and fled the country.

Although Matt Murdock was locked away in prison, "Daredevil" continued to fight crime. After Murdock escaped his jail cell, he confronted this imposter to discover he was in reality the hero Iron Fist.

MEETING OF THE MINDS

• *The New Avengers: Illuminati*
In this momentous special that would birth both the beginnings of *Civil War* and *Planet Hulk*, writer Brian Michael Bendis and artist Alex Maleev crafted the untold story of an elite group of Marvel heroes deciding to meet regularly in order to maintain a flow of information between their various Super Hero groups. Comprising Iron Man, Dr. Strange, Professor X, Mr. Fantastic, Black Bolt, and Namor the Submariner—with the Black Panther refusing his invitation—this new Illuminati met several times during the course of this special, once to discuss the Super Hero Registration Act that was about to be passed by congress.

In another of their meetings, the Illuminati decided to exile the Hulk into space to finally end his unpredictable rampages on Earth.

X-MEN: THE LAST STAND

The powerhouse cast of the original X-Men movies reunited to create this third installment, under the guidance of director Brett Ratner and screenwriters Zak Penn and Simon Kinberg. Released on May 26th, this film saw the screen debuts of Beast, brought to life by Kelsey Grammer, and Angel, portrayed by Ben Foster. Ellen Page also joined the cast as Kitty Pryde, a character who had previously only been glimpsed in cameo roles in the other X-films.

DECLARING WAR

"Congratulations, children. You just joined the resistance."

Originally aligning with his mentor Iron Man, Spider-Man soon realized he'd been misguided, and changed his allegiance to Captain America's side. He continued to fight for the rebellion even after Cap turned himself over to the authorities.

• *Civil War #1*
Accompanied by an advertising campaign challenging readers with the question, "Whose side are you on?" writer Mark Millar and artist Steve McNiven unleashed *Civil War* on the public, an epic seven-issue limited series that sparked some of the most heated fan debate in the history of Marvel Comics. Selling over 300,000 copies for its debut issue, a feat rarely seen in the marketplace of the 2000s, each issue of *Civil War* also came in a variant edition with a cover by Michael Turner, as well as in a sketch variant version featuring Turner's pencil art. The events of this tumultuous story crossed over into nearly every Marvel title of the time, and severely impacted the lives of nearly every major hero in its legendary stable.

As the government passed the Super Hero Registration Act, a new bill that required every superpowered individual to register his or her

identity with the government, Iron Man became the Act's spokesman, promoting the idea of an organized and unified sect of superhumans. Captain America, however, found the Act unconstitutional, and an invasion of privacy for those heroes requiring secret lives in order to protect their loved ones, and formed an underground militia intent on combating Stark's forces.

As the series progressed, heroes chose sides and lines were drawn in the sand, Iron Man and his band of registered heroes began arresting any unlicensed vigilantes. After the death of the hero Goliath, and a fierce battle through the streets of Manhattan, Captain America surrendered to Stark's forces, disgusted at what both sides had been reduced to. Cap's team went into hiding, choosing not to give up their fight, as Captain America was led away to a maximum security cell. Meanwhile, Iron Man took over as the director of SHIELD, ushering in a new age for the heroes of the Marvel Universe.

In a conflict with the New Warriors in Stamford, Connecticut, the villain Nitro exploded, killing hundreds of innocent men, women, and children and inspiring a grieving U.S. government to retaliate with the Super Hero Registration Act.

SPIDER-MAN UNMASKS

• *The Amazing Spider-Man* #533

With the welfare of his family always at the forefront of his mind, Peter Parker's identity was a well-guarded secret. So, he was forced to make a hard decision when asked to publicly unmask alongside his friend and mentor Iron Man, to show his support for the Super Hero Registration Act. In this story by writer J. Michael Straczynski and artist Ron Garney, Spider-Man decided to finally reveal his identity to a stunned world.

WAR ON THE FRONT LINES

• *Civil War: Frontline* #1

In this eleven-issue limited series, writer Paul Jenkins revealed the humanity behind the Civil War. Through a collection of short stories and multi-part serials he chronicled the conflict from the point of view of reporters Ben Urich and Sally Floyd. The series featured stories by artists Ramon Bachs, Steve Lieber, Leandro Fernandez, Lee Weeks, and a host of other creators including cover artist John Watson, and also detailed the hero Speedball's metamorphosis into the dark Penance.

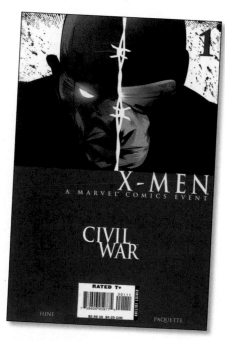

X-MEN GO TO WAR

• *Civil War: X-Men* #1

Writer David Hine and artists Yanick Paquette and Aaron Lopresti chronicled the adventures of the 198 surviving mutants, as they escaped their lives of captivity in the refugee camps set up for them by a controlling government in this four-issue miniseries.

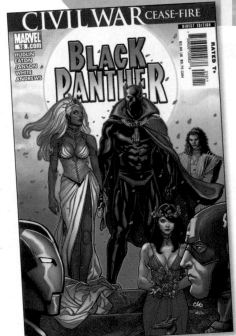

BLACK PANTHER TAKES A QUEEN

• *Black Panther* #18

After a lengthy courtship, Ororo Munroe, Storm of the X-Men, and King T'Challa of Wakanda, gathered their friends together for a brief interlude from the ongoing Super Hero Civil War—a wedding ceremony. In a story written by Reginald Hudlin with pencils by Scot Eaton and additional art by Kaare Andrews, Storm walked down the aisle in a dress designed especially for her by the costume designer of TV's *Guiding Light*, Shawn Dudley.

THE X-MEN'S NEW SEMESTER

• *X-Men: First Class* #1

In this eight-issue miniseries that later sparked its own ongoing title, writer Jeff Parker and artists Roger Cruz and Paul Smith united to tell the early adventures of the original five X-Men as they adjusted to life at Xavier's School for Gifted Youngsters.

MEANWHILE IN 2006...

MISSION TO PLUTO
The space craft New Horizons sets off on a nine-year journey to gather information on Pluto.

SADDAM EXECUTED
Former Iraqi premier Saddam Hussein is executed for crimes against humanity in Baghdad.

CONFLICT IN IRAQ CONTINUES
The US death toll in Iraq reaches 3,000.

HAMAS IS ELECTED IN PALESTINE
The Islamic militant organization Hamas wins democratic control of the government of the Palestinian Authority.

ONE BILLIONTH SONG ON iTUNES
The popularity of buying music downloads on MP3 is clear by the success of iTunes.

MILOSEVIC DIES
The former Yugoslavian leader, Slobodan Milosevic dies of a heart attack in his cell while still on trial at the Hague for war crimes.

2006 LEBANON WAR
Lebanon sees thirty-three days of conflict, largely between Hezbollah paramilitary forces and the Israeli military.

NATASCHA KAMPUSCH ESCAPES
The eighteen-year-old Austrian girl, who was kidnapped aged ten, flees from the house cellar where she was held captive for eight years.

NINTENDO RELEASES THE Wii
A new generation of gaming is launched with the Wii, a new console targeted at a broader demographic than previous video games.

ECHOES OF COLD-WAR SPY GAMES
In a plot reminiscent of the Cold War, the former KGB agent Alexander Litvinenko is poisoned with a radioactive substance in a London sushi bar.

SOCIAL NETWORKING GOES INTO CYBERSPACE
People bond with each other on the Internet as social networking sites like MySpace, YouTube, and Facebook become popular.

AND AT THE MOVIES...
Pan's Labyrinth, a young girl forgets her brutal fascist stepfather by escaping into an eerie fantasy world in Guillermo del Toro's surreal film; Casino Royale, Daniel Craig's edgy 007 takes on a terrorist banker in his first mission; The Departed, Martin Scorsese's tale of Leonardo DiCaprio's cop who goes undercover as a gangster and Matt Damon's gangster who goes undercover as a cop.

I AM THOR! AND I – WISH – TO LIVE.

2007
NEW WORLD ORDER

After the huge success of the *Civil War* miniseries, Marvel had once again realized the potential of the blockbuster crossover event to generate sales. With even *Civil War* reprints selling above and beyond expectations, it was only a matter of time before the powers that be at Marvel decided to see if lightning could strike twice for them. And with the natural procession of events set up back in the original *Illuminati* special of 2006, World War Hulk soon reared its monstrous head, creating shockwaves once again in the comic marketplace.

Meanwhile, the war had impacted on the fictional residents of the Marvel Universe as well. Despite Captain America's surrender, many of his underground forces refused to give in, and for the first time in history, the Avengers saw themselves split into two factions with each refusing to acknowledge the other as the genuine article. Spider-Man found out just why he'd been wise to fight to keep his identity hidden from the rest of the world for so long, and Captain America became a casualty of the fallout of war. But through all the carnage, familiar heroes would return, ensuring that Marvel had plenty of new surprises up its sleeve.

JANUARY

IRON FIST BREAKS THROUGH
• *The Immortal Iron Fist* #1
Already amassing much acclaim for his work on *The Uncanny X-Men*, *Captain America*, and *Daredevil*, Ed Brubaker teamed with co-writer Matt Fraction and artist David Aja to give Iron Fist another shot at an ongoing title.

FEBRUARY

Daredevil writer/director Mark Steven Johnson wrote and directed Ghost Rider's first feature film. The film opened on February 16, and starred Nicholas Cage in the title role, alongside Eva Mendes, Peter Fonda, and Wes Bentley.

MARCH

THE RETURN OF CAPTAIN MARVEL
• *Civil War: The Return*
The original Captain Marvel returned with the help of writer Paul Jenkins and artist Tom Raney in this one-shot special. He had reached out to touch a crease in the fabric of existence, only to be teleported to our conflicted present.

THUNDERBOLTS IN NEW HANDS
• *Thunderbolts* #110
Reimagined by Warren Ellis and Mike Deodato Jr. after *Civil War*, the Thunderbolts became a government-sponsored strike force bent on taking down unregistered heroes. Led by the Green Goblin, the team included returning members Songbird, Moonstone, and Radioactive Man, along with new blood Penance (formerly Speedball), Venom, Bullseye, and a new Swordsman.

APRIL

SPIDER-MAN: BACK IN BLACK
• *The Amazing Spider-Man* #539
With Spider-Man's secret identity now public, the Kingpin had hired a sniper to assassinate him. However, the bullet found its way to Aunt May instead, putting her in a coma. Infuriated by the attack, Peter donned his old black costume (first seen in *Marvel Super Heroes Secret Wars* #8, Dec., 1984) to reflect his no-holds-barred attitude. He ruthlessly followed a trail of clues back to the Kingpin, before giving his old foe a vicious beating. In this story, written by J. Michael Straczynski with pencils by Ron Garney, a vengeful Spider-Man served up a lesson to all those that would endanger his family.

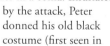

Spider-Man had originally abandoned his black costume because he felt it conveyed the wrong message. But once he saw his aunt in a coma, he decided that the gloves were off, and that a darker message was appropriate.

FALLEN HERO

"He was supposed to be the first of an army… an army of super soldiers… but it all went wrong."

• *Captain America* #25

America had never been more defeated. The Civil War was over, and the freedom fighters had lost. Captain America had turned himself over to police custody after seeing the damage that the war between these two groups of "heroes" had brought to the country he loved so much. But writer Ed Brubaker and artist Steve Epting had one final nail to put in Cap's coffin, and maybe in the coffin of the American Dream as well.

As Captain America was led in shackles up the stairs to the Federal Courthouse in Manhattan, a shot rang out. A sniper's bullet from across the street felled the hero, and chaos erupted as hundreds of spectators and reporters ran for their lives. As distraught government agent, Sharon Carter, rushed to be by the side of the man she loved, three more shots were fired by a mysterious source, ensuring Steve Roger's death. And it wasn't until much later, after Cap's pals Bucky Barnes and the Falcon had tracked down the sniper, Crossbones, and brought him to justice, that Sharon realized the truth. The second gunman, the one who'd fired those three mystery shots, had been her, albeit under Dr. Faustus' control. The whole tragic mess had been orchestrated by Cap's arch foe, the Red Skull, but Sharon Carter had done the deed. Agent 13 had killed Captain America. Surprising an unsuspecting fan base who thought the worst was over for Steve Rogers, Captain America's death captured worldwide media attention, and spawned several reprint editions.

THE SPOILS OF WAR

• *Civil War: The Initiative*

Written by Brian Michael Bendis and Warren Ellis, with art by Marc Silvestri, this one-shot special served as an introduction to the post-Civil War Marvel Universe. Debuting new teams like Omega Flight and the new lineup of the Thunderbolts, the issue also had Iron Man deciding who would make the cut in his new Avengers, and Ms. Marvel attempting to recruit Spider-Woman back onto the government's side.

THE AVENGERS EXPAND

"The World needs the Avengers. The best of the best. The best and the brightest. Symbols. Icons."

• *The Mighty Avengers* #1

The war was over. It was a time of healing and rebirth. And who better to lead the way in this brave new world than one of the architects of its design, Brian Michael Bendis. With the help of artist Frank Cho, Bendis created the Mighty Avengers, a government-sponsored team that would serve as the antithesis to the still-underground New Avengers. While Spider-Man, Luke Cage, Spider-Woman, Dr. Strange, Iron Fist, Wolverine, and the second Ronin (the newly adopted identity of the resurrected Hawkeye) all hid from the law, the Mighty Avengers were in place to enforce it. With Ms. Marvel serving as the team's leader, the Mighty Avengers were handpicked by the newly appointed Director of SHIELD, Tony Stark, aka Iron Man. The Sentry, Wonder Man, Black Widow, and the Wasp all renewed their Avengers memberships in this core team, along with newcomer, Ares, the angry god of war, and brother of the former Avenger, Hercules.

Besides existing as the first line of defense for their country and even the world, the Mighty Avengers also served as the figurehead for the newly divided American people. They stood as a team for others to look up to, and for the other Avengers teams in Iron Man's new program to base themselves on. For in the wake of the Civil War, Tony Stark had devised a fifty-state Initiative program, in which every state would get its own trained and licensed team of Super Heroes to defend it, in order to prevent future tragedies like the explosion in Stamford, Connecticut.

The first challenge the Mighty Avengers faced was an attack on Manhattan by the Mole Man and longtime Avengers' foe, Ultron.

Peter Parker returned to the silver screen on May 4 in Sam Raimi's third installment. Tobey Maguire reprised the title role, and Kirsten Dunst and James Franco returned as supporting characters Mary Jane Watson and Harry Osborn, with Franco also adopting the new identity of Spidey adversary, New Goblin.

JUNE

THE AVENGERS TAKE THE INITIATIVE

• *Avengers: The Initiative* #1
Using the *Civil War: The Initiative* special as a springboard, writer Dan Slott along with artist Stefano Caselli created this new series to spotlight the government's training program for newly registered superhuman agents. Under the tutelage of Yellowjacket, War Machine, Justice, and drill instructor the Gauntlet, new heroes were trained at the Camp Hammond military base in Stamford, Connecticut, each with the hopes of filling a slot in one of the fifty new state Avengers teams.

ALPHA MEETS OMEGA

• *Omega Flight: The Initiative* #1
When the majority of Canada's Super Hero team Alpha Flight was killed due to fallout from the House of M event, writer Michael Avon Oeming and penciller Scott Kolins filled the gap they'd left behind with *Omega Flight*, a five-issue miniseries spotlighting a new team of heroes based in Canada.

⊞ June 15 saw the release of *4: The Rise Of The Silver Surfer*, the second Fantastic Four feature film. The movie showcased the computer generated Silver Surfer character and the mysterious Galactus.

COPING WITHOUT CAPTAIN AMERICA

• *Fallen Son: Wolverine* #1
After the death of Captain America, a series of one-shots were released showing how various heroes were dealing with the tragedy. Written by Jeph Loeb with art by Leinil Yu, Ed McGuinness, John Romita Jr., David Finch, and John Cassaday, the specials dealt with the five stages of grieving: denial, anger, bargaining, depression, and acceptance.

Wolverine starred in the first of five one-shots, all spotlighting different characters including the Avengers, Spider-Man, Iron Man, and Captain America himself.

AUGUST

THE HULK DECLARES WAR

"They thought he was finally dead. But he survived. Because he is the Green Scar... the Worldbreaker... the eye of anger... The Hulk. And now he's coming home."

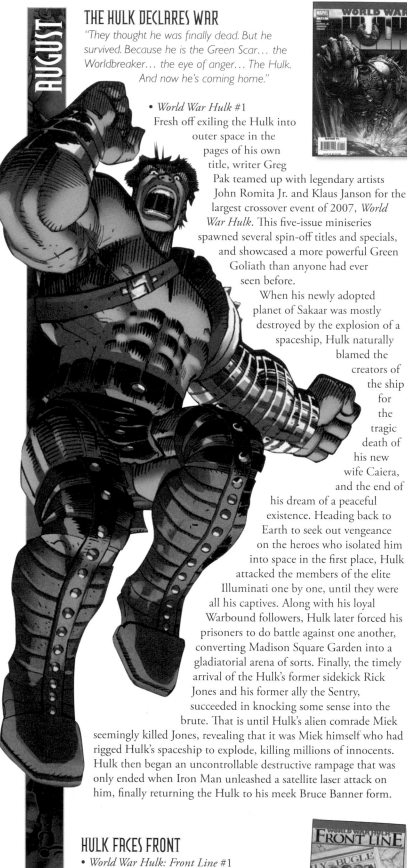

• *World War Hulk* #1
Fresh off exiling the Hulk into outer space in the pages of his own title, writer Greg Pak teamed up with legendary artists John Romita Jr. and Klaus Janson for the largest crossover event of 2007, *World War Hulk*. This five-issue miniseries spawned several spin-off titles and specials, and showcased a more powerful Green Goliath than anyone had ever seen before.

When his newly adopted planet of Sakaar was mostly destroyed by the explosion of a spaceship, Hulk naturally blamed the creators of the ship for the tragic death of his new wife Caiera, and the end of his dream of a peaceful existence. Heading back to Earth to seek out vengeance on the heroes who isolated him into space in the first place, Hulk attacked the members of the elite Illuminati one by one, until they were all his captives. Along with his loyal Warbound followers, Hulk later forced his prisoners to do battle against one another, converting Madison Square Garden into a gladiatorial arena of sorts. Finally, the timely arrival of the Hulk's former sidekick Rick Jones and his former ally the Sentry, succeeded in knocking some sense into the brute. That is until Hulk's alien comrade Miek seemingly killed Jones, revealing that it was Miek himself who had rigged Hulk's spaceship to explode, killing millions of innocents. Hulk then began an uncontrollable destructive rampage that was only ended when Iron Man unleashed a satellite laser attack on him, finally returning the Hulk to his meek Bruce Banner form.

HULK FACES FRONT

• *World War Hulk: Front Line* #1
This six-issue miniseries written by Paul Jenkins with art by Ramon Bachs looked at World War Hulk from the perspective of newspaper journalists Ben Urich and Sally Floyd as they attempted to chronicle the chaos that Manhattan had birthed.

THOR THUNDERS ON

• *Thor* #1

With his impressive run ending on *The Amazing Spider-Man*, writer J. Michael Straczynski decided to tackle another of Marvel's iconic pantheon—Thor. Thought dead since the Avengers Disassembled story line, Thor returned to Earth after struggling with his inner demons. Aided by fan-favorite artist Olivier Coipel, Thor ventured to the mortal plane and reestablished his old secret identity of Dr. Donald Blake.

ONE MORE DAY

"You will not consciously remember this bargain, or this moment, or the life you lived to this point. But there will be a very small part of your soul that will remember, that will know what you lost. And my joy will be in listening to that part of your soul screaming throughout eternity."

• *The Amazing Spider-Man* #544

When the powers that be thought it was time to reinvigorate the Spider-Man franchise by restoring some of the elements to Peter Parker's life that made Spider-Man a hit in the first place, they realized that a few of those components would prove challenging to restore. After all, Peter Parker was no longer the swinging bachelor he'd been in the past, as he was married to Mary Jane Watson. Also, during the events of Marvel's Civil War, Peter had outed his secret identity to the public, effectively changing all of his current relationships and making him a fugitive.

Editor-in-Chief Joe Quesada sought to change all that, and began to conspire just how to put those genies back in their respective bottles. His solution was One More Day, a four-issue series spanning all three Spider-Man books. J. Michael Straczynski took up the writing chores over Quesada's plot, and Quesada himself pencilled the story.

As Spider-Man's Aunt May lay dying in a hospital bed from a sniper's bullet meant for Peter, the Parkers were forced to answer the toughest question ever put to them. The demon Mephisto had taken an interest in their hopeless situation, and smelled an opportunity. Accepting Mephisto's offer of the life of their aunt in exchange for the love that Peter and Mary Jane shared, the young couple woke up alone in a world they no longer recognized. A world in which the two of them could never be together again, and never even remembered being together in the first place.

Spider-Man first turned to billionaire Tony Stark in order to obtain funds to keep his Aunt May alive. And after a violent conflict, ending with Iron Man encased in a webbing cocoon, Iron Man agreed to do just that, but in his own secretive way.

MEANWHILE IN 2007...

VIRGINIA TECH MASSACRE
In the deadliest school shooting in US history, thirty-two people are killed on a university campus when a student goes on a shooting rampage before turning the gun on himself.

FEMALE SPEAKER OF THE HOUSE
Nancy Pelosi becomes the first female speaker of the House of Representatives.

NEW PRIME MINISTER FOR BRITAIN
After ten years in power, Tony Blair resigns as Prime Minister and is succeeded by the Labour Chancellor Gordon Brown.

BENAZIR BHUTTO ASSASSINATED
After returning from exile to stand for office, former Pakistani Prime Minister Benazir Bhutto is assassinated at an election rally.

DARK PROTEST AGAINST CLIMATE CHANGE
Sydney, Australia switches off all the lights in the city from 7.30pm to 8.30pm in a statement on global climate change.

APPLE RELEASES THE iPHONE
Following the success of its iPod, Apple produces its version of the mobile phone and MP3 player in one.

SCOUT MOVEMENT CELEBRATES
The World Organization of the Scout Movement celebrates the centenary of its founding and of Lord Baden Powell's first scout camp.

A CONCERT FOR DIANA
Ten years after her death, a concert takes place at Wembley Stadium in London in honor of the former Princess of Wales.

BRIDGE STRETCHES INTO HISTORY BOOKS
The second span of the Tacoma Narrows Bridge opens in Washington, and is the longest twin suspension bridge in the world.

THE FINAL INSTALLMENT OF HARRY POTTER
The seventh and final Harry Potter book, *The Deathly Hallows*, makes publishing history when it sells over eleven million copies worldwide in the first twenty-four hours of being released.

AND AT THE MOVIES...
No Country for Old Men, the Coen brothers tell this violent tale of greed and a sociopathic hit man hunting down a missing $2 million; *Enchanted*, real and animated worlds collide in Disney's comic fairytale about a princess seeking her Prince Charming in modern-day New York; *The Bourne Ultimatum*, the last in this exciting trilogy has Matt Damon's Bourne dodging new assassins while he searches for his unknown past.

PRISONERS OF WAR

As writer Mark Millar and artist Steve McNiven's *Civil War* miniseries continued to shake the foundations of the Marvel Universe, both sides began to up the ante. Iron Man and his team of pro-registration Super Heroes were capturing unlicensed heroes by the truckload and dragging them to their impenetrable maximum security prison, designed by Mr. Fantastic and located in the removed dimension of the Negative Zone. It was here that the heroes of the resistance staged a massive attack with the help of the Invisible Woman, who had broken allegiances with her own husband. This contained fight bled out into the streets of New York City, where the rebel Cloak teleported everyone in order to escape imprisonment at the hands of Stark's team.

"YOU WANT SOME OF THIS?... AND WE'RE NOT JUST DRINK-ING... WE'RE PAYING TRIBUTE."

2008
BRAND NEW BRAND

It was a brand new day. And not just in the pages of *Amazing Spider-Man* comic books. Bruce Banner had been incarcerated, and there was a new and mysterious Red Hulk roaming the Russian countryside. Captain America had returned, even if the man beneath the mask had not; the X-Men had been rocked by the events of the "Messiah Complex" story line that had ended the previous year, spawning brand new *X-Force* and *Young X-Men* titles.

However, the main focus was on Spider-Man, as new editor Stephen Wacker arrived at the helm of flagship title *The Amazing Spider-Man*. Fresh off the weekly hit comic for DC Comics entitled *52*, Wacker utilized his expertise at working under tight deadliness to revitalize Spider-Man's comic by releasing it three times a month, with a rotating staff of creators. Hiring his Spidey "brain trust," consisting of writers Dan Slott, Zeb Wells, Marc Guggenheim, and Bob Gale, Wacker set out to create a fresh start for Peter Parker in this newly streamlined reality.

The result was a fresh world of possibility for the wall-crawler, and an infectious excitement that seemed to spread throughout the entire Marvel Universe.

JANUARY

WORLD'S GREATEST

• *Fantastic Four* #554
Mark Millar returned to the family he'd helped put through the ringer in the pages of *Civil War* as the newest writer of *The Fantastic Four*. Accompanied by one of his regular partners in crime, penciler Bryan Hitch, Millar crafted a story that saw the return of Reed Richard's ex, Alyssa Moy.

THE INCREDIBLE HERCULES

• *The Incredible Herc* #112
With Bruce Banner safely locked away in a government installation after the events of *World War Hulk*, the demi-god and former Avenger Hercules stepped up to fill the brute's massive shoes and prompt a title change to *The Incredible Hulk* comic. Written by Greg Pak and Fred Van Lente, and drawn by Khoi Pham, *The Incredible Herc* followed the adventures of Hercules and boy genius Amadeus Cho as they set out to destroy the government agency SHIELD.

FEBRUARY

THE AFTERSMASH OF WAR

• *Warbound* #1
Hulk's inner circle earned its own five-issue miniseries in this *World War Hulk: Aftersmash!* tie-in by writer Greg Pak and artists Leonard Kirk and Rafa Sandoval. On the run from the government agency SHIELD, Hulk's alien allies Korg, Elloe, Hiroim, and the nameless Brood found themselves trapped in the sealed-off small town of Gammaworld, courtesy of the Hulk's old enemy the Leader. Each issue also featured a bonus backup story fleshing out more of the Warbound's history.

BRAND NEW DAY

• *The Amazing Spider-Man* #546
With his many titles whittled down to just his flagship book, Spider-Man began a new chapter, thanks to a rotating creative team, kick-started by writer Dan Slott and penciler Steve McNiven. With his marriage to Mary Jane Watson now no more than a fading dream, Peter Parker's life began anew as he lived with Aunt May, now perfectly healthy thanks to the machinations of the demon Mephisto.

MARCH

THE NEW CAPTAIN AMERICA

• *Captain America* #34

Former sidekick Bucky Barnes donned a new costume designed by superstar painter Alex Ross in this second act of writer Ed Brubaker's and penciler Steve Epting's epic storyline "The Death of Captain America." With the mystery of the new Cap finally revealed to the hordes of fans who joined the book after Steve Rogers' surprise death, the plot thickened as the Red Skull's evil influence seemed to extend to every corner of America, causing an economic crisis.

THE TWO-FISTED TWELVE

• *The Twelve* #1

Set in the closing days of World War II, when the Super Heroes finally invaded Germany en masse, this twelve-issue limited series focused on a mostly forgotten band of heroes who had been subdued by Nazi scientists and trapped in time, until they were unearthed, in a state of cryogenic suspension, at a construction site in the present. The twelve consisted of Dynamic Man, Mister E, Master Mind Excello, Rockman, Black Widow, Captain Wonder, Fiery Mask, Blue Blade, Laughing Mask, the Witness, Electro, and the Phantom Reporter. Giving this dozing dozen the culture shock of a lifetime were writer J. Michael Straczynski and artist Chris Weston.

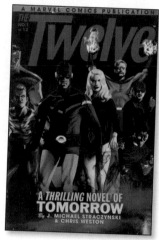

THE RED HULK

• *Hulk* #1

With Hercules stealing the spotlight in his old title, the Hulk's adventures began anew in this ongoing series by the team of Jeph Loeb and Ed McGuinness. Debuting a new, crimson-hued Hulk with a mysterious secret identity that both a team of heroes led by Doc Samson and the readers were left to deduce, Hulk began with the apparent death of classic foe the Abomination.

Readers were faced with a tantalizing mystery: the real human identity of the Red Hulk.

APRIL

X-FORCE FIGHTS BACK

• *X-Force* #1

After the events of the "Messiah Complex" crossover of late 2007, where the mutant Caliban tragically lost his life, Cyclops formed a new deadly strike force to do the dirty work that the X-Men wouldn't lower themselves to do. Featuring the team of Wolverine, X-23, Warpath and Wolfsbane, this new X-Force set out to put a permanent end to extremist group the Purifiers, thanks to writers Craig Kyle and Christopher Yost, and artist Clayton Crain.

It took the combined might of some of the X-Men's most ferocious alumni to tackle the reborn threat of their old foe Bastion.

Ⓜ March 8 saw Peter Parker's return to television with the new Kids WB animated series, *The Spectacular Spider-Man*, featuring the combined efforts of *Gargoyles* creator Greg Weisman, director Victor Cook, and character designer Sean Galloway.

MAY

Ⓜ Director Jon Favreau, along with screenwriters Mark Fergus, Hawk Ostby, Art Marcum, and Matt Holloway blasted Iron Man off on his first big screen adventure on May 2, starring Robert Downey Jr. in the lead role, alongside an impressive supporting cast.

Edward Norton both co-wrote and starred in *The Incredible Hulk*, the semi-sequel to 2003's *Hulk* film. Directed by Louis Leterrier and also written by Zak Penn, this June 13 release also starred Liv Tyler, Tim Roth, and William Hurt.

THE SECRET IS OUT

"...I know who I am... but who are you guys supposed to be, exactly?"

• *Secret Invasion* #1
With plot elements planted years earlier in the pages of comics written by Brian Michael Bendis, the infiltration of Earth by the alien race of shapeshifters the Skrulls first surfaced in the pages of *New Avengers* #31, when a dying Elektra transformed to reveal herself as one of these chameleon-like aliens. Emerging from the imagination of writer Brian Michael Bendis and artist Leinil Francis Yu, this epic miniseries began with every hero and villain's authenticity in question, and ended with a bang that shifted the entire power structure of the Marvel Universe.

Secret Invasion consisted of eight issues of heroes struggling against a barrage of alien attacks, and tied into many spinoff comics focusing on those battles in detail. By the miniseries' final issue, the invasion was ended by the unlikely heroism of Norman Osborn, formerly the renowned Spider-Man enemy the Green Goblin. During a climactic fight that saw the apparent death of longtime Avenger Wasp, Osborn fired the shot heard around the world, killing the Skrull queen and helping Earth defeat the Skrulls. This seemingly valiant act maneuvered Osborn into an extremely powerful position: he became the head of the Avengers, the Fifty-State Initiative and assumed all the powers that used to belong to the superspy agency SHIELD.

As both the Mighty Avengers and the New Avengers followed a crash-landing Skrull spaceship to the Savage Land, Dr. Hank Pym and Reed Richards examined the body of the deceased Skrull who impersonated Elektra. However, just as Mr. Fantastic let his guard down, Pym showed his true colors and attacked his friend, revealing that he was a Skrull in disguise.

THE "DEATH" OF KITTY PRYDE

• *Giant-Size Astonishing X-Men* #1
Fan-favorite X-Men member Kitty Pryde rode off into the proverbial sunset as writer Joss Whedon and artist John Cassaday wrapped up their popular run on Astonishing X-Men with this extra-large special. In this climactic chapter, Kitty seemingly sacrificed herself, using her powers to keep a giant bullet intangible so that it could continue through the cosmos without damaging any planets in its path.

UPGRADING IRON MAN

• *The Invincible Iron Man* #1
The *Iron Man* film was a smash hit at the box office, and the start of the largest and most successful Marvel movie initiative in the history of the company. Capitalizing on that popularity, Iron Man soon received a new comic book series, *The Invincible Iron Man*, courtesy of writer Matt Fraction and artist Salvador Larroca. This new title not only granted Tony Stark a powerful foe with the return of genius Ezekiel Stane, it also entranced audiences with a high-octane revitalization of the Iron Man character, endowing the hero with touches of the trademark wit that had helped make the movie such a worldwide success.

THE ULTIMATE COVER UP

• *Ultimate Origins* #1
Brian Michael Bendis delved a bit more into the backstory of the Ultimate Universe he helped create when he penned this five-issue series with artist Butch Guice. Flashing back to the days of World War II, the series revealed that mutants of the Ultimate world were not a natural genetic evolution, but the result of the government's super-soldier program.

OLD MAN LOGAN

"Get ready for the ride of your life."

• *Wolverine #66*
In the modern landscape of Super Hero comic books, future tales, flashback origins or "what if?"-style epics are rare in the pages of a character's regular title. While these self-contained, multi-part stories were often included within the main titles of the 1980s, comic companies subsequently preferred to spotlight these special tales as miniseries or graphic novels. However, when writer Mark Millar and artist Steve McNiven crafted the eight-part future tale known as "Old Man Logan," Marvel decided to include the series in its regular *Wolverine* title. The result was revitalized sales for the monthly comic, and an unexpected treat for regular readers.

One part glimpse into the dystopian future of the Marvel Universe, and one part buddy comedy, "Old Man Logan" was a fast-paced, violent romp starring an aged Wolverine embarking on a cross-country road trip with an equally time-weathered Hawkeye. When his family was threatened by the corrupt descendants of the incredible Hulk, Wolverine traveled over 3000 miles in Spider-Man's old buggy, the Spider-Mobile, battling Moloids, a Venom/dinosaur hybrid, and other twisted and deadly threats, culminating in a bloody battle as fierce as any Logan had ever experienced.

At the start of "Old Man Logan," Wolverine was retired from a life of crime fighting, living in poverty with his wife and two kids.

MEANWHILE IN 2008...

RECESSION STARTS TO BITE
The previous year's subprime mortgage crisis sparks a downturn in the US economy signaling worldwide recession. Lehman Brothers files for bankruptcy, the largest in US history.

CASTRO STANDS DOWN
Fidel Castro announces his resignation as President of Cuba, a post he has held since 1976. His younger brother Raul is elected President.

THE FIRST BIONIC EYES
At London's Moorfields Eye Hospital, two blind patients become the first people to receive bionic eyes.

CYCLONE DEATH TOLL
More than 138,000 people lose their lives in the catastrophic destruction caused by Cyclone Nargis, Burma's worst natural disaster.

ARTHUR C. CLARKE DIES
Sir Arthur C. Clark, the author of 2001: A Space Odyssey and the host of TV shows about mysterious phenomena, dies aged 90. Known, with Robert Heinlein and Isaac Asimov, as one of the "big three" science-fiction writers.

NEW RUSSIAN PRESIDENT
Dmitry Medvedev becomes President of Russia, replacing Vladimir Putin.

US PRESIDENTIAL ELECTION
The first African American candidate to be nominated by either party, Democrat Barack Obama defeats Republican John McCain to become the 44th President of the United States.

MUMBAI TERROR ATTACKS
Pakistani-based Islamist extremists stage terrorist attacks in Mumbai, India, in which 164 people are killed and over 300 injured.

MADONNA'S MILLIONS
In the year of her 50th birthday, Madonna's Sticky and Sweet world tour is the highest-grossing by a solo artist, with ticket sales of $280 million.

AND AT THE MOVIES...
In Indiana Jones and the Crystal Skull, Indy battles Soviet agents; Christopher Nolan's The Dark Knight pits Batman against The Joker; James Bond embarks on a vengeful quest in Quantum of Solace; former Bond Pierce Brosnan sings in the Abba musical Mamma Mia!; Kathryn Bigelow's The Hurt Locker follows a US Army bomb disposal squad in the Iraq War; sleeper hit is Slumdog Millionaire, about a young quiz show winner from the slums of Mumbai.

The Amazing Spider-Man #546, 2nd printing variant cover (Feb., 2008)

When Marvel revamped the Spider-Man franchise, they knew they were treading on dangerous ground. Peter Parker had such a rich history, Marvel didn't want to alienate fans by altering too much of his backstory. However, the company felt Spider-Man was in need of a fresh start, so they erased his marriage to Mary Jane Watson from continuity and brought back his old friend and sometime enemy, Harry Osborn. Fans quickly embraced this "Brand New Day" that saw Spidey return to his roots as an everyman down on his luck, in a now thrice-monthly flagship title.

"IT'S A NEW DAY. SO LISTEN CAREFULLY. THIS IS HOW IT'S GOING TO BE."

2009
DARK REIGN

It was always darkest before the dawn. Or at least that was what the heroes of the Marvel Universe had to keep telling themselves. When the corrupt Norman Osborn fired the bullet that ended the Skrull threat of *Secret Invasion*, the power structure of the entire world began to shift. Tony Stark was ousted as head of SHIELD, and Osborn renamed the organization HAMMER, even taking control of the Avengers team. Heroes already alienated by the Super Human Registration Act and the events of the *Civil War* series were now hunted by Osborn's men.

This was the status quo of "Dark Reign," a crossover event felt in the majority of Marvel's titles. While not linked by a main series or miniseries, the events of "Dark Reign" were widespread and nearly as ambitious as the world-changing battles waged in 2006-7's *Civil War*. An ominous shadow had fallen over the Marvel Universe, and the result was a refreshing batch of stories dealing with rebellion, corrupt governments, and the manipulation of public perception.

A SHOCK TO THE SENSES
• *The Amazing Spider-Man* #578
Fan-favorite writer Mark Waid stopped by the Spider-Man offices to pen an acclaimed story alongside brilliant comic artist Marcos Martin. In only two issues, the duo wove a tale full of tension as Spidey battled the Shocker in the New York City subway tunnels. Waid and Martin also introduced a major new character into Peter Parker's world, J. Jonah Jameson Sr., the father of *The Daily Bugle*'s most infamous publisher.

Ⓜ The newly formed production company Marvel Animation debuted the *Wolverine and the X-Men* animated series on January 23. The series lasted for one season and consisted of 26 episodes.

THE ULTIMATE PRICE
• *Ultimatum* #1
The Ultimate Comics Universe was in need of a shakeup, and writer Jeph Loeb and artist David Finch instigated a thorough reboot of the Ultimate titles in the pages of this five-issue, crossover miniseries. As the home of Spider-Man, the Fantastic Four, and the Ultimates, New York City played an important role in the Ultimate Universe. So when the mutant villain Magneto used his abilities to drown the city in the biggest flood it had ever seen, the damage and loss of life was tremendous—many heroes and villains wouldn't survive to see the birth of the new status quo, including mainstays like Wolverine, Professor X, Cyclops, Hank Pym, the Wasp, Doctor Doom, and even Magneto himself.

THE FINAL IRON CURTAIN
• *Iron Man: The End* #1
The classic team of David Michelinie and Bob Layton reunited on the character they had revolutionized years earlier to give Iron Man his swan song in the pages of *Iron Man: The End* special. Plotted by the legendary duo and drawn by artist Bernard Chang, this one-shot saw Tony Stark pass on his heroic mantle to young scientist Nick Travis, while focusing on his latest scientific breakthrough, an elevator into outer space.

WAR AND PIECES
• *War Machine* #1
Spinning out of the pages of the *Dark Reign: New Nation* one-shot, former Iron Man James Rhodes received his own title once again, this time with the help of writer Greg Pak and artist Leonardo Manco. This gritty series saw the now half-human cyborg that was Rhodey take on high-profile threats, including the Ultimo virus.

SCARED OF THE DARK

"I want an army of men and women ready to take back the world. And those who are not ready will be replaced."

• *Dark Avengers #1*
At the end of writer Brian Michael Bendis' *Secret Invasion* event, former Green Goblin Norman Osborn was shown talking with a clandestine alliance of elite Super Villains dubbed the Cabal. Made up of tried and true villains, including Osborn, Loki, Doctor Doom, and the Hood, along with the morally ambiguous White Queen and Namor, the Sub-Mariner, the Cabal was the secret power structure behind the post-Invasion world. As Bendis and artist Mike Deodato launched *Dark Avengers*, readers quickly realized just how drastic the landscape of that world had become.

Norman Osborn was in charge. Given power over the now-dissolved agency that was SHIELD, Osborn usurped Tony Stark's position to create HAMMER and legally hunt down all the heroes he had despised for most of his adult life. With public opinion on his side, Osborn donned the identity of the Iron Patriot, a perverse amalgam of the uniforms of his enemies Iron Man and Captain America, and recruited his own team of Avengers to help enforce his iron-fist rule. Osborn conned the Sentry and the god of war Ares into fighting by his side, as well as Marvel Boy (renaming him Captain Marvel). He filled out the rest of the team's ranks by disguising Super Villains in heroic garb. The assassin Bullseye became the new Hawkeye, Venom passed himself off as Spider-Man, and Moonstone dubbed herself Ms. Marvel. Even Wolverine's corrupt son Daken joined Osborn's cause, taking his father's moniker and wearing Wolverine's old costume. The villains had become the heroes and the heroes had become the villains. And just like that, the Avengers legacy was tainted, seemingly forever.

SPIDEY MEETS THE PRESIDENT

• *The Amazing Spider-Man #583*
While the main story of this issue, by writer Mark Waid and artist Barry Kitson, was an interesting examination of Peter Parker's relationship with his former girlfriend Betty Brant, this self-contained tale wasn't the reason readers flocked to comic stores (persuading Marvel into publishing multiple reprints). The real reason for the issue's popularity was evident on its cover, which showed Spider-Man snapping a photo of the newly elected President of the United States, Barack Obama. Besides its main tale, this landmark issue featured a backup tale by writer Zeb Wells and artist Todd Nauck, that teamed Spidey with the President in order to stop the masquerading Chameleon from being sworn in as the new Commander-in-Chief.

LIVING IN DARKNESS

• *Punisher #1*
Writer Rick Remender and artist Jerome Opena showed readers what life was like for Frank Castle in a world under Norman Osborn's thumb. In this first issue of his new, ongoing series, Punisher took on the all-powerful Sentry in a fight the vigilante actually managed to walk away from.

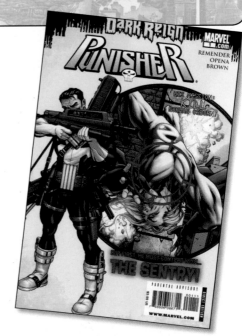

Norman Osborn altered Venom's form in order to make him seem presentable to the public as Spider-Man.

2009

"War of Kings starred many familiar faces to longtime Marvel readers, including Darkhawk, Gladiator, and Black Bolt.

MAY

COSMIC WARS
• *War of Kings* #1
Writers Dan Abnett and Andy Lanning, along with penciler Paul Pelletier, set the cosmic stage for war with this epic five-issue miniseries, which set up an interstellar battle between the alien races of the Shi'ar and the Kree, with many of Earth's heroes caught in the middle.

LOVE AND DEATH
• *New Avengers: The Reunion* #1
Death and rebirth was a concept not foreign to Super Heroes in general, and certainly not to Avengers Ronin and Mockingbird. Mockingbird had just returned to Earth from the seeming dead in the pages of *Secret Invasion*, and Ronin (formerly Hawkeye) had been granted a new lease on life by the deeds of the Scarlet Witch. In this four-issue series by writer Jim McCann and artist David Lopez, the rocky relationship between the two formerly dead and formerly married crime fighters was more stable, even if the tender moments were shared only during pauses in gunfire.

AUGUST

THE NEW WOLVERINE
• *Dark Wolverine* #75
Wolverine's misguided, cruel son Daken had made his debut in the pages of *Wolverine: Origins*, penned by Daniel Way, an intriguing series that delved into the previously mysterious past of the feral mutant. So it made sense that when Daken graduated to his father's mantle and usurped his comic book title, Daniel Way should be the pilot to guide the adventures of this Dark Wolverine. With him was co-writer Marjorie Liu and penciler Guiseppe Camuncoli, who helped chronicle Daken's machinations in the "service" of Norman Osborn.

CAPTAIN AMERICA: ALIVE AND WELL
• *Captain America* #600
Just in time for the title's 600th issue, Captain America returned to its original numbering with this oversized, blockbuster installment. Included in this issue was a feature story written by Ed Brubaker and drawn by Butch Guice, Howard Chaykin, Rafael Albuquerque, David Aja, and Mitch Breitweiser, that hinted at the possibility that Steve Rogers might still be alive, despite Captain America's recent "death." The issue also featured two shorter tales (by Roger Stern and Kalman Andrasofszky, as well as Mark Waid and Dale Eaglesham) that remembered the hero's impressive legacy, as well as a reprint of a classic Captain America/Red Skull battle from 1942 by Stan Lee and Al Avison. If that wasn't enough for every fan of the red, white, and blue hero, this issue contained a two-page origin story by Paul Dini and Alex Ross, and a column by Captain America co-creator Joe Simon.

SEPTEMBER

SPIDEY'S 600TH
• *The Amazing Spider-Man* #600
Hard on the heels of Captain America's anniversary, owing to its thrice-monthly release schedule, *The Amazing Spider-Man* reached its 600th issue with the largest collection of all-new material in the title's history. Writer Dan Slott and penciler John Romita Jr. handled the issue's main story, which saw the return of Doctor Octopus and the momentous wedding of Peter Parker's Aunt May to J. Jonah Jameson, Sr. The comic also featured a story by Spidey's legendary creator, Stan Lee, paired with artist Marcos Martin, as well as contributions from many other members of the Spider-Man brain trust.

130

THE RETURN OF THE CAPTAIN

• *Captain America: Reborn #1*

Steve Rogers borrowed a page from Kurt Vonnegut's classic novel *Slaughterhouse-Five* when he became unstuck in time in this new, six-issue, time-spanning miniseries. Written by Cap's regular scribe Ed Brubaker, and featuring the realistic artwork of Bryan Hitch and Butch Guice, this series started where *Captain America #600* left off, revealing that everyone's favorite star-spangled hero was alive, but lost in the timestream. While the world believed Cap had been shot dead on the steps of the courthouse, an investigation by Agent 13 and a team of Cap's other allies proved otherwise in this adventure, which returned Steve Rogers to his proper place in the present-day Marvel Universe.

ULTIMATE REBOOT

• *Ultimate Comics Spider-Man #1*

Briefly thought dead after the tragic events of Ultimatum, Spider-Man swung back into a new series, by longtime scribe Brian Michael Bendis and new series artist, David Lafuente. As Peter Parker tried to balance high-school drama, a job at the Burger Frog, and the chaos of life as Spider-Man, things got even crazier when his Aunt May let Johnny Storm of the Fantastic Four live at Peter's home. As the series continued, May would take in more of Peter's amazing friends, including the former X-Men member Iceman.

FANTASTIC FORAY

• *Fantastic Four #570*

New writer Jonathan Hickman began what would become a critically acclaimed run on Marvel's first family of Super Heroes with this issue, paired with artist Dale Eaglesham. In this initial issue of Hickman's time on the title, Reed Richards joined forces with many different Reeds from parallel dimensions.

SOMETHING IN THE WAY SHE MOVES

• *Spider-Woman #1*

When the long-awaited collaboration of writer Brian Michael Bendis and artist Alex Maleev on Spider-Woman's new series hit comic stores, it wasn't the only way readers could experience the post-Secret Invasion adventures of Jessica Drew. Also presented online as the first attempted, ongoing, in-continuity motion comic, Spider-Woman came to life on readers' screens, providing a new experience for fans curious to see Drew in action as an alien hunter in the service of the agency SWORD. Despite fan demand and a positive reception, the series lasted only seven issues, due to the extremely time-consuming workload on artist Alex Maleev.

Red She-Hulk was later revealed to be the Hulk's love interest, Betty Ross.

LADY IN RED

• *Hulk #15*

The world of the incredible Hulk gained a new super-strong player with the introduction of Red She-Hulk, the female equivalent of the title's mysterious protagonist. Written by Jeph Loeb and drawn by Ian Churchill, this issue saw Red She-Hulk's surprising debut during a hectic brawl between the Red Hulk's forces and the members of X-Force.

Dark Avengers #1 (March, 2009)
Writer Brian Michael Bendis navigated his way through the darkest territories of the Marvel Universe, with the help of Mike Deodato, when the pair let a band of villains borrow the heroic name of the Avengers for their own nefarious purposes. The Marvel Universe had become a world controlled by former Green Goblin Norman Osborn through the use of smoke and mirrors on a grand scale. Dark Avengers explored that fascinating reality through the adventures of its "protectors," villains disguised as some of the noblest faces in the history of super heroics. The infamous team was led by the Iron Patriot, Osborn's new identity that managed to insult two legends simultaneously: the icons Captain America and Iron Man.

2010s

In the spring of 2008, the business side of Marvel Comics changed forever. While the company had successfully licensed its properties to movie studios, resulting in blockbuster films starring the likes of Spider-Man and the X-Men, Marvel now took direct control of movie adaptations, with the debut of the hit *Iron Man*. Followed shortly by *The Incredible Hulk*, *Iron Man* introduced the world to Marvel Studios, a powerful player on the Hollywood scene able to self-finance its own films. Marvel Studios began to pump out hit after hit at the box office, leading to the release of *The Avengers* in 2012 and the establishment of a cinematic Super Hero universe.

Meanwhile, Marvel Comics decided to revitalize its own universe. Once more celebrating the iconic nature of its characters, Marvel initiated the "Heroic Age." By the end of 2010, five writers had been chosen to pilot this era of comics as the company's "architects." Writers Brian Michael Bendis, Jason Aaron, Ed Brubaker, Matt Fraction, and Jonathan Hickman were handed the keys to the Marvel Universe, promising readers an exciting ride in the years to come.

2010

THE AGE OF HEROES

It all ended with a punch in the face. Norman Osborn's corrupt empire finally fell during the events of the *Siege* miniseries, when Spider-Man socked his longtime foe on the jaw. The good guys reclaimed their Super Hero status, and fans saw the return of the traditional Marvel Universe, one they hadn't really witnessed since the *Civil War* series in 2006.

While many readers had enjoyed the turmoil and unrest of the dark landscape of the last four years of storytelling, Marvel understood that the majority of fans were now ready for a return to the familiar. So Marvel introduced the "The Heroic Age," an official return to the traditional status quo. This event, celebrating the return of Super Heroes to the forefront, was ushered in by a series of banners that ran along the top of many new comic book titles. Marvel also issued many variant covers that featured iconic representations of their most classic crime fighters. The wars were over and the heroes had won.

At least, for now…

JANUARY

RUNNING THE GAUNTLET

• *The Amazing Spider-Man* #612
Spider-Man's classic rogues were back, updated for his Brand New Day relaunch, in "The Gauntlet," a twenty-two-part saga that began with this issue by writer Mark Waid and artist Paul Azaceta. Before Peter Parker could get a breather, he'd face Electro, Sandman, Mysterio, Morbius, the Juggernaut, the Lizard, a new Rhino, and Vulture.

MAXIMUM KINGPIN

• *PunisherMAX* #1
The adventures of Frank Castle were once again taken to the max with this new series by writer Jason Aaron and artist Steve Dillon. Featuring all the violence and disturbing themes the MAX imprint was known for, this bloody series saw a new take on the origin of the Kingpin.

MARCH

UNDER SIEGE

"It's time to take back this country."

• *Siege* #1
Norman Osborn had gone too far. It was time for his "Dark Reign" to come to an end. Almost two years had elapsed since the end of the Secret Invasion event and Osborn's rise to power. The heroes of the Marvel Universe had been forced to operate as outlaws against a corrupt, overbearing system. They had been waiting for a chance to reassert the proper status quo, and in this four-issue series by writer Brian Michael Bendis and artist Olivier Coipel, they would finally be given that opportunity.

Manipulated by the nefarious Norse god Loki, Osborn staged an attack on the home of the gods, Asgard, which had recently relocated to the airspace above Broxton, Oklahoma. Despite being ordered to stand down by the President of the United States, Osborn went ahead with the attack, which led to a brutal battle between Captain America's Avengers and Osborn's Dark Avengers. The resulting death toll was high, and included such powerhouses as Ares, Sentry, and even, seemingly, Loki himself. When the dust settled, the heroes were still standing, and a new Heroic Age had dawned in the Marvel Universe.

The Avengers finally triumphed over the machinations of Norman Osborn and Loki.

MAY

ULTIMATE UPGRADES

• *Ultimate New Ultimates* #1
Jeph Loeb returned to the Ultimate Universe to script this five-issue miniseries alongside artist Frank Cho. This series not only returned Thor to the land of the living, it also featured a now super-powered version of the Ultimate Defenders.

On May 7, director Jon Favreau and actor Robert Downey Jr. returned to pilot Iron Man back into theaters with *Iron Man 2*, featuring a screenplay by Justin Theroux.

JUNE

THE DEATH OF NIGHTCRAWLER

• *X-Force* #26
The fan-favorite mutant Nightcrawler paid the ultimate price for his adventures with the X-Force in this tragic tale by writers Christopher Yost and Craig Kyle, and artist Mike Choi. In this chapter of the "Second Coming" storyline, Nightcrawler sacrificed himself in order to save the life of Hope Summers.

CAGE FIGHT

The New Avengers: Luke Cage #1
Luke Cage stepped into the spotlight with his own three-issue miniseries, by writer John Arcudi and artist Eric Canete. Set in the final days of Norman Osborn's "Dark Reign," the story saw Cage square off with Spider-Man's foe Hammerhead, as well as one of his own old enemies, Lionfang.

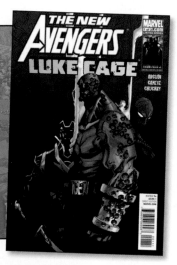

JULY

LOGAN AND PETER'S EXCELLENT ADVENTURE

• *Astonishing Spider-Man & Wolverine* #1
Spider-Man and Wolverine had shared many classic team-up stories over the years, and even served side by side on teams like the New Fantastic Four and the New Avengers. However, the two had never really seen eye to eye. In this six-issue series, writer Jason Aaron and artist Adam Kubert examined the duo's complex relationship in an offbeat story that saw them time-travel to the cretaceous period, the far-flung future, and the Old West. In what turned out to be a bizarre reality TV show produced by the infamous Mojo, the two heroes found some common ground.

JULY

THE HEROIC AVENGERS

"Our president asked me what the world needs now... I told him the world needs what it always needs. Heroes."

• *The Avengers* #1
Norman Osborn was out and Steve Rogers was in. Handpicked by the US President, the former Captain America was charged with creating the Super Hero landscape in the aftermath of the dramatic *Siege* event on Asgard. Central to this new Heroic Age were Rogers' choices for the primary branch of the Avengers. With nearly every Super Hero to choose from, Rogers chose the best of the best, under the guidance of his right-hand woman, Maria Hill: Thor, Hawkeye (returning to his classic mantle after giving up the role of Ronin), Spider-Man, Wolverine, Captain America (James Barnes), Spider-Woman, and Iron Man. The team immediately faced the threat of Kang, and were forced to recruit the former Marvel Boy, now called the Protector, to embark on a time-spanning adventure.

In this new, ongoing series by writer Brian Michael Bendis and artist John Romita Jr., the Avengers were rocked by threat after threat, forced to fight their old teammate Wonder Man. They also faced former crime boss the Hood, who had undergone a quest to retrieve the gems of the fabled, all-powerful Infinity Gauntlet. The Avengers triumphed over these challenges and, with the recruitement of the Red Hulk, it was clear that the Avengers were once again the most powerful team in the Marvel Universe.

STEVE ROGERS' SECRET

• *Secret Avengers* #1
As the newly appointed "top cop of the world" one of Steve Rogers' first decisions was to form a team of Secret Avengers in this new series by longtime Captain America writer Ed Brubaker and artist Mike Deodato. This clandestine strike force of black-ops experts included Valkyrie, Black Widow, Agent 13, War Machine, Beast, Moon Knight, Ant-Man (Eric O'Grady), and Nova (Richard Rider).

THE NEW NEW AVENGERS

• *The New Avengers* #1

The New Avengers had been a force for the underground resistance since the beginning of the Super Hero Civil War. But now, in the wake of Steve Rogers' promotion to head of the Avengers, the team was finally made legitimate in this series by writer Brian Michael Bendis and penciler Stuart Immonen. To make room for this title, as well as the other new "Heroic Age" Avengers comics including *Secret Avengers*, *The Avengers*, and the youth-based new title *Avengers Academy*, the former four Avengers titles (*Dark Avengers*, *The Mighty Avengers*, *The New Avengers*, and *Avengers: The Initiative*) were cancelled, making it apparent to readers that this was indeed the start of a bold new era.

As the series began, Luke Cage was put in charge of the team, having proved himself during the New Avengers' previous incarnation. Ms. Marvel, Spider-Man, Wolverine, the Thing, Jessica Jones Cage, Mockingbird, Iron Fist, and Hawkeye helped round out the rest of the roster, although Hawkeye would soon depart to focus on his adventures with the main branch of the Avengers. Norman Osborn's former first in command Victoria Hand was also brought into the fold as the team settled in at the Avengers Mansion, leaving the main Avengers branch to establish Avengers Tower as their home base. The Avengers franchise was renewed and, as usual, more than ready for action.

THE GRIM HUNT

• *The Amazing Spider-Man* #634

Sick and exhausted from running a gauntlet of his fiercest foes, Peter Parker was in no condition to be hunted by the Kraven family. But in this four-part storyline by writers Joe Kelly and Zeb Wells and artists Michael Lark, Marco Checchetto, and Stefano Gaudiano, Spider-Man was nearly killed so that the original Kraven the Hunter could be resurrected.

THE YOUNG AND THE RESTLESS

• *Young Allies* #1

When a group of young villains attacked New York City, veteran hero Firestar partnered with Gravity, the new Nomad and Toro, and Arana (now calling herself Spider-Girl after her predecessor was killed during the events of the "Grim Hunt") to combat the threat as a group of Young Allies in this six-issue series by writer Sean McKeever and penciler David Baldeón.

ONE MOMENT IN TIME

• *The Amazing Spider-Man* #638

Editor-in-Chief Joe Quesada returned to Spider-Man's world to answer some of the continuity questions fans had been wondering about since the "One More Day" event of 2007. This emotional, four-part story scripted by Quesada and illustrated by Paolo Rivera explained that Peter Parker and Mary Jane Watson dated in the past, but never married.

TWILIGHT OF THE X-MEN

• *X-Men* #1

If box-office returns and book sales were any indication, vampires were a hot commodity. So it was only a matter of time before the mutants of the X-Men found themselves fighting off a plague of the infamous bloodsuckers. The bloody battle began in this newly relaunched title featuring a script by Victor Gischler and pencils by Paco Medina.

DISAPPEARING INTO SHADOWS

• *Shadowland* #1

Usually the star of solo adventures, Daredevil was thrown into the crossover spotlight thanks to this five-issue miniseries event written by Andy Diggle and drawn by Billy Tan. After accepting leadership of notorious ninja clan the Hand, Daredevil built his own kingdom of sorts in New York City's Hell's Kitchen, calling the fortress Shadowland. As Daredevil's personality darkened (as did his uniform, changing from red to black), many of his allies began to suspect that there was something wrong with the Man Without Fear. They discovered that Daredevil had been possessed by a force of evil known as the Beast of the Hand. After a battle with a host of Super Heroes, Daredevil bested his inner demon and disappeared into the darkness.

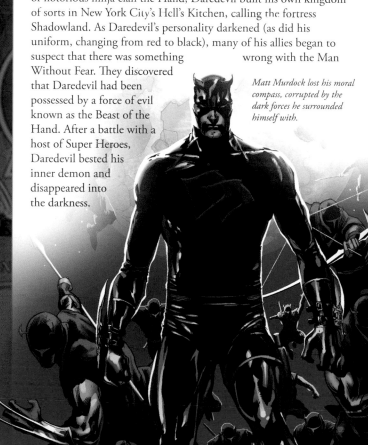

Matt Murdock lost his moral compass, corrupted by the dark forces he surrounded himself with.

Marvel Animation debuted the critically acclaimed animated series, *The Avengers: Earth's Mightiest Heroes*, on October 20, beginning a series of fifty-two episodes.

NOVEMBER

WOLVERINE GOES TO HELL
• *Wolverine* #1

Popular Wolverine scribe Jason Aaron took another stab at the character with the help of artist Renato Guedes in this debut issue that saw the start of a new storyline crossover event entitled "Wolverine Goes to Hell." The issue also featured a backup tale, starring the Silver Samurai, by Aaron and Jason Latour.

ALL IN THE FAMILY
• *Daken: Dark Wolverine* #1

Writers Daniel Way and Marjorie Liu continued the adventures of Wolverine's wayward son Daken in this series illustrated by Giuseppe Camuncoli. This new ongoing comic, along with the new *Wolverine* relaunch and another fledgling title *X-23*, helped carve Wolverine out his own family of comics in Marvel's lineup.

DECEMBER

FROST AND THE FÜHRER
• *Ultimate Thor* #1

The ultimate God of Thunder received his own four-issue miniseries, thanks to writer Jonathan Hickman and artist Carlos Pacheco. In this time-spanning story, Asgard faced the threat of a deadly alliance between Frost Giants and Nazi forces.

FACING APOCALYPSE
• *Uncanny X-Force* #1

When a secret society attempted to jumpstart the Age of Apocalypse in the X-Men's reality, Wolverine joined forces with Deadpool, Psylocke, Fantomex, and Archangel for this newest incarnation of the X-Force, written by Rick Remender and illustrated by Jerome Opeña.

THE RETURN OF CARNAGE
• *Carnage* #1

Thought dead since the beginning of the original New Avengers series of 2005, Carnage made his disturbing return in a five-issue miniseries by writer Zeb Wells and artist Clayton Crain. As Spider-Man and Iron Man did their best to handle the deadly menace of the old Spider-Man foe, readers glimpsed the first appearance of a new symbiote-powered character, Scorn.

The Avengers #1 (July, 2010)

When it came to revitalizing one of Marvel's largest team franchises, writer Brian Michael Bendis pulled out all the stops. Teamed with powerhouse artist John Romita Jr., Bendis pulled together some of the biggest icons in the Marvel pantheon to form the Avengers, and immediately had them face some of their most daunting foes. In fact, in the first six issues of the title, the Avengers faced Apocalypse, Ultron, Galactus and even a future version of the Hulk, any one of whom would be regarded as a major level threat all on his own. The overall effect was truly a blockbuster return for Marvel's greatest heroes.

2011 TO THE POINT

One of the things that makes Super Hero comics so unique is the fact that, from nearly the very beginning of the history of the industry, each tale set in a particular comic book universe built on the stories that preceded it. The Marvel Universe has been expanding and evolving since the late 1930s; for this reason, it can be difficult for new readers to find good entry points to begin their comic book reading. Over the years, Marvel has tried many different methods to attract new readers. One way is to restart a series with a new first issue. Another is to release a zero issue that details the title character's origin. In 2011, Marvel tried a new initiative, calling it Point One.

With *The Invincible Iron Man #500.1*, the subsequent issue to that hero's oversized 500th anniversary special, Marvel began to release Point One stand-alone specials that could be easily understood by new readers. Point One issues were the perfect place for teasing new storylines—*The Amazing Spider-Man #654.1* showcased the newest incarnation of Venom for the first time—or ushering in bold new eras for some of Marvel's biggest characters.

JANUARY

BIG TIME

• *The Amazing Spider-Man* #648
Spider-Man's "Brand New Day" had come to a close after more than a hundred issues, clearing the way for the series' new regular writer, Dan Slott, and a new direction for Spider-Man's flagship title. With the assistance of artist Humberto Ramos, this issue saw Peter Parker finally achieve his dream job: a high-paying gig developing new technology for the innovative company Horizon Labs.

WORLDWIDE SPIDER WEB

• *Spider-Girl* #1
Writer Paul Tobin and penciler Clayton Henry helped the teenage heroine formerly known as Araña into her new role as Spider-Girl in this eight-issue series. Using the innovative device of Spider-Girl's Twitter feed for captions, Spider-Girl was updated for a new generation of readers.

MARCH

THE DEATH OF THE HUMAN TORCH

• *Fantastic Four* #587
Wrapped in an ominous black polybag with a large "3" printed on it, the conclusion to the five-part "Three" storyline in *Fantastic Four* prepared fans for the worst from the get-go. Written by Jonathan Hickman and illustrated by Steve Epting, this issue saw founding Fantastic Four member Johnny Storm, the Human Torch, sacrifice himself so that the world would be spared an invasion by Annihilus's insectoid hordes. The issue's ending was poignant and powerful, as the Thing did his best to comfort Johnny's niece and nephew during the aftermath of the battle. Happily, the Human Torch's death would not prove to be permanent...

While the team did everything in its power to stop the forces of Annihilus, only Johnny Storm's sacrifice could save the day.

LOOKING TO THE FUTURE

• *FF* #1

The famous initials of Marvel's first family, the Fantastic Four, took on new meaning when the team adopted the name of the Future Foundation, in this ongoing series by writer Jonathan Hickman and artist Steve Epting.

In the wake of the death of Johnny Storm, the Human Torch, the Fantastic Four was no more. But Johnny Storm was a never-say-die type of person, and in his holographic will, he requested that the Fantastic Four continue without him. Johnny even had a replacement in mind, his old friend and sometime rival, Peter Parker, the Amazing Spider-Man.

While Spider-Man quickly accepted the position on the team, despite his other commitments to two different teams of Avengers and his work at Horizon Labs, he soon realized that the Fantastic Four he'd signed up for was a thing of the past. The team had become the Future Foundation, an organization dedicated to changing the world for the better. Not only did the team now wear white and black uniforms rather than their traditional blue costumes, but it also consisted of a think tank of some of the world's brightest—and youngest—shining stars. The Fantastic Four had evolved, and Spider-Man was along for the ride.

Ⓜ The Mighty Thor received the blockbuster treatment in his first feature film, which hit screens on May 6. *Thor,* starring Chris Hemsworth as the title character, was directed by Kenneth Branagh and featured a screenplay by Ashley Miller, Zack Stentz and Don Payne, based on a story by Mark Protosevich and J. Michael Straczynski.

VEINS OF VENOM

• *Venom* #1

Peter Parker's former high-school bully Flash Thompson took center stage in his first-ever ongoing series as the new Venom. Wearing the symbiote suit at the behest of the US government's Project Rebirth, Flash was finally able to imitate his hero Spider-Man, in this debut issue by writer Rick Remender and artist Tony Moore.

Ⓜ Marvel made its way to Broadway with the musical *Spider-Man: Turn Off The Dark.* Despite some hiccups, a revised and improved version of the show debuted on June 14.

The X-Men movie franchise saw a revitalization on June 3 at the hands of director Matthew Vaughn with the release of
Ⓜ the film *X-Men: First Class.* Vaughn co-wrote the screenplay along with Ashley Miller, Zack Stentz and Jane Goldman, with additional story credits going to Sheldon Turner and Bryan Singer.

NOTHING TO FEAR

• *Fear Itself* #1

With Marvel Studios debuting two more pieces of their Avengers franchise with the release of *Thor* and *Captain America: The First Avenger,* it made sense for Marvel Comics to capitalize on the mainstream attention given to these two heroes with a blockbuster event. Enter *Fear Itself,* a seven-issue miniseries on a grand scale. Placing both Cap and Thor at the forefront of this crossover was writer Matt Fraction and artist Stuart Immonen.

The story began when the Red Skull's daughter, Sin, released an evil force on Earth by uncovering a powerful mystic hammer. Unleashing a chain of events that freed the corrupt brother of the Norse god Odin—a being calling himself by Odin's title, the All-Father—Sin received a power upgrade, as did many of Marvel's already powerful heavy hitters. With mind-controlled servants, including Hulk and Juggernaut, at his side, the evil All-Father sought to instill fear in the people of Earth, thereby boosting his own power. In the end, an army led by Captain America bested the villains, although it cost the heroes dearly. When the smoke cleared, it seemed that both Thor and Captain America's old sidekick, James Barnes, were among the dead.

A MIGHTY QUEST

• *The Mighty Thor* #1

The religious and philosophical ramifications of gods living among humans were explored by writer Matt Fraction and artist Olivier Coipel in this new series starring Thor. This debut issue also featured Thor, Sif, and Loki on an adventure in search of the mystical Worldheart, as well as an ominous appearance by the Silver Surfer.

Ⓜ Director Joe Johnston took audiences back to World War II for the July 22 release of *Captain America: The First Avenger.* Starring Chris Evans as the patriotic title hero, and written by Christopher Markus and Stephen McFeely, this film helped complete Marvel's cinematic movie universe, and pave the way for an upcoming Avengers film.

MOON KNIGHT MAKEOVER

• *Moon Knight* #1

The critically acclaimed team of writer Brian Michael Bendis and artist Alex Maleev, who revitalized Daredevil and Spider-Woman, took on their next vigilante in Moon Knight. Bendis and Maleev moved the hero to the streets of Los Angeles and examined his multiple personalities, forcing Moon Knight to live with the conflicting personalities of Spider-Man, Wolverine, and Captain America inside his head.

THE DEATH OF SPIDER-MAN

• *Ultimate Comics Spider-Man* #160

When the Ultimate Comics imprint was first created by Marvel in 2000, the idea behind it was to attract new readers to their most popular characters, without the heavy burden of decades' worth of continuity. Marvel re-envisioned Spider-Man, X-Men, and the Avengers (as the Ultimates) as brand-new heroes just starting their adventures. With the extra incentive of top-drawer, exciting talent, the imprint was a hit, doing exactly what it set out to do.

But ten years later, the Ultimate line had built up its own complex continuity. The imprint wasn't quite as easy to jump into, and needed something to set it apart from the mainstream Marvel Universe. To accomplish that goal, writer Brian Michael Bendis did the unthinkable and killed the character he had done so much to bring to life. Bendis, along with returning penciler Mark Bagley, killed Peter Parker.

When the Green Goblin escaped from the Triskelion, he took his own team of powerhouse Super Villains with him: Electro, Doctor Octopus, Sandman, the Vulture and Kraven. After taking a bullet for Captain America in a related conflict, Spider-Man was then forced to face this lineup of his most dangerous foes, as the Goblin brought the fight to Peter's neighborhood and the home of his beloved Aunt May. Peter finally defeated the villains with the help of Iceman and the Human Torch, but his injuries proved too great and he died in the arms of Mary Jane Watson.

SPIDER-ISLAND

• *The Amazing Spider-Man* #666

New York City has always featured prominently in Spider-Man's life—so writer Dan Slott decided to give the Big Apple an upgrade. Virtually the entire population of Manhattan gained spider powers, thanks to the machinations of the villainous Jackal and his partner in crime, the Queen. While this prologue chapter by artist Stefano Caselli (who also drew the epilogue chapter in *The Amazing Spider-Man* #673) only hinted at the dangers to come, the following six issues—drawn by Humberto Ramos—threw Peter Parker into a world where his exceptional abilities no longer made him that special. By the end of this mammoth crossover event, Peter would learn that it was the man rather than the spider than had made him a hero for all these years.

BRAVO FOR CAPTAIN AMERICA

• *Captain America* #1

Acclaimed writer Ed Brubaker was back to chronicle yet another chapter of Captain America's life, this time with the help of penciler Steve McNiven, in this new series that pitted the hero against a mysterious face from his past, a covert agent dubbed Codename: Bravo.

CYCLOPS VS. WOLVERINE

• *X-Men: Schism* #1

Allies and brothers-in-arms for years, Wolverine and Cyclops reached the breaking point of their relationship in this five-issue miniseries by writer Jason Aaron and pencilers Carlos Pacheco, Frank Cho, Daniel Acuña, Alan Davis, and Adam Kubert. When Wolverine witnessed mutant teenagers being treated like soldiers, he took many of Cyclops' forces away from his stronghold in Utopia to rediscover the peaceful dream of Charles Xavier back in New York.

DERRING-DO

• *Daredevil* #1

Blind swashbuckling lawyer Matt Murdock returned to his somewhat lighter roots thanks to the brilliant combination of writer Mark Waid and artist Paolo Rivera (with the equally talented Marcos Martin penciling later issues) for this new ongoing series. With an emphasis on visual storytelling and exploring the details of Daredevil's hypersensitive powers, Murdock was taken in a less gritty direction, facing threats from Marvel's Super Villain community, as well as realistic challenges, such as issue seven's powerful story of Murdock leading a troop of blind children through a snowstorm.

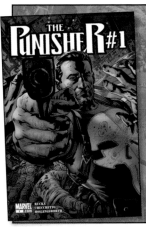

ANOTHER ROUND OF PUNISHMENT

• *The Punisher* #1

Writer Greg Rucka and artist Marco Checchetto started a new chapter of Frank Castle's life with a bang as his new series began with a violent gun battle at a wedding reception. Realistic and as violent as Punisher readers would expect, this new series examined the Punisher's life from his point of view as well as from that of local law-enforcement officers.

THE SOUND AND THE FURY

• *Ultimate Comics: The Ultimates* #1

The newest take on the extremely busy world of Nick Fury and the Ultimates arrived in the form of this ongoing series by writer Jonathan Hickman and artist Esad Ribic, showcasing Fury juggling the many crises that face the Ultimate Universe.

THE NEW SPIDER-MAN

• *Ultimate Comics Spider-Man #1*

Ultimate Spider-Man was dead. Long live Ultimate Spider-Man.

While Peter Parker had met his demise at the end of the first volume of *Ultimate Comics Spider-Man*, a replacement soon stood up to accept his mantle in the form of young Miles Morales. While fans first glimpsed Miles in action in Spider-Man's traditional costume in the fourth issue of the six-issue *Ultimate Comics Fallout* miniseries (October, 2011) in a short story by writer Brian Michael Bendis and artist Sara Pichelli, they didn't discover the origin of the new hero until this debut issue by the same writer/artist team.

This series began in a flashback set eleven months prior. When a test subject spider escaped the confines of Osborn Industries and bit the hand of Miles Morales, Miles discovered that he could adhere to walls, sting opponents, and blend in with his environment so as to become virtually invisible. But seeing the way mutants are treated in the modern world, Miles was reluctant to accept his new legacy. When Peter Parker died, Miles discovered that with great power comes great responsibility and, after an impressive fight with Electro, the young man soon donned a black and red version of the world-famous Spider-Man suit.

Following increased reader interest due to real-world news coverage, the Ultimate Comics imprint had finally gone back to its roots. Just like a decade ago, *Ultimate Comics Spider-Man* was a fresh and inviting version of the longtime Marvel character, easily accessible for new readers.

ULTIMATE AND AMAZING FRIENDS

• *Ultimate Comics X-Men #1*

Writer Nick Spencer and artist Paco Medina helped to launch this ongoing series, starring new and established mutant characters, as well as recent Spider-Man supporting characters such as Kitty Pryde, the Human Torch, and Iceman.

HEADMASTER WOLVERINE

• *Wolverine and the X-Men #1*

Writer Jason Aaron and Chris Bachalo chronicled the challenges Wolverine faced as headmaster of the newly established Jean Grey School For Higher Learning in Westchester County, New York, in this new, ongoing title that dealt with the fallout from the *X-Men: Schism* miniseries. Previous headmaster Cyclops would subsequently continue fighting for mutantkind in the pages of the newly relaunched *Uncanny X-Men* series by writer Kieron Gillen and penciler Carlos Pacheco that would debut in January 2012.

Wolverine and Beast were just a few of the faculty members at the Jean Grey School.

Daredevil #4 (Dec., 2011)

When Daredevil originally debuted in the pages of the original Daredevil # 1 (April 1964), the character wasn't the grim avenger of the night he later became. Over the years, the hero darkened in personality, as did the world he inhabited. In fact, many of the artists and writers associated with DC Comics' grim and gritty Batman franchise were equally associated with the history of Marvel's Man Without Fear. However writer Mark Waid and artists Paolo Rivera and Marcos Martin decided to return to Stan Lee's original tone for Daredevil in this revamp, bringing a bit of light back into the blind world of Matt Murdock. This new team used innovative storytelling techniques to give a fresh perspective to the decades-old hero.

"THERE ALWAYS HAS TO BE DESTRUCTION... BEFORE THE REBIRTH."

2012
INFINITY AND BEYOND

Over the last few years, the digital comics market had started to grow exponentially. With the rise in popularity of handheld devices like iPads and Kindles, comic book companies recognized the potential for digital comics to be the "new newsstand." Comics could once again become impulse buys for new readers unwilling to hunt down a local comic book store.

Marvel was quick to recognize this growing market, and began offering a free digital download with purchase of their titles. With the release of *Avengers Vs. X-Men*, their biggest event of 2012, Marvel further raised the bar on digital interaction. On many pages of that series, an AR symbol could be found. This new Augmented Reality feature allowed readers to see characters come alive and view other bonus content simply by scanning the image into their mobile devices. In addition, Marvel released Infinite Comics, with the help of renowned writer Mark Waid. These digital-first comics used moment-to-moment story beats to control the pacing of a tale in a way traditional print comics simply could not. If the future of the comic book industry was indeed the digital marketplace, Marvel was going to great lengths to make sure that it not only kept up with the trends, but helped create them.

JANUARY

AMAZING AND AVENGING
• *Avenging Spider-Man* #1
Spider-Man's life as a team player was explored in this new ongoing series that paired the web-slinger with his Avengers teammates. The series began with a three-part story that cast the web-slinger alongside the Red Hulk in a battle to free the Mole Man, by writer Zeb Wells and artist Joe Madureira.

FOUR ONCE MORE
• *Fantastic Four* #600
The Human Torch returned to the Fantastic Four just in time to see the team reach a new milestone. By writer Jonathan Hickman and artists Steve Epting, Carmine Di Giandomenico, Ming Doyle, Leinil Francis Yu, and Farel Dalrymple, this oversized issue revealed that Johnny Storm had been resurrected by the forces of Annihilus.

FEB

Actor Nicolas Cage drove Ghost Rider back into theaters with the February 17 release of *Ghost Rider: Spirit of Vengeance*, directed by Mark Neveldine and Brian Taylor, and written by Scott Gimple, Seth Hoffman, and David S. Goyer.

APRIL

THE ARRIVAL OF WINTER
• *Winter Soldier* #1
After the events of *Fear Itself*, the world believed James Barnes was dead. And that's exactly the way the hero preferred it as he began a new string of top-secret adventures as the Winter Soldier, in this series by writer Ed Brubaker and Butch Guice.

 Marvel Animation reignited the animated Spider-Man franchise with a new cartoon based on the highly acclaimed Ultimate Spider-Man series. Also called *Ultimate Spider-Man*, the cartoon debuted on April 1.

MAY

READERS ASSEMBLE!
• *Avengers Assemble* #1
Just in time for the debut of Marvel Studios' blockbuster *Avengers* feature film came *Avengers Assemble*, an ongoing series jumpstarted by writer Brian Michael Bendis and artist Mark Bagley that pitted the Avengers against the now-upgraded Zodiac. The cover of this first issue featured Iron Man, Thor, Hawkeye, Black Widow, the Hulk, and Captain America—the same team starring in the blockbuster film. This series was meant as a perfect jumping-on point for new readers, a way for them to get in on a title from the start.

MAY

RVX

• *Avengers Vs. X-Men #0*

While Marvel Studios was busy scoring at the box office, Marvel Comics was not to be outdone. With the release of *Avengers Vs. X-Men #0*, Marvel embarked on a thirteen-issue crossover event that would shake up its entire Super Hero universe. Supported by various innovative digital tie-ins, including an ad that, when scanned with a compatible digital device, allowed Marvel's new Editor-in-Chief Axel Alonso to walk onto the pages of each reader's comic, *Avengers Vs. X-Men* promised a battle royal involving nearly every major Marvel hero.

To birth a series with such an epic feel, a large creative team was recruited. Marvel teamed all its world-building "architects" for the project: writers Brian Michael Bendis, Jason Aaron, Ed Brubaker, Jonathan Hickman, and Matt Fraction. Serving as artists for the series were heavy-hitters Frank Cho, John Romita Jr., Olivier Coipel, and Adam Kubert.

With this creative team in place, the series explored the ramifications of the return of the Phoenix Force, a powerful entity familiar to longtime X-Men fans. The Phoenix Force corrupted Cyclops of the X-Men and, when he and his team began to shape the world in their image, the Avengers fought against their former allies. They finally bested Cyclops with the help of the X-Men's own protégée, Hope Summers, although it cost the life of Charles Xavier, Professor X of the X-Men. Aided by the probability-altering powers of the Avengers' Scarlet Witch, Hope shattered the Phoenix Force, creating a new generation of mutants all over the world.

While many characters fought during AVX, two of the most important players turned out to be the Scarlet Witch and Hope Summers.

MAY

Ⓜ Marvel Studios released their biggest hit to date in the form of their highly anticipated film *Marvel's The Avengers* on May 4. The movie was written by director Joss Whedon, alongside screenwriter Zak Penn, and starred Robert Downey Jr., Chris Evans, Mark Ruffalo, Chris Hemsworth, Scarlett Johansson and Jeremy Renner as Super Hero teammates.

JUNE

KNOCK-DOWN, DRAG-OUT

• *AVX: VS. #1*

Fans had been debating battles between their favorite Marvel heroes for decades, so when *Avengers Vs. X-Men* debuted, they rushed to see the results of many of these fantasy bouts. However, with only thirteen-issues to tell a globe-spanning story, the main miniseries didn't have room to delve into the specifics of the epic battles being waged. Enter *AVX: VS.*, a six-issue companion series with shifting creative teams, showcasing at least two big fights per issue. The initial issue of this fast-paced series featured Iron Man triumphing over Magneto in a tale by writer Jason Aaron and artist Adam Kubert, as well as the Thing defeating Namor in a story by writer Kathryn Immonen and artist Stuart Immonen.

JULY

Ⓜ *The Amazing Spider-Man*, a reboot of the Spider-Man film franchise, premiered on July 3 starring Andrew Garfield as Peter Parker. The aptly-named Marc Webb was the movie's director, with James Vanderbilt, Alvin Sargent, and Steve Kloves tackling the film's screenplay.

AUGUST

DARK THUNDERBOLTS

• *Dark Avengers #175*

Luke Cage went from Thunderbolt to Dark Avenger when he was put in charge of a new team in this issue by writer Jeff Parker and artist Declan Shalvey. Filling out Cage's ranks were: Hulk's son Skaar, cyborg Thor double Ragnarok, Hawkeye's brother Trick Shot, unhinged Scarlet Witch impersonator Toxie Doxie, and the monstrous spider-creature Ai Apaec.

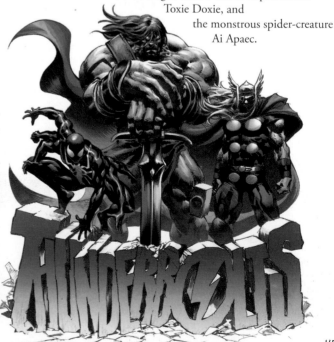

NORTHSTAR'S WEDDING

• *Astonishing X-Men* #51

For decades, Marvel Comics had stood against bigotry and hatred, often using the plight of the X-Men as a metaphor for the struggles faced by minority groups. So when same-sex marriage became legal in New York State in 2011, it didn't take long for Marvel to stand up once again for equal rights by having two of its gay characters marry in Manhattan in classic comic-book fashion. Performing the ceremonies for Northstar and new husband Kyle Jinadu in front of a multitude of X-Men and Alpha Flight members in this heartfelt issue was writer Marjorie Liu and penciler Mike Perkins.

MS. MARVEL GETS A PROMOTION

• *Captain Marvel* #1

A supporting character of the original Captain Marvel, and a longtime fan favorite, Carol Danvers had been through several costume overhauls and name changes over the years. She went from being called Ms. Marvel, to Binary, to Warbird, and back again, but she never fully accepted her role as the official replacement to the alien hero Mar-Vell. In this issue by writer Kelly Sue DeConnick and artist Dexter Soy, Carol finally seized hold of her destiny as the new Captain Marvel, adopting a new costume of impermeable fabric designed by Tony Stark.

STRAIGHT SHOOTER

• *Hawkeye* #1

Clint Barton's time away from the Avengers was explored in this new series by writer Matt Fraction and artist David Aja. Containing stories far removed from the event-style super-confrontations of the Avengers, this title focused on Clint's more realistic adventures, such as dealing with a corrupt New York City landlord. A brilliant, character-driven piece, *Hawkeye* was immediately gripping, taking full advantage of colorist Matt Hollingsworth's beautiful, muted color palette, which enhanced Aja's artful storytelling. The result was a very different kind of Marvel comic that was every bit as entertaining as its blockbuster companions.

DEVIL'S END

• *Daredevil: End of Days* #1

Matt Murdock's career was brought to an end in this eight-issue miniseries set in the not-too-distant future. The product of the collected talents of many Daredevil luminaries, including writers Brian Michael Bendis and David Mack, and artists Klaus Janson and Bill Sienkiewicz, this Citizen Kane-like tale followed reporter Ben Urich as he investigated Daredevil's final fight, when the hero was apparently killed by his longtime enemy Bullseye in a brutal battle caught on video.

AVENGING XAVIER

• *Uncanny Avengers* #1

In the fallout of the *Avengers Vs. X-Men* event, Captain America found himself in a world that was more anti-mutant than ever. Realizing that the Avengers hadn't done enough to help mutants over the years, Cap set out to create a new breed of Avengers, in this ongoing series by writer Rick Remender and artist John Cassaday. Placing Cyclops' brother Havok in charge of this new group, Cap recruited several other mutants, including Rogue, Wolverine and Scarlet Witch, pairing them with traditional, non-mutant powerhouses like Thor, to create a formidable team. They soon needed every ounce of that strength when the Red Skull stole the powerful mind of deceased Professor X to use as a weapon.

TEAM ADDITIONS

• *A+X #1*

Spinning out of *Avengers Vs. X-Men* was this new title with a shifting creative team. Taking the opposite approach of the conflict of *Avengers Vs. X-Men*, this series focused on two team-up stories in each issue, featuring X-Men and Avengers working alongside one another. The initial issue featured a Captain America/Cable pairing by writer Dan Slott and artist Ron Garney, as well as a Hulk/Wolverine team-up by scripter Jeph Loeb and penciler Dale Keown.

GODS AND MONSTERS

• *Thor: God of Thunder #1*

Writer Jason Aaron and artist Esad Ribic gave Thor more than he bargained for in this ongoing series, in which the hero met the threat of Gorr the God Butcher in a story that spanned Thor's past, present, and future.

Ribic's artwork vividly conveyed the majestic side of Thor.

2013 MARVEL NOW

In the landscape of the modern Super Hero comic book, crossovers and large-scale events have proven to be a tried and true method of generating sales and excitement throughout the readership. Oftentimes the aftermath of these events can spawn an even larger audience, if the changes to the comic book universe are bold enough.

In October 2012, Marvel decided to reinvigorate its titles with a bold move. The company took the success of the *Avengers Vs. X-Men* maxiseries as its springboard, shuffled creative talent around, and restarted many of the highest-profile titles. Dubbed "Marvel NOW!," these books began to hit comic stores near the end of 2012 and were an instant crowd pleaser. With big-name writers and artists tackling properties previously foreign to them, the revamp resulted in fresh takes on classic characters. At the same time, the Marvel NOW! relaunch managed to keep fans excited and positive about the future.

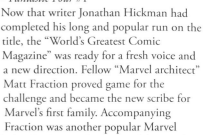

FANTASTIC VOYAGE
• *Fantastic Four* #1
Now that writer Jonathan Hickman had completed his long and popular run on the title, the "World's Greatest Comic Magazine" was ready for a fresh voice and a new direction. Fellow "Marvel architect" Matt Fraction proved game for the challenge and became the new scribe for Marvel's first family. Accompanying Fraction was another popular Marvel mainstay, penciler Mark Bagley. In the very first issue of this newly restarted title, Fraction and Bagley created a smooth transition from Hickman's run by having Mr. Fantastic discover that he and the rest of the Fantastic Four seemed to be dying from the long-term effects of the cosmic rays that had first given them their superpowers. To discover a cure, Reed Richards gathered up his family and headed on a journey through space and time, charting a bold new path for the heroes.

A STRONG FOUNDATION
• *FF* #1
Already handling the writing chores for *Fantastic Four*, it made sense that Matt Fraction take over writing the rebooted *FF* title as well, this time alongside artist Michael Allred. Together, they informed readers about the activities of the Future Foundation while the Fantastic Four were away exploring the cosmos, spotlighting the Foundation's reluctant new head, Scott Lang, the second man to take up the Ant-Man mantle.

MR. ROGERS' NEW NEIGHBORHOOD
• *Captain America* #1
Steve Rogers' past and present were examined in this volume of Cap's adventures by writer Rick Remender and artist John Romita Jr. Moving in a slightly more off-beat direction than the one taken by writer Ed Brubaker during his long run on the character, this first issue saw Cap fight a villain named the Green Skull before traveling on an abandoned subway train to Arnim Zola's stronghold in Dimension Z.

EXTREMIS CIRCUMSTANCES
• *Iron Man* #1
Writer Kieron Gillen and penciler Greg Land donned their best suit of iron to begin their run charting the adventures of Tony Stark. Clad in black and gold armor, Iron Man found his life haunted once again by the threat of Extremis, following the death of his colleague Maya Hansen.

JANUARY

GET CYCLOPS

• *All-New X-Men* #1

Writer Brian Michael Bendis had finished his time on the Avengers titles, having been one of the main pilots for the Marvel Universe for years. With this new, ongoing series, Bendis shifted his focus to a Marvel franchise that he hadn't had the chance to explore in detail. With penciler Stuart Immonen providing the book's striking visuals, Bendis began his tenure on the X-Men, centering on the team's founding members: Cyclops, Beast, Iceman, Marvel Girl, and Angel. In this engrossing storyline, Beast traveled back in time to visit his younger self and the rest of his original team. Now that the Cyclops of the present had taken the mutant cause to an almost militant extreme, Beast decided that the only way to combat the threat of his old ally was to recruit a Cyclops that was younger, less jaded, and on the right side of the law.

BRUCE BANNER, AGENT OF SHIELD

• *Indestructible Hulk* #1

The Hulk received the Marvel NOW! relaunch treatment in this issue penned by Mark Waid and illustrated by Leinil Francis Yu. Packed with action as the Hulk took down the Mad Thinker, this issue established Bruce Banner as the newest employee of the superspy agency SHIELD.

XAVIER'S LEGACY

• *X-Men Legacy* #1

The many personalities of Legion, the unbalanced son of Charles Xavier, were put in the spotlight in this revamp of the X-Men Legacy title by writer Simon Spurrier and penciler Tan Eng Huat. The series set off at a fast pace when one of Legion's inner demons killed the inhabitants of a Himalayan commune, forcing the rest of the world to view the mutant as a murderous fugitive.

EXPANDING THE AVENGERS

• *Avengers* #1

The latest epic in the continuing saga of the Avengers began in this new Marvel NOW! series by writer Jonathan Hickman and artist Jerome Opeña. Captain America, the Hulk, Thor, Hawkeye, Black Widow, and Iron Man responded to an attack on Earth emanating from Mars. They were shocked to be immediately, and almost effortlessly, overpowered by new foes Ex Nihilo and his allies Aleph and Abyss. Only Captain America made it back to Earth after the battle, and the hero realized that there was just one way to counter such a dire threat: the Avengers had to increase their ranks.

JANUARY

THUNDERBOLT ROSS

• *Thunderbolts* #1

The Red Hulk, aka retired General "Thunderbolt" Ross, recruited an unlikely array of hardened killers into a new breed of Thunderbolts, thanks to writer Daniel Way and artist Steve Dillon. Using leverage when necessary, Ross organized a team including heavy hitters Venom, Deadpool, Elektra, and the Punisher.

THE DEATH OF PETER PARKER

• *The Amazing Spider-Man* #700

It was the end of an era. This issue marked not only the apparent final issue of Spider-Man's flagship title, but also the supposed conclusion of the adventures of Peter Parker as everyone's friendly neighborhood wall-crawler. In this oversized anniversary edition celebrating fifty years of Spider-Man, Doctor Octopus won a battle with the web-slinger after swapping minds with the hero. As a result, Peter Parker's mind seemingly passed away with Doctor Octopus' frail form, while Octopus lived on in the healthy body of Peter Parker. This shocking conclusion to Spider-Man's story was delivered to audiences by writer Dan Slott and penciler Humberto Ramos. The issue also included two other stories, one by writer J. M. DeMatteis and penciler Giuseppe Camuncoli, and the other by writer Jen Van Meter and artist Stephanie Buscema, as well as a letter column moderated by Stan Lee himself.

FEBRUARY

INSIDE THE ILLUMINATI

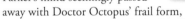

• *New Avengers* #1

Writer Jonathan Hickman continued his chronicle of the Avengers in this series with penciler Steve Epting. Starring the newest incarnation of the Illuminati, Marvel's most elite team of Super Heroes, this issue began with a spotlight on Black Panther.

SPIDER-MAN 2.0?

• *The Superior Spider-Man* #1

While Doctor Octopus apparently succeeded in killing Peter Parker after swapping minds with the hero, he was unable to destroy Peter's sense of responsibility. Since the two shared the same memories, Peter was able to transfer his greatest life lesson into Doctor Octopus' consciousness before seemingly passing on. This new series by writer Dan Slott and artist Ryan Stegman examined Doc Ock's life as Spider-Man as the villain tried to turn over a new leaf, with the help of the "ghost" of Peter Parker, who still lingered in his mind.

MARVEL COMICS
COVER ART

▲ *AVENGERS #1*

February 1998
Artist: George Pérez

When *Avengers* was relaunched in 1998, Marvel put two of
its best at the helm—writer Kurt Busiek and artist George
Pérez. The latter produced a stunning cover for the debut
issue (shown here in full), featuring a host of potential
Avengers bursting out of the cover. Pérez had originally
made his name illustrating the title in the 1970s, but he
produced some of his best work on the new series.

AVENGERS #2 ▶

March 1998
Artist: George Pérez

George Pérez got to draw numerous
Avengers once again for the second
cover of the relaunched comic—but this
time with a twist. The evil Morgan le Fay
had altered reality into an Arthurian
world, transforming the heroes into
feudal versions of themselves. This
made for a very unusual cover image.

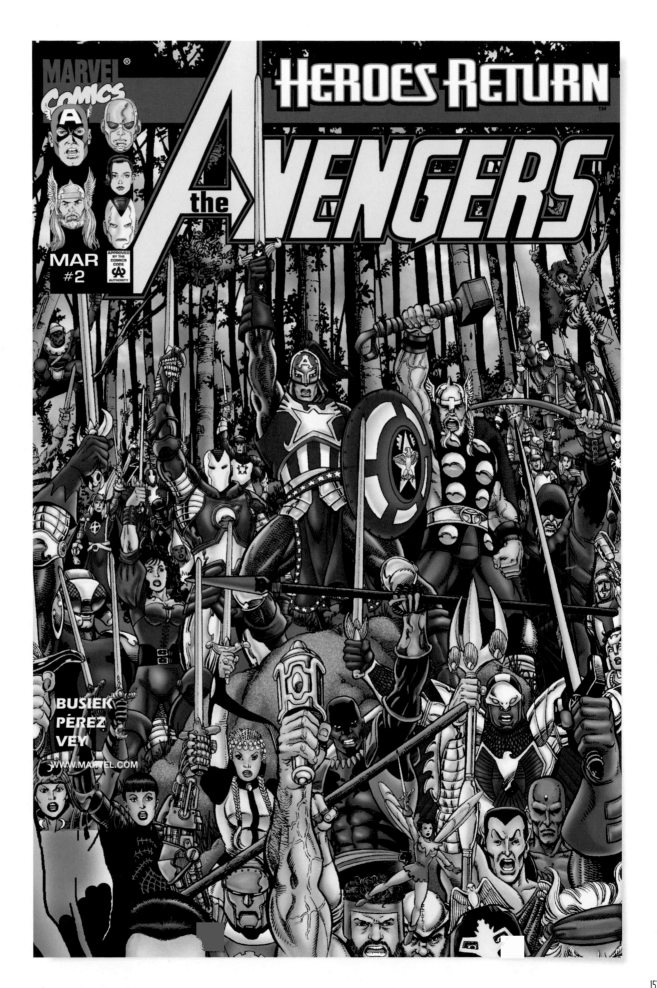

David Finch produced a dark and thoughtful cover for the final part of the "Avengers Disassembled" epic, which saw the Avengers destroyed from within by an insane Scarlet Witch. The sight of Captain America surrounded by his friends' weaponry suggested that even more Avengers could die.

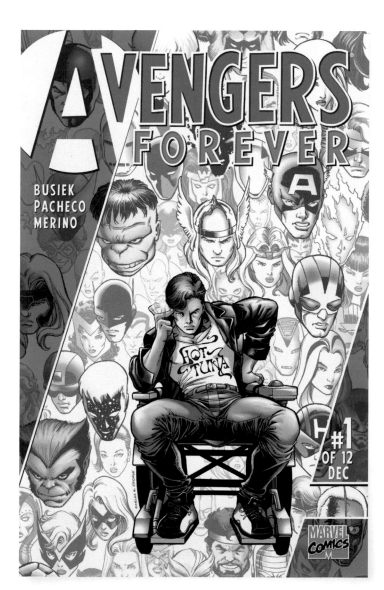

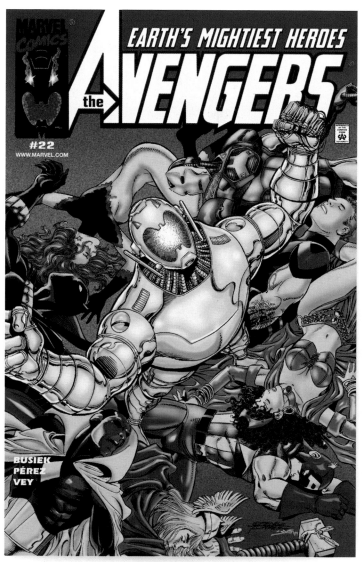

▲ *AVENGERS FOREVER* #1

December 1998
Artist: Carlos Pacheco

Avengers Forever was Kurt Busiek's complex, 12-part epic that brought together Avengers from across the timeline. The first issue's cover, by Carlos Pacheco, is a simple, but effective image featuring Rick Jones, the Hulk's old sidekick, contemplating a new line-up of the Avengers.

▲ *AVENGERS* #22

November 1999
Artist: George Pérez

Ultron, a robot created by Dr. Hank Pym in *Avengers* issue #55 (August 1968), has always been one of the team's deadliest enemies. This cover by George Pérez is one of the most menacing Ultron covers to date, showing the ferocious robot standing victorious over the defeated heroes.

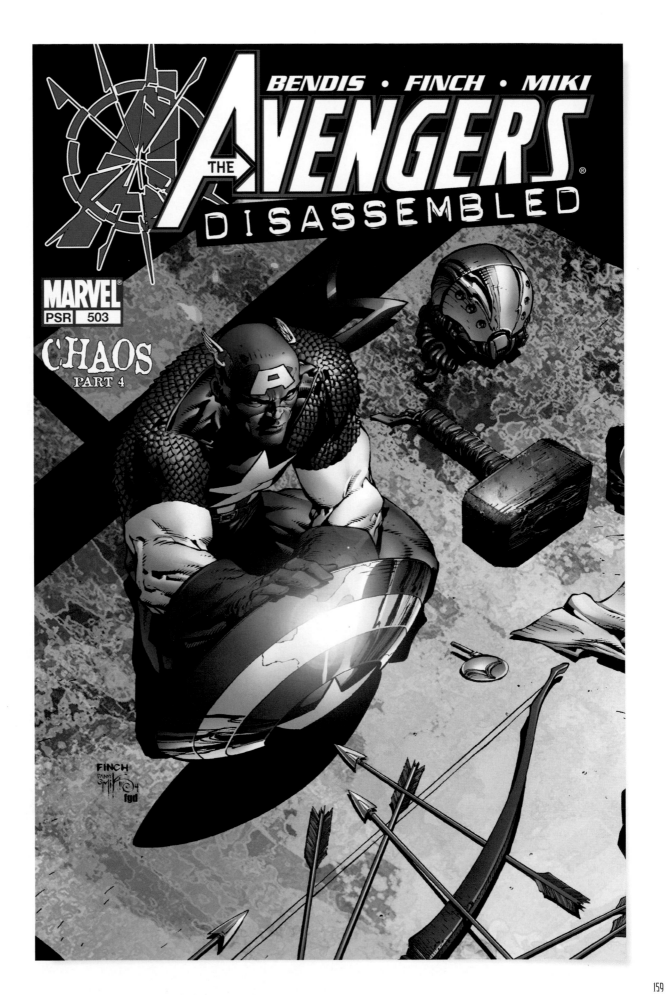

AVENGERS FINALE

January 2005
Artist: Neal Adams

Legendary artist Neal Adams produced a stunning piece of work for the cover of the final *Avengers* comic (before the series was relaunched.) The dynamic nature of Adams' early work was back in full force with this image of the team charging into action. The story itself acted as an epilogue to the "Avengers Disassembled" storyline.

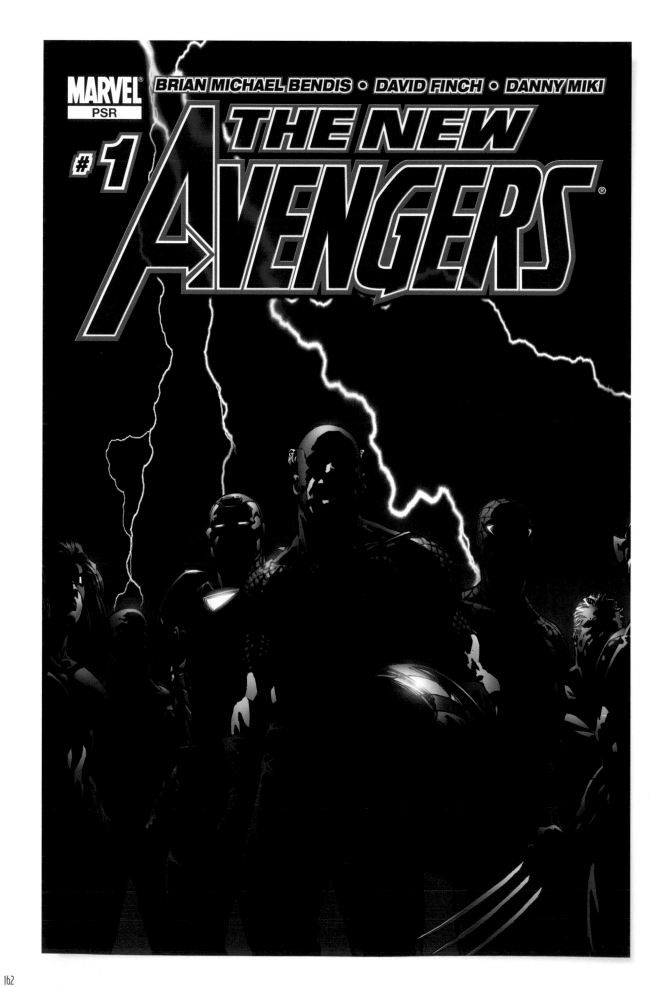

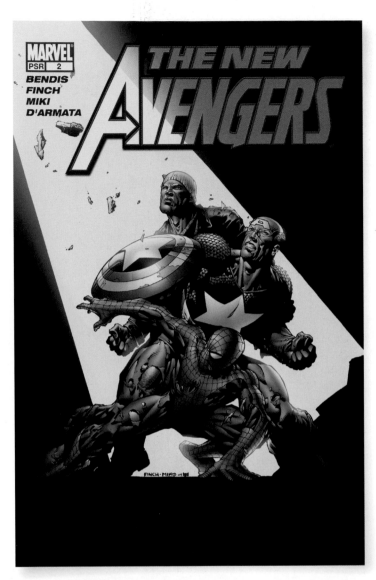

▲ *THE NEW AVENGERS* #2

February 2005
Artist: David Finch

With Spider-Man now a member of the
Avengers, he soon became a regular on
the covers. The second issue is another
dramatic and tense-looking work from
Finch. The image reflects the main story,
as the heroes joined forces in an attempt
to stop a mass breakout from the Super
Villain penitentiary known as the Raft.

▲ *THE NEW AVENGERS* #27

April 2007
Artist: Leinil Francis Yu

Leinil Francis Yu produced this stylish
cover during his brief run as artist on
The New Avengers. His striking image
shows new hero Ronin (Clint Barton
taking over the role from Echo) facing
off against an overwhelming horde of
ninja assassins led by Elektra.

◀ *THE NEW AVENGERS* #1

January 2005
Artist: David Finch

This was the book that made the
Avengers one of Marvel's bestsellers,
and created an entire franchise,
with various Avengers-related titles
spinning off its success. The cover for
issue #1 is darker and moodier than
those of the previous title, and Finch
instills a real sense of heroic power
and mystery into the characters by
showing them in half-shadow.

▲ *AVENGERS: THE INITIATIVE* #1

June 2007
Artist: Jim Cheung

Jim Cheung produced the art for a unique cover—or rather two covers—that could be put together to reveal one big image of the Avengers Initiative. Following on from the Civil War, which split Marvel's Super-Hero community in two, the new series focused on young heroes as they trained to be potential Avengers.

THE NEW AVENGERS: ILLUMINATI #1 ▶

February 2007
Artist: Jim Cheung

One of the most shocking revelations writer Brian Michael Bendis introduced to the Avengers was that six of Marvel's most respected heroes had formed a secret group—the Illuminati. Jim Cheung illustrated the series, his first cover bringing the heroes together in an atmospheric work that hints at the group's hidden affiliation.

▲ *AVENGERS CLASSIC* #1

August 2007
Artist: Art Adams

Art Adams created a stunning piece of work for the
debut issue of *Avengers Classic*, a series that reprinted
Avengers tales from their first issue (with some modern
material added). Adams manages to incorporate just
about every hero who had ever been an Avenger for his
cover. It was interesting to see Adams' artistic take on
the original team, including Iron Man, Thor, and the Hulk.

▲ *SECRET AVENGERS* #16

October 2011
Artist: John Cassaday

Famed writer Warren Ellis produced a
tightly written series of one-shot stories
for *Secret Avengers*, each graced with a
cool, highly stylized cover by John Cassaday.
In his first cover, Cassaday rotated his
artwork from portrait to landscape, a
radical move that perhaps reflected the
strange time-travel story within.

▲ *SECRET AVENGERS* #17

November 2011
Artist: John Cassaday

John Cassaday surpassed himself with the
next *Secret Avengers* cover. This relatively
simple artwork shows Steve Rogers
(during a spell where he wasn't Captain
America), in front of an almost demonic-
looking truck running him down. Using a
limited color palette, Cassaday imbued the
cover with a sense of danger and tension.

▲ *SECRET AVENGERS* #18

December 2011
Artist: John Cassaday

John Cassaday portrayed the martial-arts hero Shang-Chi seemingly using his skills to split someone's head in two on this much-acclaimed cover. The shocking image set the scene for another skilled Warren Ellis story, with interior art by David Aja.

▲ *SECRET AVENGERS* #19

January 2012
Artist: John Cassaday

As Warren Ellis' run on *Secret Avengers* continued, John Cassaday illustrated another stunning cover. This time he placed the team in a cold, desolate Eastern European landscape, their shadows overlapping the logo, to highlight the covert nature of the team. The story featured the heroes taking down a gangster who was using special drugs to increase his strength.

When it was decided to pit the Avengers against the X-Men, Marvel knew they would need an A-list artist for this crossover event. Jim Cheung had broken into the world of comics as a teenager via Marvel UK and has gone on to become one of the industry's top artists. He provided the cover art for *Avengers vs. X-Men* [or *AVX*], showing both teams on the verge of war in a stunning piece of work.

◀ AVENGERS #1

July 2010
Artist: John Romita Jr.

The *Avengers* was relaunched following the end of the "Dark Reign," a period in Marvel continuity during which the unstable Norman Osborn gained political control of America's heroes. Steve Rogers, Osborn's more honorable successor, formed several new Avengers teams. Romita Jr.'s cover reflects the nobility of the main team and was the defining image of the new "Heroic Age."

◀ UNCANNY AVENGERS #1

December 2012
Artist: John Cassaday

Combining both the X-Men and Avengers into one team was a simple yet brilliant idea. John Cassaday, who had become one of the biggest names in the business by this time, illustrated the cover for the debut issue. Cassaday showcased the line-up and even incorporated the logo into his work, using it to separate the X-Men and Avengers.

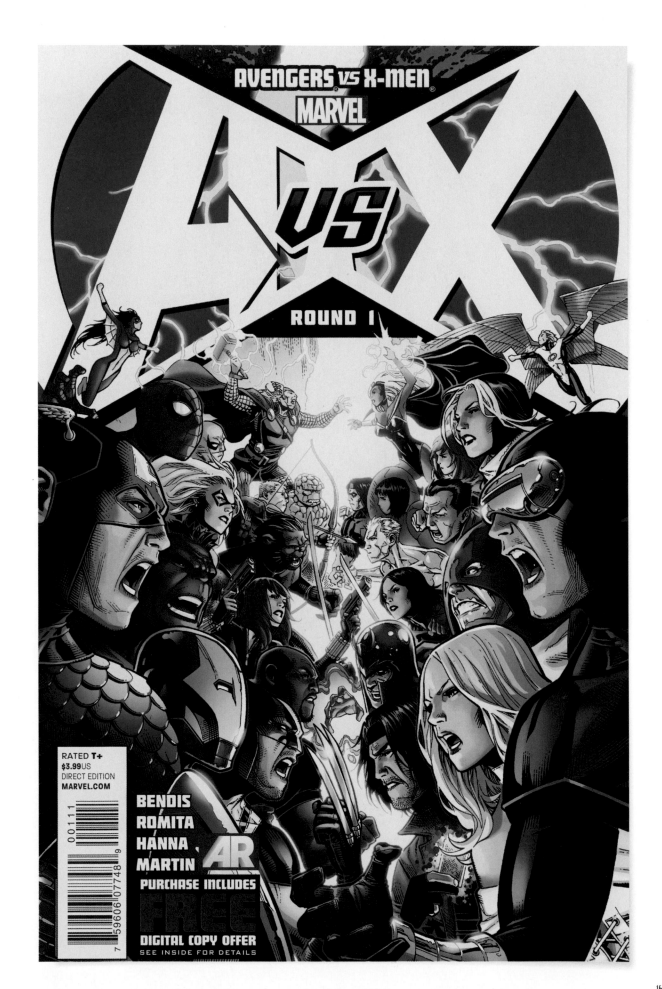

◀ *CAPTAIN AMERICA ANNUAL #8*

September 1986
Artist: Mike Zeck

By the mid-1980s, Wolverine was firmly established as one of Marvel's favorite heroes, and an appearance by him on a cover would usually lead to an increase in sales. This was one of the most spectacular Wolverine covers outside of his own title. Mike Zeck's dynamic style gives the piece a dangerous energy fit for a Super Hero of Wolverine's standing.

◀ *CAPTAIN AMERICA #405*

August 1992
Artist: Rik Levins

One of the strangest *Captain America* adventures saw Steve Rogers become a werewolf called "Capwolf." The Rik Levins cover has a simple layout, but the image of Capwolf is a striking and strangely intriguing one, typical of the title's experimental stories during the mid-90s.

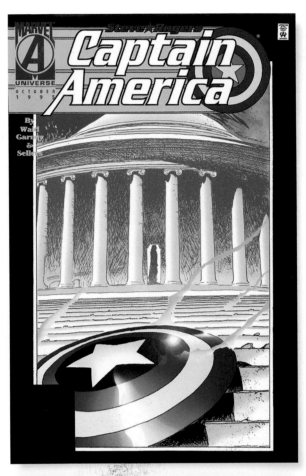

◀ *CAPTAIN AMERICA #444*

October 1995
Artist: Ron Garney

Writer Mark Waid and artist Ron Garney provided what many consider to be the best *Captain America* stories of the decade. Garney's covers were both stylish and eye-catching—and this one is a fine example. The discarded shield outside the White House hints at Cap's meeting with the President, and his eventual exile.

◀ *CAPTAIN AMERICA #451*

May 1996
Artist: Ron Garney

Ron Garney's stark cover reflected Steve Rogers taking up a new costume in this issue—one without the familiar stars and stripes emblazoned on it (seen here seemingly discarded and blowing in the wind). The striking image also obliquely refers to Cap's exile beyond US soil.

◄ CAPTAIN AMERICA #14

February 1999
Artist: Andy Kubert

Andy Kubert's terrifying portrait of the Red Skull made this Cap cover one of the most iconic of the decade. Writer Mark Waid's first run on *Captain America* had been cut short when the title was outsourced for a year to creators from publisher Image Comics. However, when the title returned, Marvel brought Waid back and relaunched the series from a new issue #1. It proved to be a huge success.

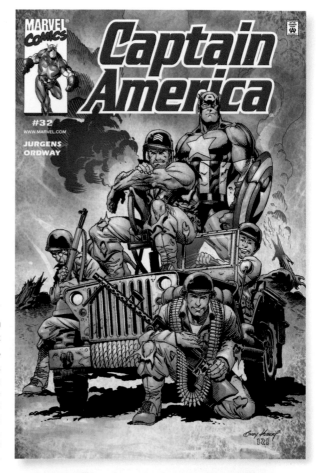

CAPTAIN AMERICA #32 ►

August 2000
Artist: Andy Kubert

Andy Kubert got to draw Nick Fury and his Howling Commandos for this classic Captain America cover. Kubert's father, the legendary artist Joe Kubert, had made his name illustrating Sergeant Rock for DC Comics, and Andy's image has definite echoes of his father's work.

CAPTAIN AMERICA #1 ►

June 2002
Artist: John Cassaday

The after-effects of the real-life 9/11 terrorist attacks that had taken place the previous year were felt in this issue as Cap was sent to the Middle East to find those responsible. Cassaday's stunning cover is über-patriotic and militaristic, reflecting a country—and indeed a world—trying to come to terms with the attacks.

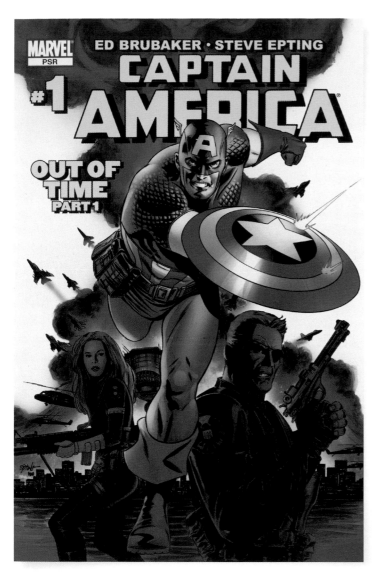

▲ *CAPTAIN AMERICA* #1

January 2005
Artist: Steve Epting

Writer Ed Brubaker and artist Steve Epting created one of the all-time great *Captain America* sagas, "Out of Time." Epting's covers were exceptional montages, resembling high-end movie posters. This cover highlights a change in storytelling style, as Cap's adventures became more like a top-class spy-thriller than a traditional Super-Hero adventure.

▲ *CAPTAIN AMERICA* #6

June 2005
Artist: Steve Epting

Ed Brubaker's story gave a new twist to Bucky Barnes' role as Cap's old sidekick, making him a deadly assassin rather than teenage poster boy. Epting's cover for this issue focuses on Cap's exploits in World War II. It is another movie-style montage, the stark red Nazi flags providing a sinister backdrop.

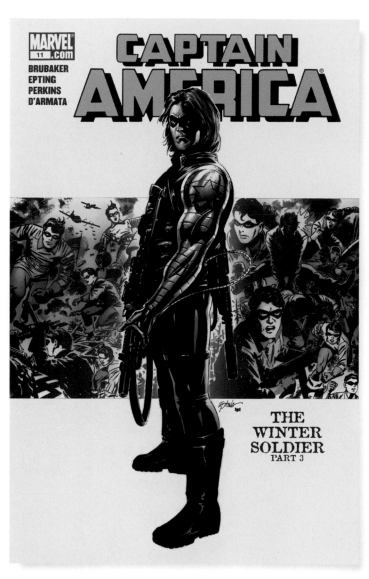

▲ *CAPTAIN AMERICA* #11

November 2005
Artist: Steve Epting

"The Winter Soldier" (Bucky Barnes, who had become a Soviet assassin since his days as Cap's sidekick) is the main focus on this issue's cover, with a montage of Bucky's war-time exploits behind him. The character and story was the inspiration for 2014's second *Captain America* movie.

▲ *CAPTAIN AMERICA* #25

April 2007
Artist: Ed McGuinness

Ed McGuinness' simple but emotionally charged cover illustrated a story that made headlines across the world—the assassination of Captain America. The headlines on the background image echo famous assassinations of real-life American heroes, making the cover all the more emotively powerful.

▲ *CAPTAIN AMERICA REBORN #6*

March 2010
Artist: Bryan Hitch

Bryan Hitch is one of the most talented artists in the business and provided a stunning wraparound cover for the final issue of the series that had revealed Steve Rogers was still alive, but lost in time. Hitch's art is as bombastic as the final chapter's action-packed conclusion. It also shows the original Captain America taking his rightful place at the forefront of Marvel's heroes.

CAPTAIN AMERICA #34 ▶

March 2008
Artist: Alex Ross

When Bucky Barnes took on the role of Captain America from the seemingly dead Steve Rogers it was always going to be a big deal. Alex Ross produced a stunning painted cover showing the new Captain America—complete with a brand new costume. Bucky had been the Winter Soldier, a deadly assassin, and continued to use guns as Captain America. It was the portrayal of Cap with a gun that shocked many readers.

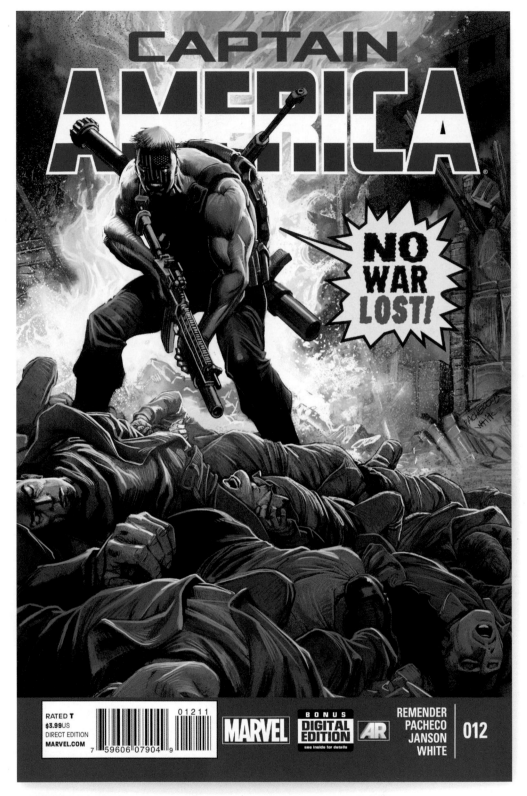

▲ *CAPTAIN AMERICA* #12

December 2013
Artist: Carlos Pacheco

Crazed war-veteran and failed Super Soldier Nuke
had first been seen in the classic *Daredevil* issue
#232 (July 1986) and had seldom been used since
the end of that story. He was, however, center stage
in this story, and never looked as menacing as he
does on Carlos Pacheco's powerful cover, which
shows him standing over the bodies of his victims.

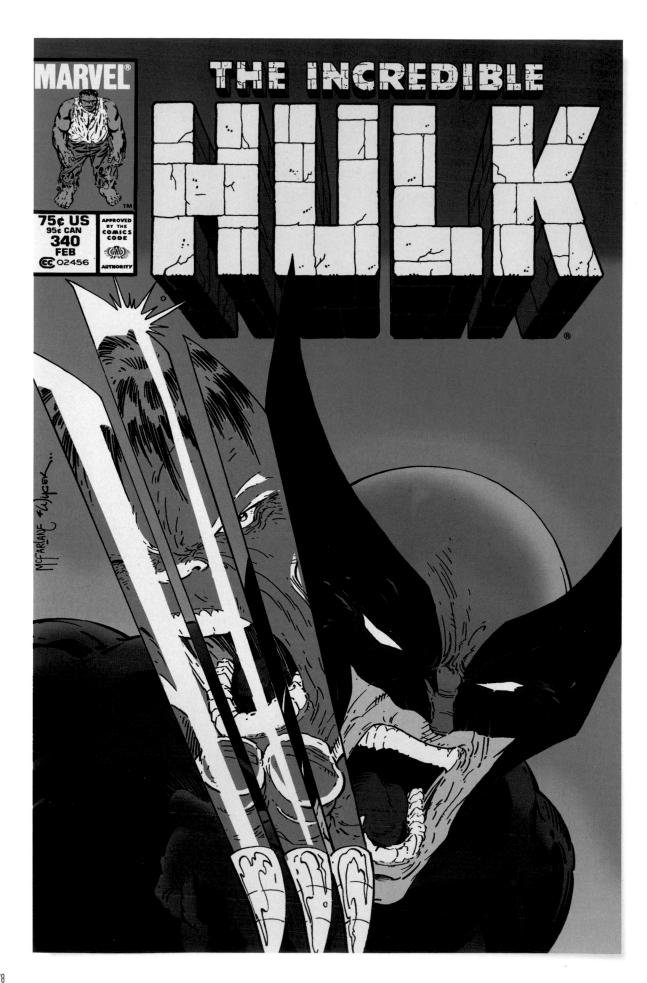

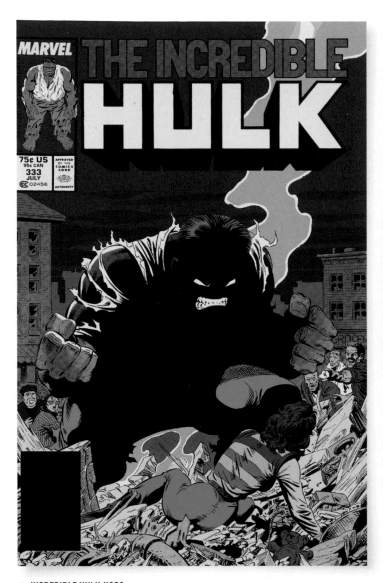

▲ INCREDIBLE HULK #333

July 1987
Artist: Steve Geiger

The Hulk had rarely looked as angry as he did on this cover, illustrated by Steve Geiger. Bruce Banner had just learned shocking secrets of his past. The trauma he felt was transferred to his monstrous alter ego, which Geiger brilliantly reflects in his depiction of a glowering Hulk.

▲ INCREDIBLE HULK #345

July 1988
Artist: Todd McFarlane

Todd McFarlane frequently reinvented (or simply broke) the rules of cover design in order to create an eye-catching image. This cover is a classic example—McFarlane made the logo part of the cover artwork, so he could have the gray, enraged Hulk smashing it up.

◀ INCREDIBLE HULK #340

February 1988
Artist: Todd McFarlane

Todd McFarlane's work on the Hulk (with writer Peter David) revitalized the hero and propelled McFarlane to the big league. This classic cover is a shining example of what made his run so popular. Since Wolverine's first appearance in *Incredible Hulk* issue #181 in November 1974 (after a cameo in issue #180), Hulk–Wolverine fights have always been a big deal. This artwork, with the gray Hulk cleverly reflected in Wolverine's claws, showcases one of the best.

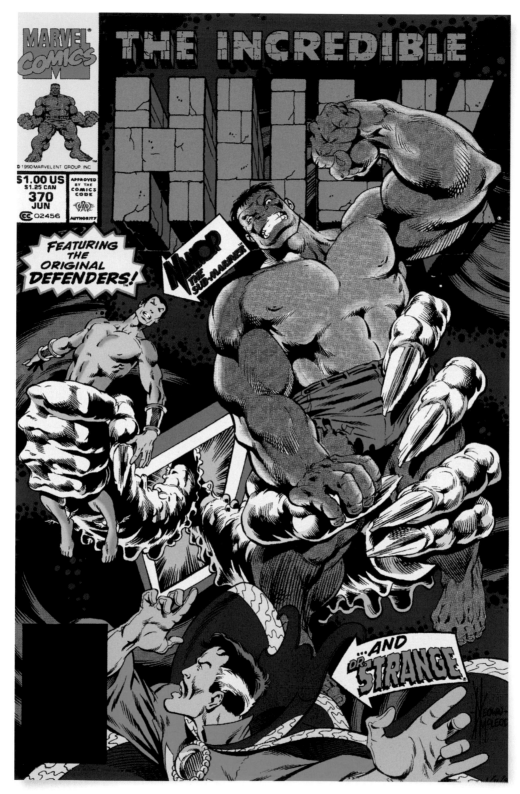

▲ *INCREDIBLE HULK* #370

June 1990

Artist: Dale Keown

Dale Keown followed Todd McFarlane as artist on *Incredible Hulk* and, working with writer Peter David, created what is considered by fans to be one of the title's best runs. Keown also produced a number of fantastic covers, including this one, which brings the original Defenders together for the first time in years.

▲ *INCREDIBLE HULK* #373

September 1990
Artist: Dale Keown

Peter David remains one of the best writers to
chronicle the Hulk's adventures, bringing a
sense of humanity to the character. This
classic cover by Keown, featuring the Hulk and
Betty Ross (Bruce Banner's main love interest)
sharing a few laughs, best exemplifies that
aspect of David and Keown's time on the title.

INCREDIBLE HULK #379 ▶

March 1991
Artist: Dale Keown

One of the standout covers from Keown's run on *Incredible Hulk*, this issue marked the start of a new Hulk "persona," as Bruce Banner's intellect and the Hulk's physical form became one. The change was reflected in the title logo, which showed glimpses of previous incarnations of the Hulk. Keown's portrayal was about a mixture of power and intellect, the new Hulk managing to be both more human and more dangerous.

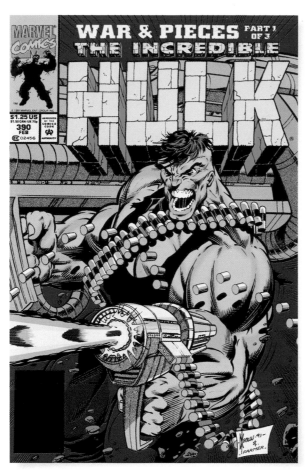

◄ *INCREDIBLE HULK* #390

February 1992
Artist: Dale Keown

Guns were big business in the 1990s. At times, it seemed like every hero was suddenly carrying really big, over-the-top weaponry. The new incarnation of the Hulk also got in on the action with this issue when he became involved in a Middle-Eastern conflict. The sight of the Hulk at war was a new and shocking image.

◄ *INCREDIBLE HULK* #395

July 1992
Artist: Dale Keown

The Punisher became very popular in the late 1980s and early 1990s, and he guest-starred in a number of Marvel titles. Keown's image of the vigilante, reflected in the glasses of a mean-looking Hulk, suggested that this was going to be a deadly confrontation. The story saw the Hulk return to Las Vegas to avenge the death of a friend.

◄ *INCREDIBLE HULK* #409

September 1993
Artist: Gary Frank

In this issue, British-born artist Gary Frank got to illustrate the characters with whom he had made his name—Motormouth and Killpower. These characters had been created by Marvel UK and illustrated by Frank before he succeeded Dale Keown on *Incredible Hulk*. It was one of the few occasions when Marvel UK characters appeared on the cover of a mainstream US title.

◄ *INCREDIBLE HULK* #418

June 1994
Artist: Gary Frank

Rick Jones married his girlfriend Marlo in this issue that came with a die-cut cover. The early 1990s saw many special-treatment covers. Just about anything and everything was tried, from die-cuts to foil. Such covers added a whole new element of design to the books. Lifting the die-cut cover of *Incredible Hulk* issue #418 reveals the guests at Rick and Marlo's wedding.

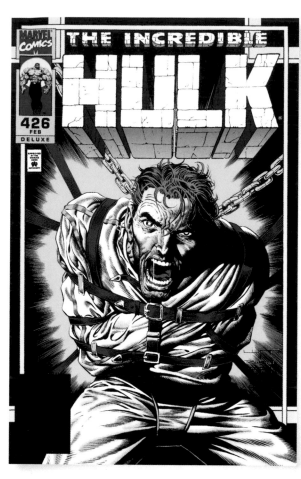

◄ *INCREDIBLE HULK* #426

February 1995
Artist: Liam Sharp

Liam Sharp produced this startling cover during his short run on *Incredible Hulk*. Sharp's close-up of a straightjacketed Banner screaming out at the reader hinted at the shock inside the issue, as Hulk's ferocious consciousness dominated Banner's comparatively puny frame.

◄ *INCREDIBLE HULK* #60

November 2003
Artist: Mike Deodato Jr.

The Hulk's second volume took the green-skinned beast back to his roots as a vicious monster fueled by anger. Artist Mike Deodato Jr. gave this new, brutal incarnation a sense of raw power, showcased on the cover. Deodato experimented with the design and layout to create a memorable image of an enraged Hulk breaking through a wall— and the title logo.

INCREDIBLE HULK #94 ▶

June 2006
Artist: José Ladrönn

Writer Greg Pak created one of the best Hulk stories of the decade with his "Planet Hulk" saga. The third part's cover, drawn by José Ladrönn, was later used for the story's graphic novel collection. It shows the Hulk in his new role as a gladiator in an alien arena. The image gave the character a dramatic new visual twist, and this latest incarnation proved extremely popular.

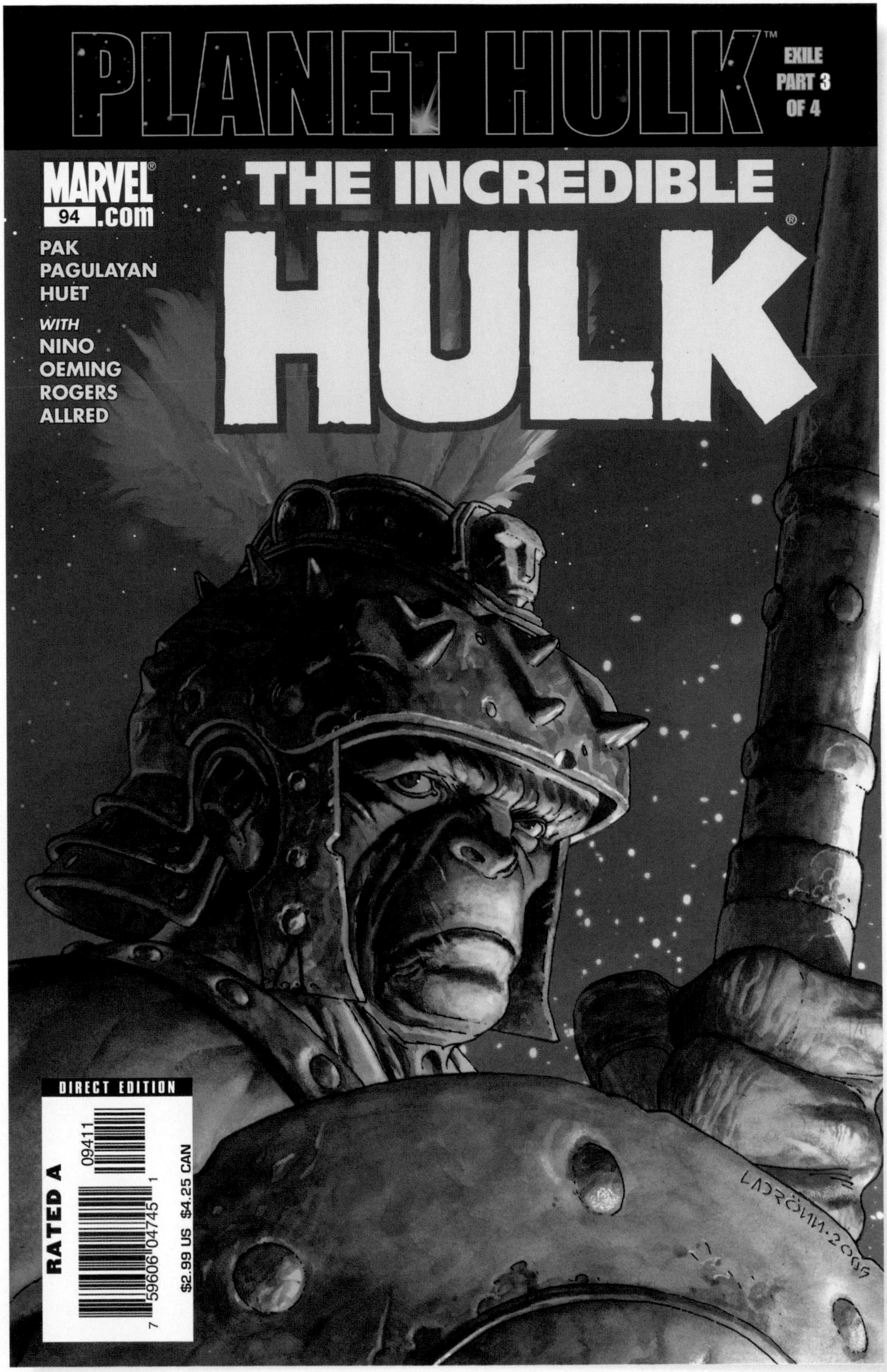
PLANET HULK
EXILE PART 3 OF 4
MARVEL
94 .com
THE INCREDIBLE
HULK
PAK
PAGULAYAN
HUET
WITH
NINO
OEMING
ROGERS
ALLRED
DIRECT EDITION
RATED A
$2.99 US $4.25 CAN
LADRÖNN·2005

▲ *WORLD WAR HULK* #1

August 2007
Artist: David Finch

The Hulk was returning to Earth to seek revenge on
the so-called heroes who had exiled him into space
and—he believed—destroyed his adopted planet.
David Finch's powerful cover illustration shows a
Hulk that is more barbarian than monster, a terrifying
creature filled with rage. It left readers wondering
just what would happen when he reached Earth...

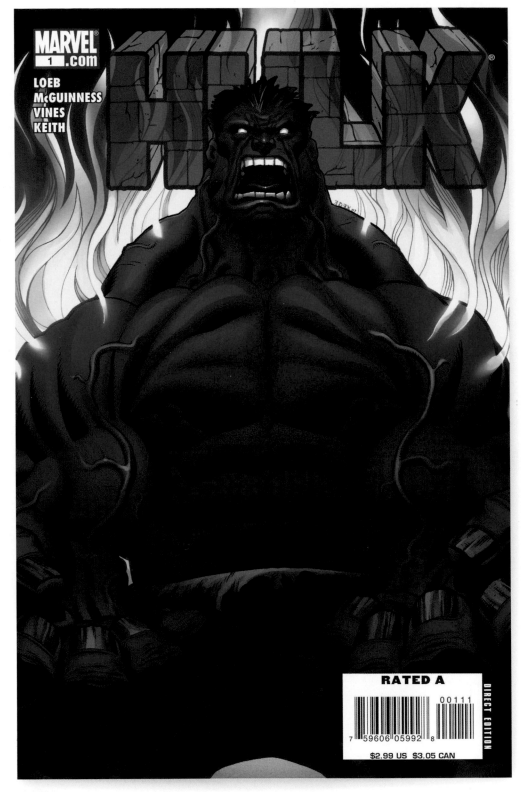

▲ *HULK* #1

January 2008
Artist: Ed McGuinness

Ed McGuinness was the perfect choice to create a new incarnation
of the Hulk: His art is always larger than life, and he specializes
in portraying muscular characters. McGuinness helped to create
a memorable first issue cover image; the change of color (and
creation of this new Hulk, later revealed to be none other than
Thunderbolt Ross) ensured that readers were desperate to
find out what had happened to the green-skinned behemoth.

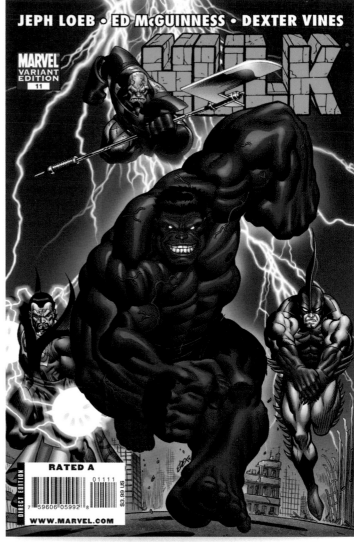

▲ *HULK* #11

April 2009
Artist: Ed McGuinness

Cover variants proved to be big news in the 2000s, and the second part of the "Defenders/Offenders War" story showed how alternative covers could be used to complement the main one. In this case the original cover shows the green Hulk and the Defenders while the variant shows the Red Hulk and the Offenders in a mirrored pose, providing a dramatic contrast between the two groups.

HULK & THING: HARD KNOCKS #1–4 ▶

November 2005–February 2006
Artist: Jae Lee

Artist Jae Lee created beautiful covers for this four-part series about the long rivalry between the Hulk and the Thing. The story, written by Bruce Jones, depicted the Hulk and the Thing talking over their old fights before coming to blows once again. Lee's close-up covers look like stills from the fight and also proved to be four of the most dramatic covers to feature the two heroes.

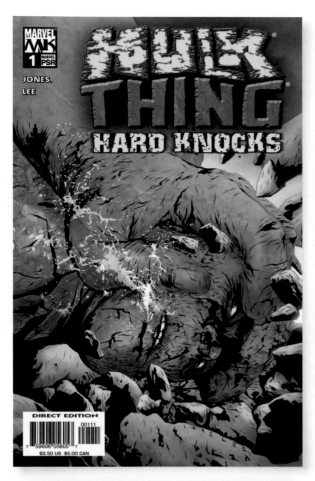

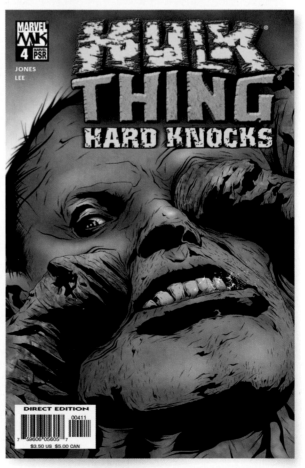

◄ *HAWKEYE* #1

October 2012
Artist: David Aja

Marvel's covers became increasingly stylized in the 2010s as artists pushed the boundaries of design. Writer Matt Fraction and artist David Aja produced one of the most adventurous Marvel comics in decades with *Hawkeye*. Each issue had a fabulous slick cover, and this debut issue set the standard for what was to follow. Aja eventually won a prestigious Eisner award for his work on this series.

◄ *HAWKEYE* #3

December 2012
Artist: David Aja

David Aja's art, coupled with Matt Fraction's stories, led to the new *Hawkeye* series gaining rave reviews. Aja's third cover shows the weapons of two Hawkeyes—Clint Barton and Kate Bishop (Hawkeye of the *Young Avengers*). The image uses the same black, white, and purple color scheme of the early covers, which gave the book a distinctive look and set it apart from its competition.

◄ HAWKEYE #4

January 2013
Artist: David Aja

Issues #4 and #5 of *Hawkeye* are both fine examples of David Aja's stylistic and intelligent covers. The two-part story was called "The Tape" and involved Hawkeye trying to recover a politically sensitive video tape. The first part, in extreme contrast to most other Marvel Comics covers, simply shows a VHS cassette with sound waves below it, and lots of white space. It is enigmatic in its simplicity.

◄ HAWKEYE #5

February 2013
Artist: David Aja

The cover for the second part of "The Tape" was a dramatic and grisly contrast to that of part one. The blood splatters also signified the end of the "purple" cover phase. In a medium that usually employs action-packed, detailed covers, Aja's designs for *Hawkeye* were truly a breath of fresh air.

HAWKEYE #9 ▶

May 2013
Artist: David Aja

This cover focuses on another Hawkeye, Kate Bishop. The young archer was becoming far more than a supporting character in the series, and this issue focused on her adventures rather than those of Clint Barton. Aja shows a keen sense for design on the cover, playing with both the logo and the brand to create a special cover image of Kate Bishop.

HAWKEYE #11 ▶

July 2013
Artist: David Aja

Pizza Dog takes center stage on the cover of one of the most inventive issues of *Hawkeye*. The image, showing the bloody pawprints left by Hawkeye's dog, reflects the fact that the whole issue is told from the dog's perspective. It was a unique cover for a unique series.

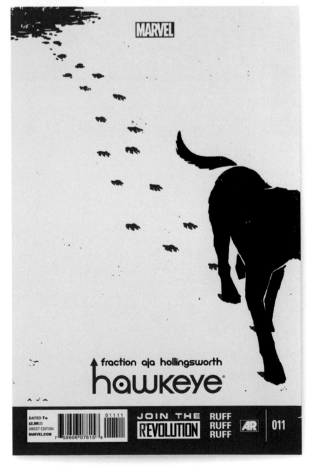

◀ HAWKEYE #8

April 2013
Artist: David Aja

While most comic-book covers often utilize bright visuals, few use one color in such a dominant way as this "Valentine special" issue of *Hawkeye*. The central image of Cherry (one of Clint Barton's many ex-girlfriends) on a blood-red background really conveys a feeling of violence and danger. With such bold use of color and imagery, artist David Aja pushed the boundaries of design in ways not seen since the days of Jim Steranko.

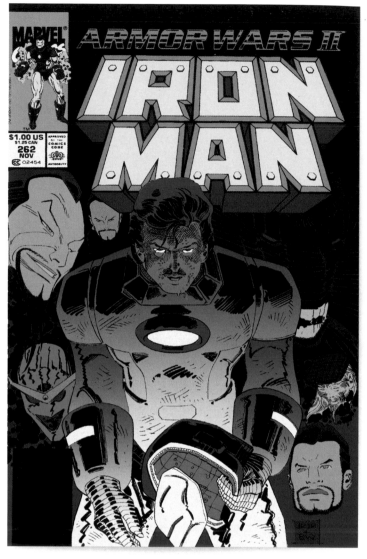

▲ *IRON MAN #232*

July 1988
Artist: Barry Windsor-Smith

The "Armor Wars" epic—in which Tony Stark tried to reclaim stolen Stark technology—ended with this epilogue. Barry Windsor-Smith created a beautiful, but disturbing cover, which shows Tony Stark's corpse-like body suspended from cables, hinting at the nightmarish story inside.

▲ *IRON MAN #262*

November 1990
Artist: John Romita Jr.

The follow-up to "Armor Wars" continued in this issue behind a stunning John Romita Jr. cover. The cover art reflected the turmoil that Stark was undergoing, as the villainous Kearson DeWitt took control of his nervous system, literally manipulating Stark's every move, while others prepared to make their own moves against the hero.

IRON MAN #282 ▶

July 1992
Artist: Kevin Hopgood

British-born artist Kevin Hopgood introduced the character War Machine to the Iron Man universe in this issue. The comic had never seen armor quite like the War Machine's. The militaristic design and gray coloring of the armor made this an impactful cover. The artist had fun with typography by having War Machine's name as graffiti over the Iron Man title.

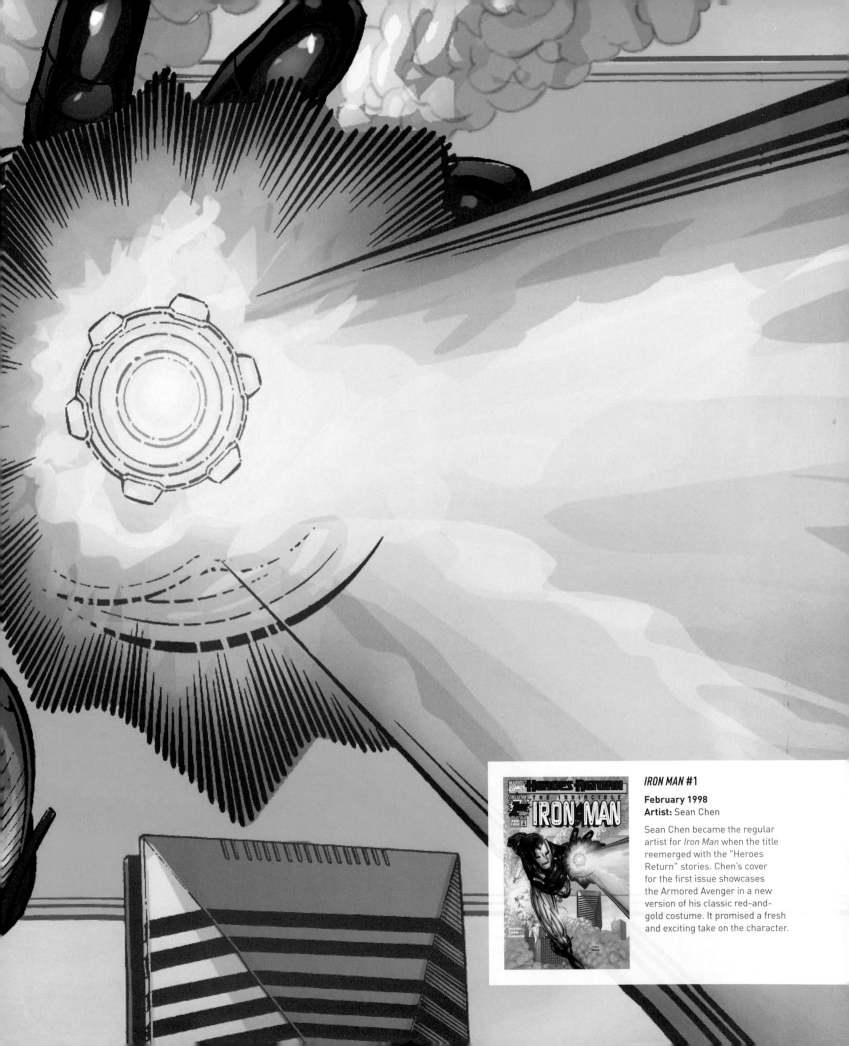

IRON MAN #1

February 1998
Artist: Sean Chen

Sean Chen became the regular artist for *Iron Man* when the title reemerged with the "Heroes Return" stories. Chen's cover for the first issue showcases the Armored Avenger in a new version of his classic red-and-gold costume. It promised a fresh and exciting take on the character.

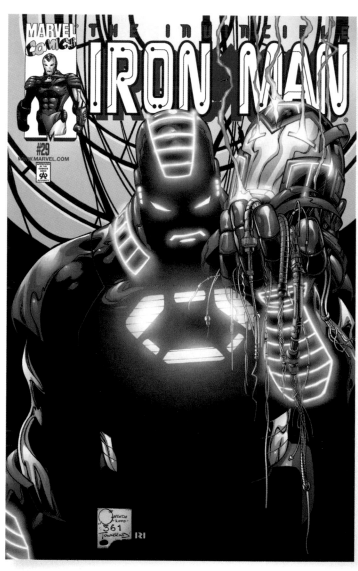

▲ *IRON MAN #29*

June 2000
Artist: Joe Quesada

Future Marvel Editor-in-Chief Joe Quesada
created this story about Iron Man's latest
armor becoming sentient and turning against
its creator. Quesada also provided the cover
for his story—his dramatic image instills the
sentient armor with a suitably menacing feel
as it gripped one of Stark's old helmets.

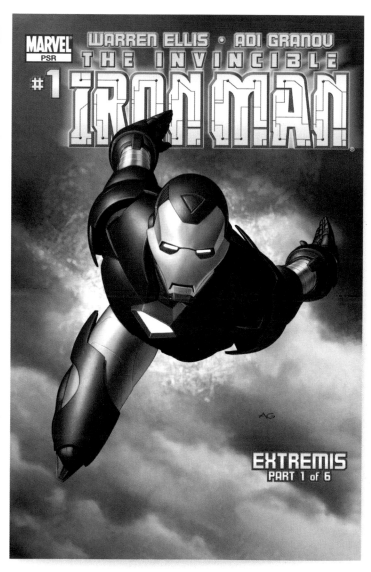

▲ *IRON MAN #1*

January 2005
Artist: Adi Granov

Writer Warren Ellis and artist Adi Granov
teamed up to relaunch *Iron Man*, creating
a story that would later provide the
inspiration for the third *Iron Man* movie.
Granov created a striking incarnation
of the hero, his realistic take on the
Armored Avenger staring straight out
at the reader from the cover.

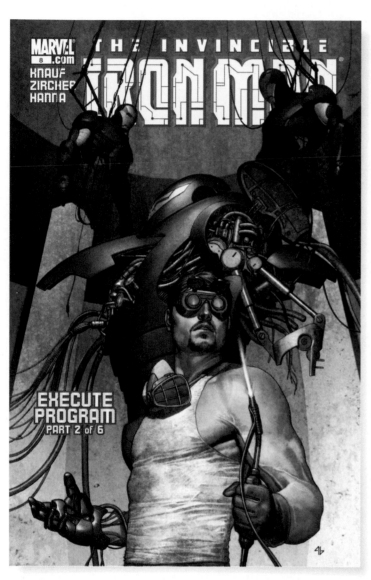

▲ *IRON MAN #8*

July 2006
Artist: Adi Granov

Adi Granov's stylish run on *Iron Man* continued with a cover focusing on Tony Stark in inventor mode. Granov also worked as an artist for the first *Iron Man* movie, and elements of his version of Tony Stark on this cover clearly influenced the movie incarnation.

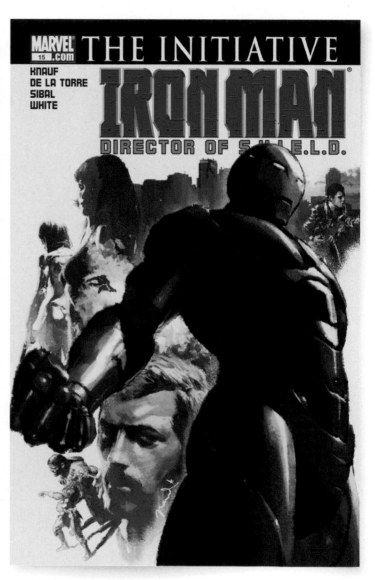

▲ *IRON MAN: DIRECTOR OF S.H.I.E.L.D. #15*

April 2007
Artists: Gerald Parel and Adi Granov

This explosive cover heralded a new direction for Iron Man's adventures as his alter ego, Tony Stark, became head of S.H.I.E.L.D. Stark's adventures had always been more realistic than many other heroes, and this cover reflects his new dual role as hero and super spy.

▲ *INVINCIBLE IRON MAN #20*

January 2010
Artist: Salvador Larroca

This slightly surreal cover perfectly captured a turning point in the life of Tony Stark and Iron Man as the hero struggled to reboot his mind after he had wiped it to stop Norman Osborn from learning his secrets. All five parts of this storyline reflected Stark's inner struggle. This first part showcased Stark's concern that he would never regain his lost knowledge.

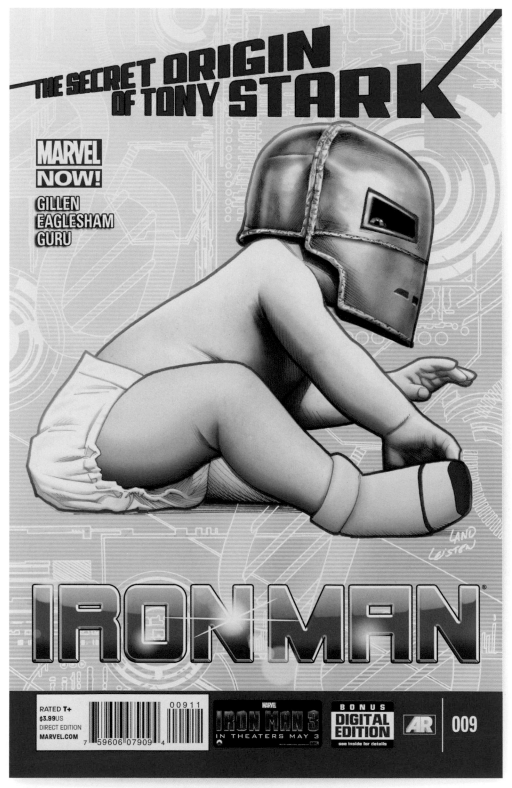

▲ *IRON MAN #9*

June 2013
Artist: Greg Land

Few covers can claim to be truly original, but this Greg Land piece, showing an infant Tony Stark, managed it. It signalled the start of one of the most shocking *Iron Man* stories of all time, as writer Kieron Gillen's story seemed to suggest alien intervention leading up to Stark's birth—only to reveal that Tony had been adopted and that the Stark's natural son, Arno, was still alive.

◄ *SHE-HULK #8*

December 2004
Artist: Mike Mayhew

Under writer Dan Slott, She-Hulk enjoyed
one of her most creative—and humorous—
runs. These aspects are both exemplified
in this Mike Mayhew cover, showcasing
She-Hulk's office life. With cameos by
Matt Murdock (Daredevil) and Howard
the Duck, it artfully mixes the mundane
with the chaotic in the Marvel universe.

▲ *SHE-HULK #1*

May 2004
Artist: Adi Granov

Writer Dan Slott created some excellent
stories during his time on the title, each
one behind a stunning cover. On the debut
cover to the hero's new series, Adi Granov
manages to portray both the power and
beauty of She-Hulk in this issue. In fact,
this became one of the most frequently
seen images of the character.

▲ *SHE-HULK #10*

October 2006
Artist: Greg Horn

Dan Slott's *She-Hulk* was relaunched in 2005.
The new series continued the title's tradition
of great covers, and one of the favorites was
this Greg Horn piece depicting the hero's
relationship with John Jameson, a.k.a. the
Man-Wolf. The pulpy 1950's horror-movie
look of the cover was an accurate reflection
of the comic's knowing humor.

▲ *THOR* #1

July 1998
Artist: John Romita Jr.

When Thor's own series was relaunched
following the end of the "Heroes Reborn"
saga, John Romita Jr. was brought in as
the artist. His powerful style was the
perfect match for Thor, who has rarely
looked as godlike as he does on this
stunning wraparound cover.

THOR #1 ▶

September 2007
Artist: Olivier Coipel

The first new *Thor* comic since
2004 needed to feature something
special on the cover. Artist Olivier
Coipel's interpretation of the
powerful God of Thunder shows
a new, darker look for Thor than
had been seen previously.

▲ *THOR* #601

June 2009
Artist: Marko Djurdjevic

This issue boasts one of the most beautiful covers in *Thor*'s history, and one of the greatest modern interpretations of Thor's home, Asgard. Marko Djurdjevic captured Thor's anger and melancholy at being exiled from Asgard in one moody, expressionistic piece. This art style had a big influence on the first *Thor* movie (2011).

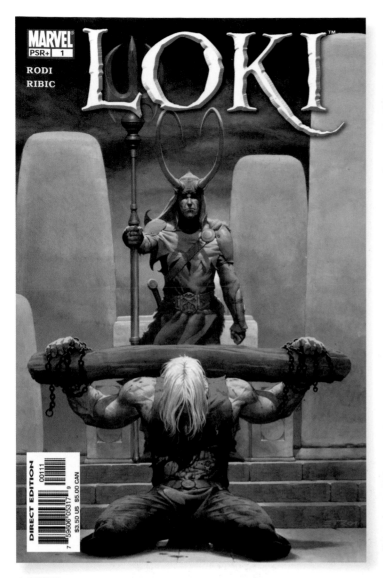

▲ *LOKI* #1

September 2004
Artist: Esad Ribic

Thor's evil adopted brother, Loki, gained his very own miniseries, with Esad Ribic creating beautifully painted covers for all four issues. Each one showcased Loki's troubled relationship with the Thunder God. The first, showing Loki looming menacingly over his captured brother, set the scene for the Loki-centric series.

▲ *JOURNEY INTO MYSTERY* #625

September 2011
Artist: Stephanie Hans

Stephanie Hans' romantic-looking cover belies writer Kieron Gillen's dark and ultimately tragic fantasy told within. Far from being a romantic tale, issue #625 told the story of a young Loki attempting to save the world from the Serpent, an ancient Asgardian God of Fear.

◄ *THOR: AGES OF THUNDER* #1

June 2008
Artist: Marko Djurdjevic

Thor: Ages of Thunder recounted tales of Thor's Asgardian adventures. Artist Marko Djurdjevic created a suitably mythic-looking cover for this one-off issue, showing the Thunder God standing triumphantly on a defeated Frost Giant. Other one-shots, telling more tales of Thor's Asgardian life, soon followed, each with a highly detailed Djurdjevic cover.

FANTASTIC FOUR #348 ▶

January 1991
Artist: Art Adams

This issue's cover (and the story inside) brought together four of Marvel's most popular heroes of the time—Ghost Rider, the Hulk, Spider-Man, and Wolverine—into an all-new *Fantastic Four*. Add artist Art Adams producing some of his finest work, and you have a classic *Fantastic Four* cover. The heroes joined forces to rescue the original team, who had been captured by a rogue Skrull.

◀ FANTASTIC FOUR #345

October 1990
Artist: Walt Simonson

Could the Fantastic Four really be dead? That was the question raised by the image of a triceratops with torn FF costumes hanging out of its mouth. The strapline was changed from the usual "World's Greatest Comic Magazine" to "Prehistory's Greatest Comic Magazine" to reflect the time-travel nature of the story as Simonson's inventive run on the title continued.

◀ FANTASTIC FOUR #349

February 1991
Artist: Art Adams

Art Adams produced another outstanding piece of work for this cover, lining the original Fantastic Four up alongside a new team that had formed to save them following their capture in the previous issue. The sight of all the heroes together, alongside the Mole Man, marching out towards the reader resulted in an eye-catching cover.

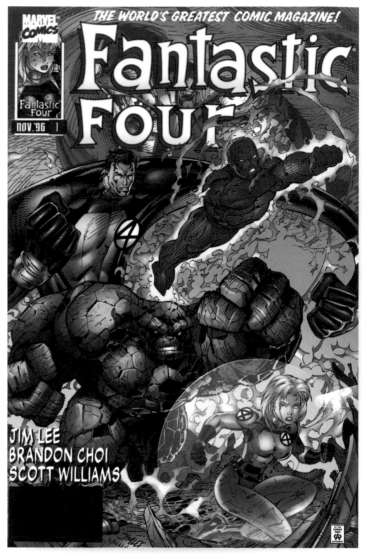

▲ *FANTASTIC FOUR* #350

March 1991
Artist: Walt Simonson

"Ain't nothing like the real Thing!" Ben Grimm's word balloon said it all on this anniversary issue cover—the founding member of the Fantastic Four was once again transformed into the FF's powerhouse. Simonson's image of the Thing standing over girlfriend Sharon Ventura, with Doctor Doom looming large in the background, suggested that this was going to be another epic clash between the FF and their archenemy.

▲ *FANTASTIC FOUR* #1

November 1996
Artist: Jim Lee

In 1996, four of Marvel's biggest titles were taken over by creators from rival publisher Image Comics and relaunched as part of the "Heroes Reborn" imprint. Jim Lee was the biggest name in comics at the time and he took on the *Fantastic Four*, updating their origin and giving the art a sleek, modern-day feel, as can be seen on the first issue. It brought the bestselling, artistic energy of Image Comics—and especially Jim Lee—to the FF.

▲ *FANTASTIC FOUR* #1

January 1998
Artist: Alan Davis

Marvel's "Heroes Return" branding saw the
company bring top creators to their major titles
as they returned to Marvel after a year of being
produced by Image Comics. Alan Davis' style was
perfect for the *Fantastic Four*, as he brought a
vitality and spirit of adventure to Marvel's First
Family, as exemplified by his first cover.

◀ *FANTASTIC FOUR #60*

October 2002
Artist: Mike Wieringo

Mike Wieringo's cover art for the *Fantastic Four* conveyed a sense of wonder that only the best FF artists brought to the title, while Mark Waid's scripts ensured a series of great stories. Such was Marvel's confidence in this new creative duo that they released the issue for only 9 cents.

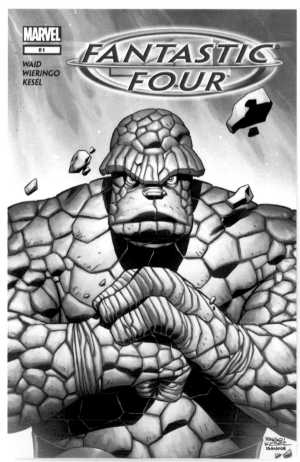

◀ *FANTASTIC FOUR #61*

November 2002
Artist: Mike Wieringo

The Thing was perhaps the most human of Marvel's monstrous heroes, and artist Mike Wieringo's interpretation manages to encapsulate this theme perfectly. He evokes not only The Thing's amazing strength, but also his inner nobility.

◄ FANTASTIC FOUR #67

May 2003
Artist: Mike Wieringo

This issue was a prologue to "Unthinkable," a highlight of Mark Waid and Mike Wieringo's time working on the *Fantastic Four*. Wieringo's striking cover portrays a powerful and despotic Doctor Doom burning with energy gained through selling the soul of his true love to demons.

◄ FANTASTIC FOUR #558

August 2008
Artist: Bryan Hitch

Doctor Doom has been the subject of many great covers, but Bryan Hitch's startling close-up of Latveria's dictator presented a new aspect to the character. It is one of the only times Doom has looked scared on a cover, making the reader instantly want to find out exactly what, or who, Doom feared so much.

▲ *FANTASTIC FOUR #583–586*

November 2010–February 2011
Artist: Alan Davis

The strapline on each of these four issues gave an ominous "Countdown to Casualty," as the Fantastic Four approached a time when one of them would die. Issue #583 depicts the team standing around an empty grave, while the following issues show Ben, Sue, and Reed in strange—and possibly deadly—situations. Writer Jonathan Hickman's critically acclaimed run on the FF was nearing a key moment, and, tellingly, the hero who did not get a cover of his own was the one destined to die—the Human Torch.

▲ *FANTASTIC FOUR #587*

March 2011
Artist: Alan Davis

Alan Davis' dramatic cover image for the fifth installment of the "Three" story arc depicts each member of the Fantastic Four in deadly peril, arranged around an ominously cracked 4 insignia. The result was one of the most tense covers in the FF's long history. To further increase the tension, the issue came in a black sealed bag emblazoned with a 3 insignia.

◀ FANTASTIC FOUR 1234 #1

October 2001
Artist: Jae Lee

Working with writer Grant Morrison, Jae Lee brought his unique vision to the Fantastic Four on a four-part miniseries, which focused on the bonds that united the team. Lee's illustration of Yancy Street, once home to Ben Grimm, established the dark, moody tone of the series. As Ben desperately tried to alter his own past so that he never became the Thing, evil Doctor Doom was masterminding the team's destruction.

FF #12 ▶

January 2012
Artist: Steve Epting

The FF—or Future Foundation—replaced the Fantastic Four both as a team and a comic in the 2010s. The FF was actually an organization for young, gifted minds, founded by Mr. Fantastic. Epting's simple cover shines the spotlight on these great young characters (and a reformed, intelligent Dragon Man), and brought a fresh energy to the book.

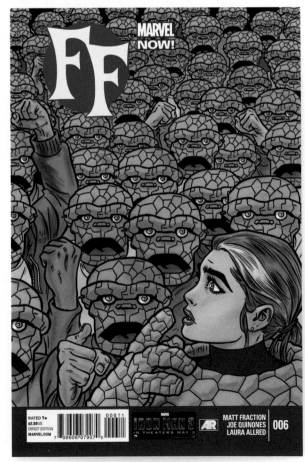

FF #6 ▶

June 2013
Artist: Mike Allred

The FF gained a second volume, written by Matt Fraction and illustrated by Mike Allred. The new series was strange, funny, and sometimes bizarre—as exemplified by this crazy cover showing new FF member Darla Deering (aka Miss Thing) being stalked by a masked Yancy Street Gang, who resented her taking on the role of the Thing.

February 2006
Artist: Mike Deodato Jr.

Comic fans always love team-ups and this issue had one of the coolest. Black Panther joined forces with the Falcon, Shang Chi, and Luke Cage to take on Shang Chi's estranged father Han (a criminal mastermind). Deodato's cover brought all the main players together in one stylish image that also reflected the villain's Asian powerbase.

◀ *BLACK PANTHER #58*

June 2003
Artist: Liam Sharp

The Black Panther was one of Marvel's first African heroes and Liam Sharp used the Panther's African background to add some beautiful design elements to his cover. The bright African sun helps to frame the Panther and gives the image an almost mythical element.

◀ *BLACK PANTHER:*
THE MOST DANGEROUS MAN ALIVE #525

January 2012
Artist: Francesco Francavilla

When Black Panther took over Daredevil's title from issue #513, the new series produced a number of adventurous cover designs. The covers that Francavilla produced for "The Most Dangerous Man Alive" story-arc had a real pulp-fiction detective-story look, right down to the faded colors. The cover featured the Panther's latest adversary, the Kingpin.

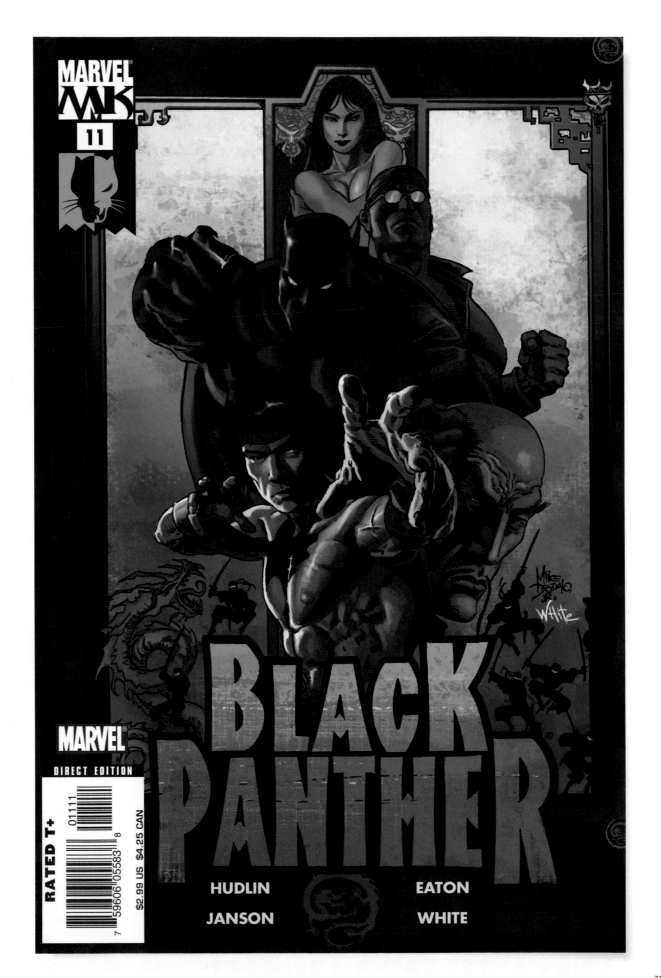

BLACK PANTHER #1

April 2005

Artist: John Romita Jr.

For the creation of the *Black Panther* issue #1 cover, John Romita Jr. started the process the traditional way, creating a number of rough character poses (1) before moving onto pencils. Once these were approved, the finished pencils (2) were inked by the legendary Klaus Janson (3) before passing on to Dean White for coloring (4). White colored the cover on computer, but gave it a natural, painterly feel to reflect the subject of the piece. The finished art was then sent digitally to Marvel, whose design team added the Marvel branding, before turning the cover into a high-resolution format ready for print (5). With the advent of direct sales to comic shops, covers are now produced months in advance of the final comic-book art, so that they can be used for advanced promotion.

1. Sketch
2. Pencil
3. Ink
4. Color
5. Final cover

1.

2.

3.

4.

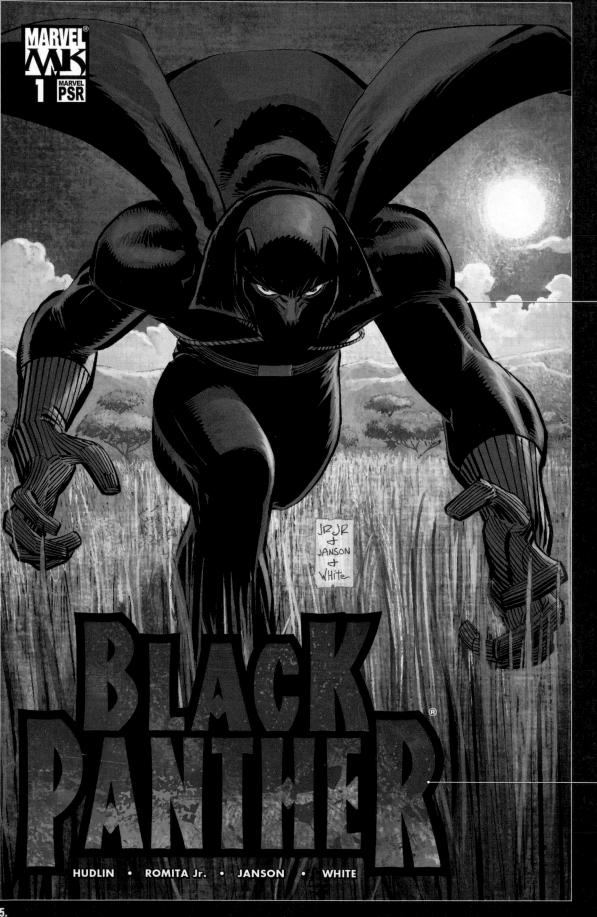

Romita's pose for the Black Panther portrayed the hero as a hunter. He also reinstated the cloak to the hero's costume.

The Black Panther logo was updated for the new series, wi_ subtle textures that reflect the story's African setting.

HUDLIN • ROMITA Jr. • JANSON • WHITE

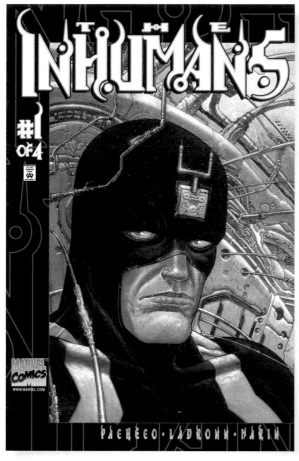

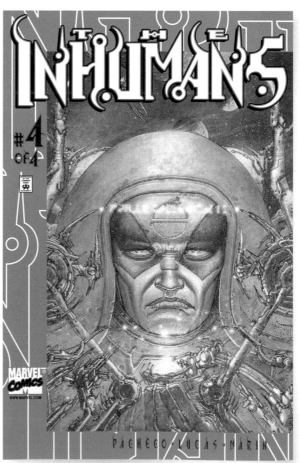

INHUMANS #1 ▶

November 1998
Artist: Jae Lee

The cover of the first issue of this 12-part series is a powerful one. It portrays the Inhuman royal family with their king, Black Bolt, in the forefront, flanked by his wife Medusa and his closest allies. The Inhumans look both regal and alien, thanks to Lee's dark and stylish work.

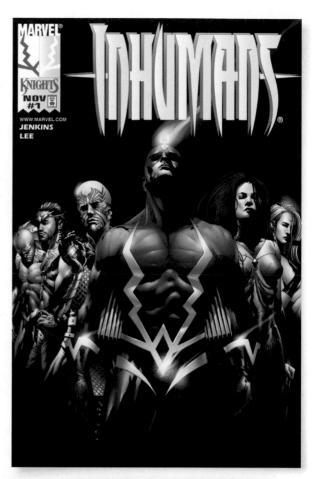

INHUMAN #1 ▶

April 2014
Artist: Joe Madureira

Top artist Joe Madureira returned to Marvel to illustrate Inhuman. The cover shows the Inhumans covertly living side-by-side with humanity. They were Inhumans who—like the title's hero, Dante—had no knowledge of their true genetic origins until exposure to the Inhumans' Terrigen Mists brought out their Inhuman abilities. This issue marks the increased importance of the Inhumans in the wider Marvel Universe.

◀ *THE INHUMANS* #1–4

June–October 2000
Artist: José Ladrönn

The third volume of *The Inhumans* was a four-part miniseries, written by Rafael Marin and illustrated by José Ladrönn. Each cover reflects the alien nature of the Inhumans' origins, a focal point of the series, with a close-up of one or two of the main Inhumans—Black Bolt, Medusa, and Karnak and Triton. Issue #4 featured the Inhumans' enemy Ronan the Accuser.

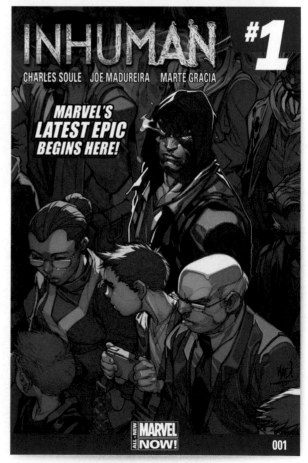

▲ *MARVELS #1*

January 1994
Artist: Alex Ross

Every now and again, an artist bursts onto the comic scene and changes the very nature of the business. Alex Ross did just that with the launch of *Marvels*, widely considered to be the best miniseries of the decade. The painted cover image was based on the classic version of the first Human Torch from *Marvel Comics issue* #1.

▲ *MARVELS #2*

February 1994
Artist: Alex Ross

Each issue of *Marvels* dealt with a different era of Marvel history, with Kurt Busiek's brilliant scripts giving Alex Ross a chance to shine. The second issue concentrated on the early days of Marvel's modern heroes. Ross' painted cover depicts the rise of the X-Men, with a beautiful version of Angel escaping a baying mob.

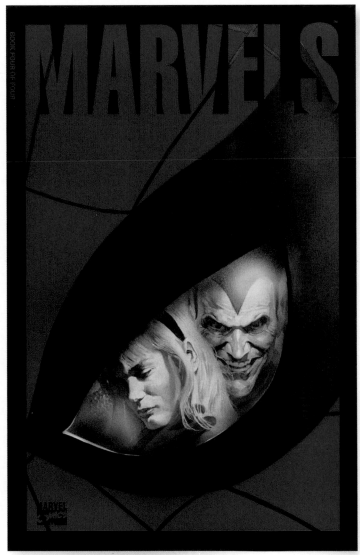

▲ **MARVELS #3**

March 1994
Artist: Alex Ross

The third book in the *Marvels* series focused on the arrival of Galactus (originally told in the classic *Fantastic Four* issue #48 of 1966). For the cover, Ross painted a striking portrayal of Galactus' herald, the Silver Surfer, with the Fantastic Four's Human Torch and the city of Manhattan reflecting off his alien skin.

▲ **MARVELS #4**

April 1994
Artist: Alex Ross

The conclusion of *Marvels* centered around one of the company's greatest (and most tragic) stories—the death of Gwen Stacy. Many consider this to be the best cover of the series, with its portrayal of the Green Goblin and Gwen as seen in the reflection of Spider-Man's eyepiece.

◄ *NEXTWAVE: AGENTS OF H.A.T.E.* #1

March 2006
Artist: Stuart Immonen

With *Nextwave*, writer Warren Ellis and
artist Stuart Immonen created a series
that both celebrated and mocked the
Super-Hero genre. The cover to its debut
issue firmly established that the title
was different from regular Marvel books.
The stylish design mixes an image of
The Great Wave off Kanagawa by Japanese
painter Hokusai with the superteam,
topped off by the book's satirical tagline,
"healing America by beating people up."

▲ *THE ULTIMATES* #1

March 2002
Artist: Bryan Hitch

One of the most important Marvel comics of the 2000s, *The Ultimates*
was a reimagined version of the Avengers, set in Marvel's new
"Ultimate Universe." Bryan Hitch's cover for the debut issue
emphasized the role of Captain America and the first issue focused
almost entirely on Cap in World War II. Writer Mark Millar and artist
Bryan Hitch created a masterful series, influencing many of the
Marvel movies that followed, especially Marvel's *The Avengers* (2012).

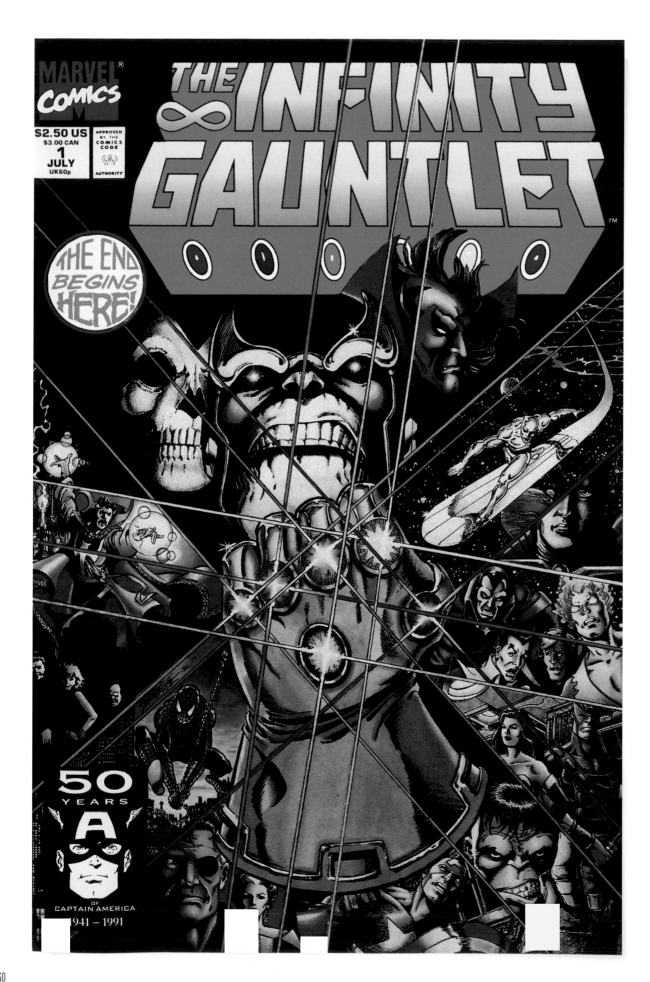

The Marvel Universe is changing. In the wake of a tragedy, Capitol Hill proposes the Super Hero Registration Act, requiring all costumed heroes to unmask themselves before the government. Divided, the nation's greatest champions must each decide how to react—a decision that will alter the course of their lives forever!

WHOSE SIDE...
...ARE YOU ON?

MARK MILLAR

STEVE MCNIVEN

DEXTER VINES

MORRY HOLLOWELL

CIVIL WAR
A MARVEL COMICS® EVENT IN SEVEN PARTS

MARVEL
RATED T+
DIRECT EDITION
00111
7 59606 05921 8
$3.99 US $5.75 CAN

1

CIVIL WAR #1 ▲

July 2006
Artist: Steve McNiven

Marvel created a new design style for the launch of *Civil War*, the company's 2006 saga that made headlines across the world. Steve McNiven's striking cover for the first issue hints at the drama to come, while the white border and careful placement of text revealed the increasing role that design was playing in Marvel's covers as they sought new ways to make their comics stand out.

◄ *THE INFINITY GAUNTLET* #1

July 1991
Artist: George Pérez

Award-winning artist George Pérez was at the helm for *The Infinity Gauntlet*, one of Marvel's first comic-book blockbusters. Pérez's stunning cover for the first issue displays a host of Marvel's Super Heroes around the central image of Thanos. The cover established the star-spanning nature of the series, with heroes such as Silver Surfer and the Hulk caught up in Thanos' attempt to impress Death by wiping out half of the universe.

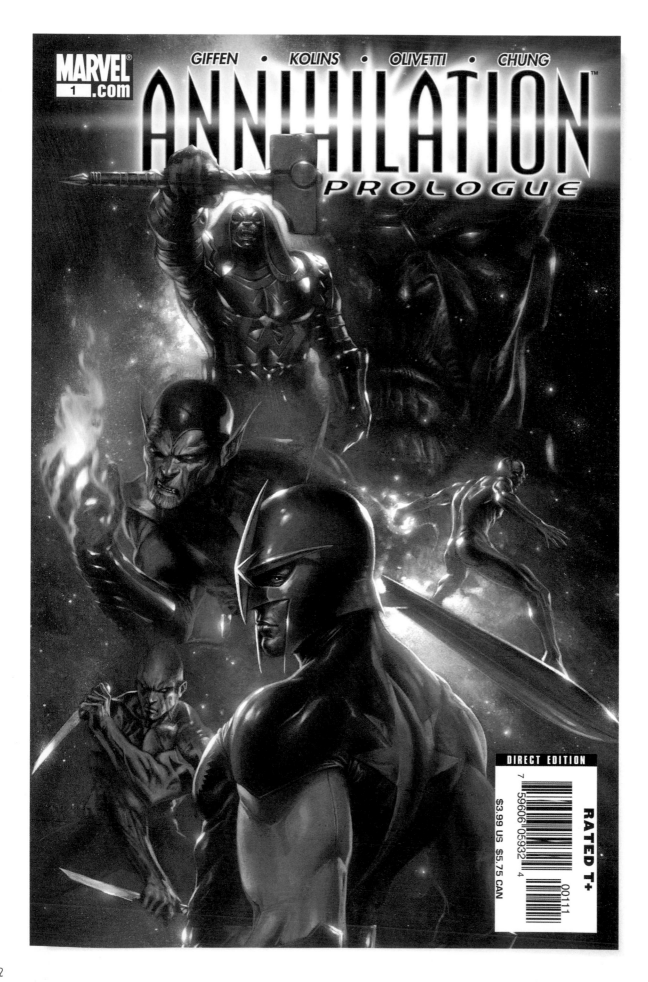

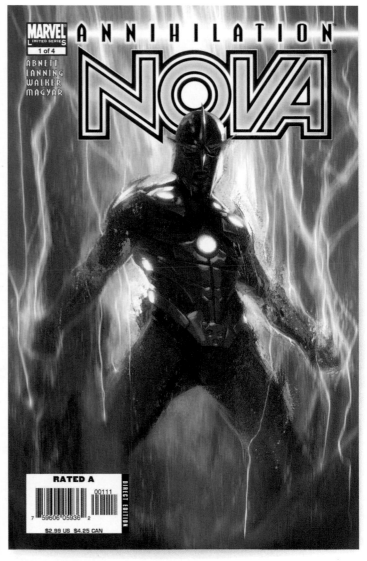

▲ *ANNIHILATION #1*

October 2006
Artist: Gabriele Dell'Otto

The Annihilation event continued with another
Gabriele Dell'Otto painted cover featuring some
of Marvel's most powerful heroes and villains.
With Annihilus at the center of the image and the
face of Galactus looming large in the background,
the first issue cover firmly established that this
was an event on a truly cosmic scale.

▲ *ANNIHILATION: NOVA #1*

June 2006
Artist: Gabriele Dell'Otto

Nova was relaunched in 2006 as part of the
Annihilation event. Gabriele Dell'Otto's dramatic
cover of Nova standing alone reflected the hero's
new role as the only survivor of the Nova Corps,
following its destruction by the Annihilation
Wave (a vast alien army led by Annihilus).

◄ *ANNIHILATION: PROLOGUE #1*

May 2006
Artist: Gabriele Dell'Otto

Annihilation was the series that made
Marvel's cosmic heroes popular again,
as they starred in one vast intergalactic war
story. Each issue in the multi-part epic had
amazing painted covers that were more like
those found on science fiction novels than
comics. Gabriele Dell'Otto set the standard
high with this movie-poster style montage,
heralding the start of the epic.

◀ *ANNIHILATION: CONQUEST—STARLORD* #1

September 2007
Artist: Nic Klein

The success of *Annihilation* led to a follow-up, *Annihilation: Conquest*, which saw Marvel's cosmic heroes facing a new threat—the Phalanx. The series had started with a prologue that led into several miniseries, including one featuring Starlord. Artist Nic Klein created an action-packed pose for the first cover, depicting the hero blasting his guns out at the reader.

◀ *NOVA* #22

April 2009
Artist: Juan Doe

Writers Andy Lanning and Dan Abnett re-established *Nova* as one of Marvel's greatest cosmic heroes and—by this issue—left the hero close to death after his powers had been stripped from him by the alien entity Worldmind. This issue heralded the return of the Nova Corps, with Juan Doe turning the cover into a stylish recruitment poster for the new corps.

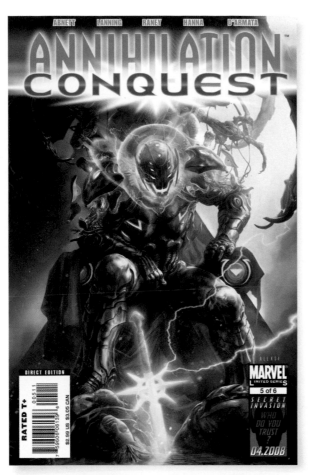

◄ *ANNIHILATION: CONQUEST* #5

May 2008
Artist: Aleksi Briclot

As *Annihilation: Conquest* continued its run, this cover revealed the true bad guy of the series—leader of the Phalanx, Ultron. Aleksi Briclot's image of the Avengers' old enemy sitting astride a throne was one of the most powerful interpretations of the villain. The series also featured the characters who would become the new Guardians of the Galaxy.

◄ *ANNIHILATION: CONQUEST* #6

June 2008
Artist: Aleksi Briclot

Some of Marvel's greatest cosmic heroes appeared together for this final part of *Annihilation: Conquest*. Briclot's cover, with its dramatic use of color and lighting, gives the reader the sense that the heroes, led by Adam Warlock, are about to face their greatest battle yet against Ultron and the Phalanx.

Artist Sara Pichelli perfectly captured the chaotic swagger and the bold attitude of the new group of guardians on this cover. The illustration shows the mismatched heroes in an art style that set the group apart from existing teams of Super Heroes.

◀ *GUARDIANS OF THE GALAXY #1*

July 2008
Artist: Clint Langley

Andy Lanning and Dan Abnett masterminded a modern-day relaunch for *Guardians of the Galaxy*. The new guardians were a disparate group of alien heroes. Chris Langley's cover quickly established the fast-paced style of the new series, and created a look that would carry the team to the big screen in 2014.

◀ *GUARDIANS OF THE GALAXY #1*

May 2013
Artist: Steve McNiven

Guardians of the Galaxy was relaunched again as part of 2013's Marvel Now! branding. Artist Steve McNiven used a team shot on the cover to introduce the heroes, featuring Star-Lord front and center. This new series boosted the groups' standing in the Marvel Universe to coincide with the release of the *Guardians of the Galaxy* movie in 2014.

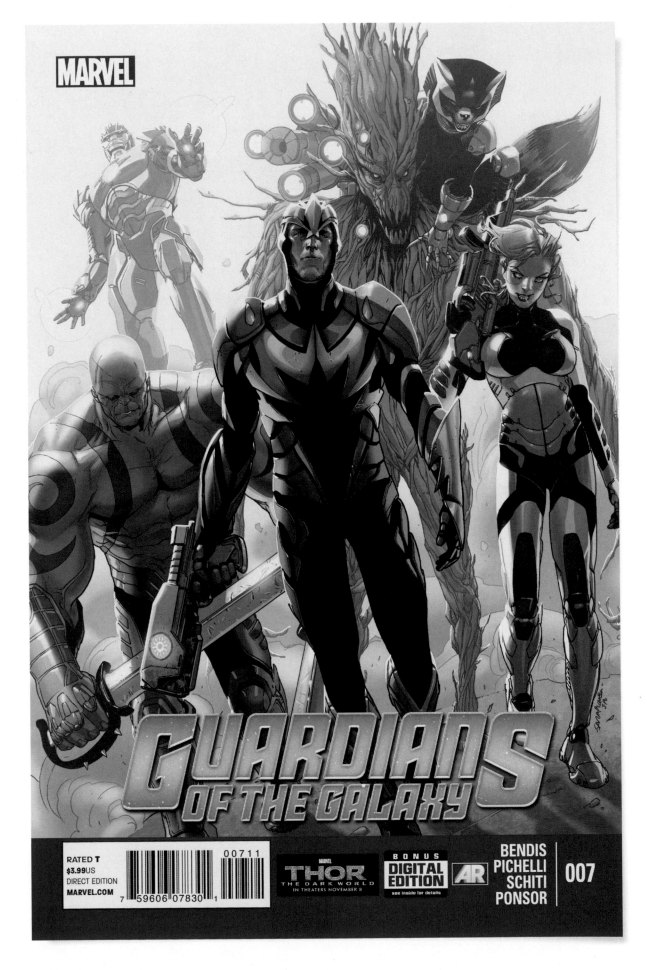

◄ *SECRET INVASION* #1

June 2008
Artist: Gabriele Dell'Otto

Marvel's big event of 2008 saw Earth invaded by shape-changing Skrulls. Gabriele Dell'Otto's cover for the first issue depicts humanity's greatest heroes in shadow, the Skrull outlines of their faces just visible. It was a clear message that no hero could be trusted and, as far as this storyline was concerned, anyone could be a Skrull.

◄ *MS. MARVEL* #25

May 2008
Artist: Greg Horn

The Skrull "Secret Invasion" spread beyond the central series, with various Marvel titles featuring Skrull-themed covers. Greg Horn's painting of a Skrull Ms. Marvel hints that the title's lead character might be an alien—a fact that was central to the storyline as those closest to the heroine started to doubt her.

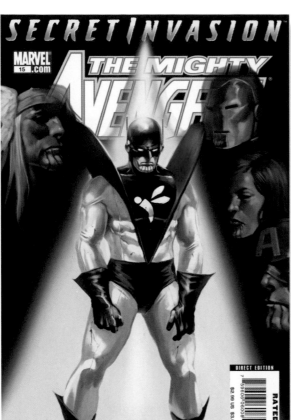

◄ *MIGHTY AVENGERS* #15

August 2008
Artist: Marko Djurdjevic

As the "Secret Invasion" continued, some heroes found out that they had been Skrulls all along—and in some cases, never even realized it. One of the biggest shocks was the revelation that Yellowjacket was a Skrull. Djurdjevic's cover shows that not only was Yellowjacket a Skrull, but he was one who had started to enjoy his life as an Avenger too much and was replaced by his Skrull masters. It also acted as a homage to *Avengers* issue #213 (November 1981), in terms of the layout and character poses.

◄ *GUARDIANS OF THE GALAXY* #4

October 2008
Artist: Clint Langley

The "Secret Invasion" of Earth was now in full force and soon even Marvel's star-spanning heroes were affected by it. Covers such as this one, by artist Clint Langley, helped to convey one of the main ideas of "Secret Invasion"—that behind their masks any hero could be a Skrull, even an interplanetary one such as Star-Lord.

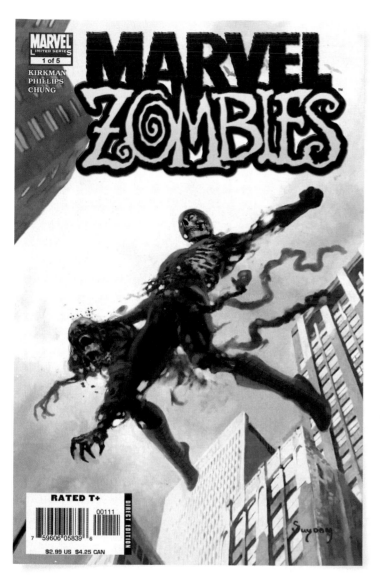

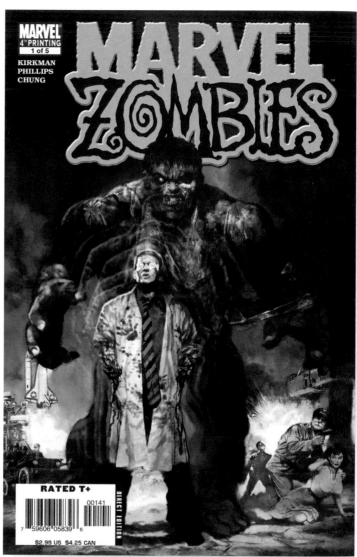

▲ *MARVEL ZOMBIES* #1

February 2006
Artist: Arthur Suydam

Arthur Suydam's zombified paintings of classic
Marvel covers were a big reason for the success of
Marvel Zombies (a title written by *The Walking Dead*
creator Robert Kirkman). The original cover of the
first issue in the series was a homage to *Amazing
Fantasy* issue #15 (August 1962) and the first
appearance of Spider-Man.

▲ *MARVEL ZOMBIES* #1 (FOURTH PRINTING VARIANT)

April 2006
Artist: Arthur Suydam

Cover variants became increasingly popular in the
2000s, with avid collectors seeking out every version
of a cover. This fourth printing of *Marvel Zombies*
issue #1 featured a homage to *Incredible Hulk* issue
#1 (May 1962). A zombie Hulk was one of the
standout characters of the series, his stomach
bloated with the friends he had eaten.

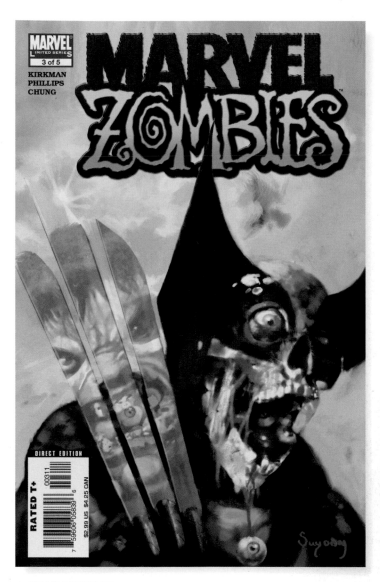

▲ *MARVEL ZOMBIES #3*

April 2006
Artist: Arthur Suydam

This *Marvel Zombies* cover was another homage, this time to Todd McFarlane's classic *Incredible Hulk* issue #340 (February 1988; *see p178*). Additions such as the bloody eyeballs in Wolverine's mouth conveyed the setting of this story—a world filled with zombie Super Heroes—and are also what made Suydam's work so very eye-catching.

▲ *MARVEL ZOMBIES #4*

May 2006
Artist: Arthur Suydam

This homage to *The X-Men* issue #1 (September 1963)—with a grisly Cyclops holding his own severed head in his arms and Beast's arms falling off—is a perfect example of the humor that made *Marvel Zombies* a smash hit. Suydam's zombies lived on long after the series, appearing as variants on many other Marvel titles.

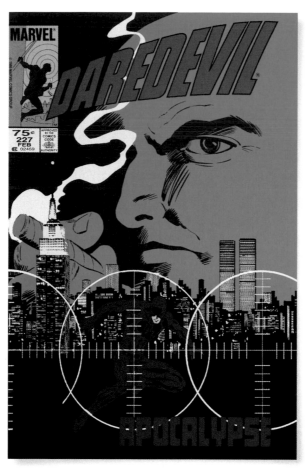

◄ *DAREDEVIL* #227

February 1986
Artist: David Mazzucchelli

After a three-year absence, comic-book megastar Frank Miller returned to *Daredevil* as a writer to mastermind one of the hero's greatest stories. Known as "Born Again," the story arc saw the Kingpin learn Daredevil's secret identity, and then set out to ruin him. David Mazzucchelli produced stunning art for both the cover and the story.

◄ *DAREDEVIL* #228

March 1986
Artist: David Mazzucchelli

Each cover of the "Born Again" saga had a religiously themed tagline. "Purgatory" was the perfect summation of Daredevil's suffering in this dark issue. The cover image reflects the chaotic, terrified state of Matt Murdock's mind, the cracks revealing how close to insanity the hero is as a result of the Kingpin tearing apart his life.

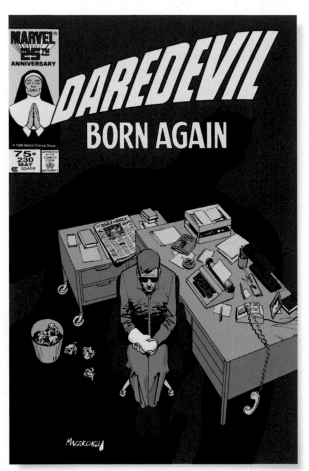

◄ DAREDEVIL #230

May 1986
Artist: David Mazzucchelli

This key issue in the "Born Again" saga featured reporter Ben Urich on the cover. Daredevil's shadow looms over Urich as he tries to come to terms with death threats caused by his connection to the hero. The saga saw most of the main characters going through their own personal hells to be born again as better people.

◄ DAREDEVIL #232

July 1986
Artist: David Mazzucchelli

Mazzucchelli's penultimate cover for the "Born Again" saga saw the debut of Nuke, a villainous product of the secret Super Soldier program that had created Captain America. As Nuke's tattooed face peers over at Daredevil on the cover, the story's religious themes were given a military twist in the cover line, "God and Country."

▲ *DAREDEVIL #252*

March 1988
Artist: John Romita Jr.

John Romita Jr. created this powerful cover for a
"Fall of the Mutants" crossover issue of *Daredevil*,
featuring the Man Without Fear trying to maintain
order and stop the bad guys during a blackout.
Working with writer Ann Nocenti, Romita Jr.
created a well-respected run on the title. The cover
beautifully demonstrates his maturing art style.

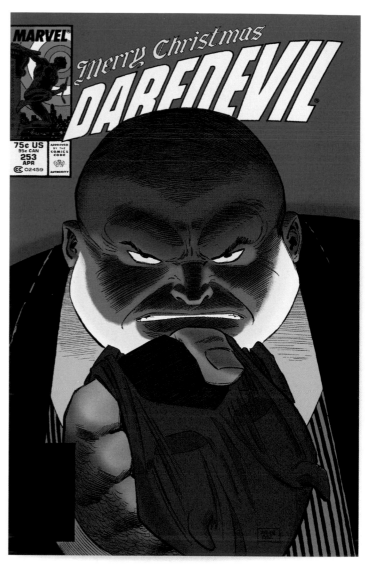

▲ *DAREDEVIL #253*

April 1988
Artist: John Romita Jr.

Romita Jr. gave Kingpin a real sense of power and
menace on this cover, a Christmas-themed issue of
Daredevil that seemed lacking any seasonal cheer.
Romita Jr.'s interpretation of the character caught
the eye of Frank Miller, who would go on to work
closely with Romita Jr. five years later on the
Daredevil: The Man Without Fear series.

DAREDEVIL #1 ▶

November 1988
Artist: Joe Quesada

When Daredevil was given to Joe
Quesada's Marvel Knights imprint to
relaunch, Marvel's future boss took on
the artistic chores himself, illustrating
filmmaker Kevin Smith's challenging
story. Quesada created some stunning
covers for the series, starting with this
acrobatic image. The "Guardian
Angel" saga (which began with this
issue) won several awards, including
an Eagle Award for Best Story.

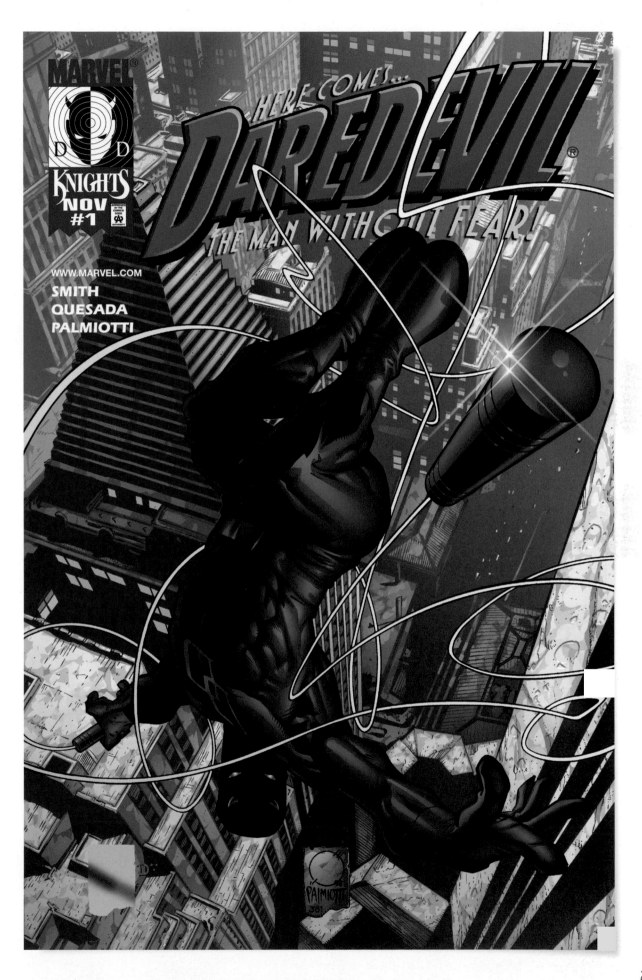

1.

2.

3.

JOHN ROMITA JR.

John Romita Jr. has been one of Marvel's top artists for over 40 years. From producing pages for Marvel UK as a young man, to his more recent work on Marvel's leading titles, John Romita Jr. has drawn just about every Marvel character going. While at first his art echoed the clean, commercial style of his father, Romita's art evolved during his run on *Daredevil* (1988–1990), becoming more confident, powerful, and increasingly filled with energy. It was a style that propelled him to the very top of his field. As art legend Joe Kubert said, "His style is one immediately recognizable, and the movement combined with impact and clarity of his storytelling is what cartooning is all about."

1. *WOLVERINE #20*

December 2004

This early sketch of Wolverine saw John Romita Jr. experiment with a different angle for the hero compared to the one finally used *(see p296)*. His loose pencil style still shows the raw power of his finished work.

2. *AMAZING SPIDER-MAN #43*

September 2002

Romita Jr. enjoyed two successful runs on *Amazing Spider-Man* and this cover exemplifies what made his second spell on the title so popular. It is a brooding, atmospheric work, perfectly bringing out the arachnid in Spider-Man, who was perched behind a ledge as a storm raged behind him.

3. *UNCANNY X-MEN #207*

July 1986

This cover showcases the dynamism of Romita's art during his first run on *Uncanny X-Men*. It also shows his use of inventive design and layout skills as Wolverine's claws tear dramatically through the cover.

4. *DAREDEVIL: THE MAN WITHOUT FEAR #1*

October 1993

Romita Jr. himself considers his work with Frank Miller on this title to be some of his best. This cover shows the highly detailed line-work Romita had developed during this period, as well as his ability to convey raw emotion and drama in his art.

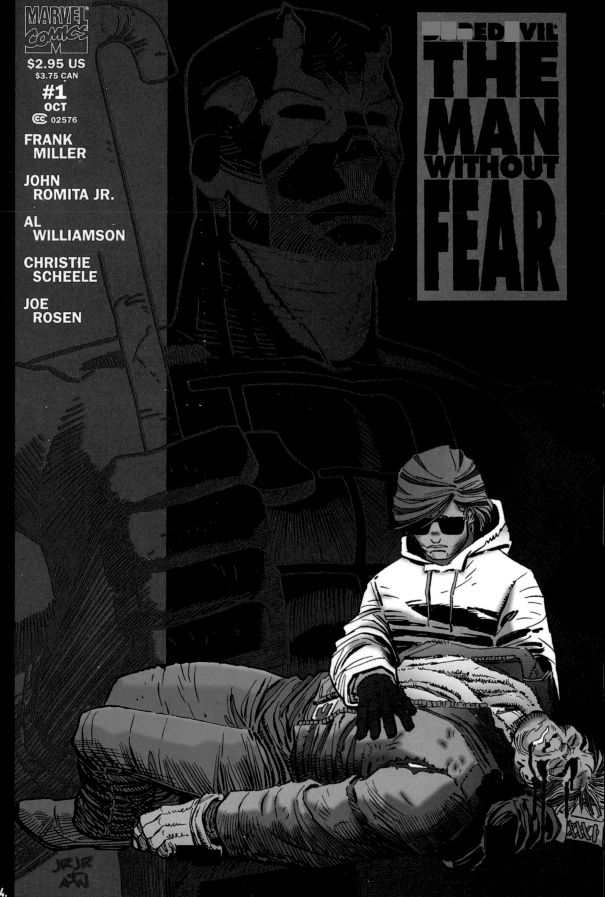

July 2000
Artist: Joe Quesada

The Marvel Knights imprint gained a team book with this issue, which brought together Shang Chi, Punisher, Dagger, Daredevil, and the Black Widow. The team had a more urban feel than other groups, and although they weren't officially a team, the heroes fought together against a number of foes. Joe Quesada illustrated the cover to the first issue and used the rope of Daredevil's Billy Club to add a sense of movement and energy to the atmospheric image.

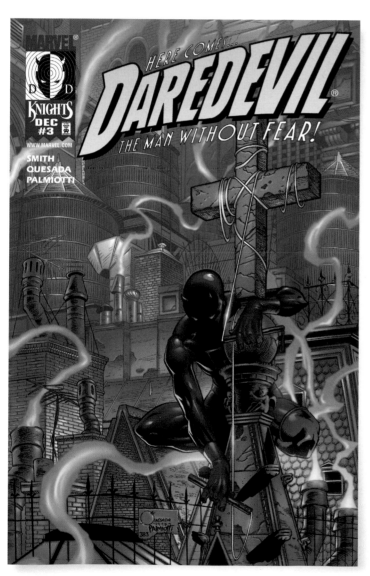

▲ *DAREDEVIL #3*

January 1999
Artist: Joe Quesada

This atmospheric Joe Quesada cover captures the story's religious elements. Matt Murdock's Catholicism had often played a major part in the comic's storylines. His beliefs were once again laid bare as the hero tried to protect a young baby he would soon come to believe could be the Messiah—or the Antichrist.

▲ *DAREDEVIL #8*

June 1999
Artist: Joe Quesada

Smith and Quesada's "Guardian Devil" epic came to a close this issue, which acted as an epilogue to the main saga. Quesada's cover, showing Spider-Man and Daredevil, was a calm change of pace after the tension and shocks of the previous issues. It reflects the melancholy nature of the climax, as Matt mourned Karen Page.

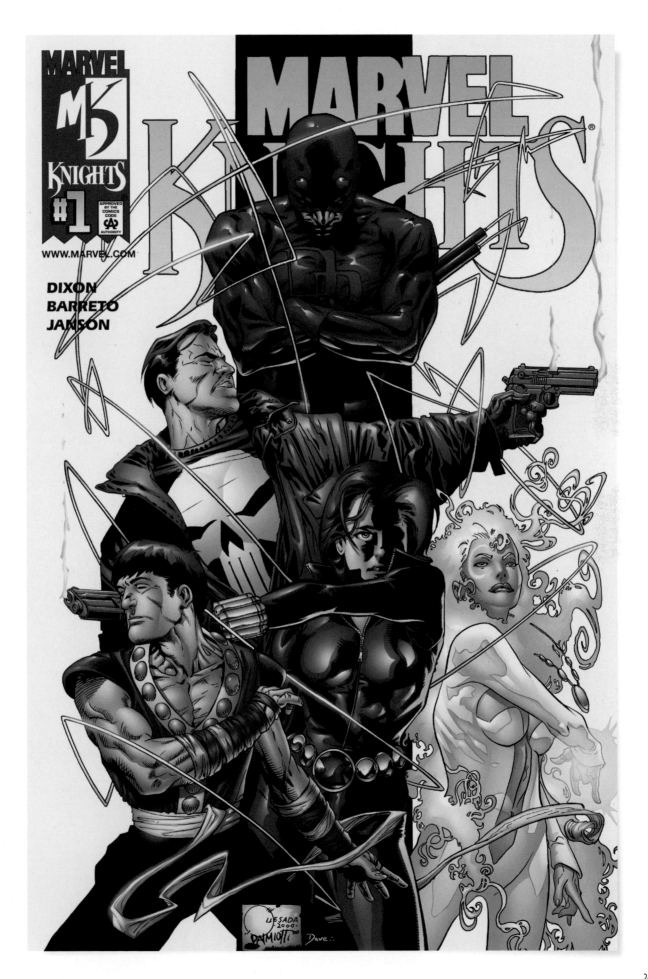

249

▲ *DAREDEVIL #16*

May 2001
Artist: David Mack

David Mack mixed collage and painting techniques to create high-impact covers for his short run on *Daredevil.* He also illustrated this four-part story, "Wake Up." Mack brought his unique vision to Brian Michael Bendis' tale of a young boy named Timmy and his turmoil after seeing his father, the villain Leap Frog, fight his hero Daredevil.

▲ *DAREDEVIL #17*

June 2001
Artist: David Mack

Mack's second cover for the "Wake Up" story focused on the young protagonist, Timmy. The artist produced another dream-like montage for the cover, highlighting Timmy's admiration of heroes such as Daredevil and Spider-Man. Mack's painterly style brought storybook elements to the cover, which reflects Timmy's childish world view.

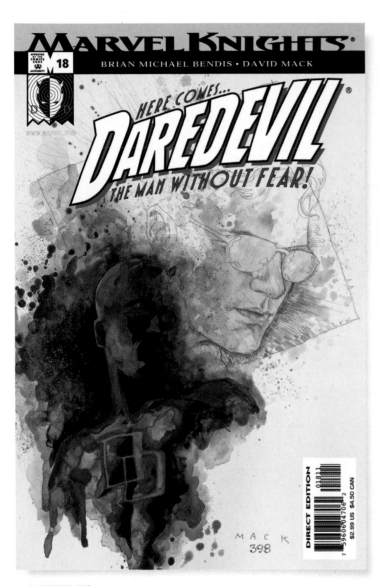

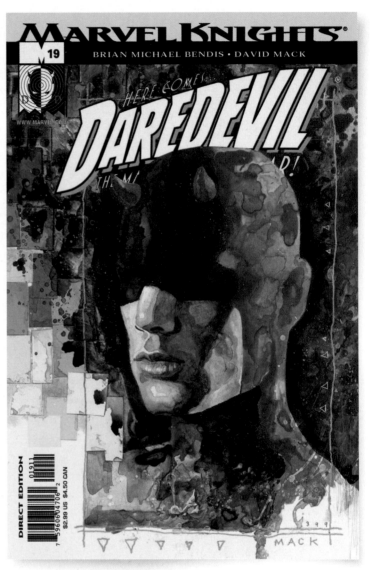

▲ *DAREDEVIL #18*

July 2001
Artist: David Mack

David Mack created another thoughtful cover as "Wake Up" reached its penultimate chapter. This time Mack produced a portrait of the Man Without Fear and his alter ego. The heroic depiction of the character reflects Timmy's obsession with the hero, which proved to be the main focus of the issue.

▲ *DAREDEVIL #19*

August 2001
Artist: David Mack

"Wake Up" concluded with this issue and with one of David Mack's best covers. The elegant portrait of Daredevil has a grace and thoughtfulness not seen on many comic covers. In the story's thought-provoking climax, reporter Ben Urich learned of Timmy's troubled past and his shock at seeing Daredevil viciously defeat Leap Frog.

◄ *DAREDEVIL* #32

June 2002
Artist: Alex Maleev

Writer Brian Michael Bendis and artist Alex Maleev had a long and award-winning run on *Daredevil*, creating several twists along the way. This issue's cover reflects one of the biggest twists—the FBI started to suspect that Matt Murdock was Daredevil. Maleev had a fine arts background and his covers were often experimental, blending drawing with digital and photorealistic techniques.

◄ *DAREDEVIL* #46

June 2003
Artist: Alex Maleev

Typhoid Mary, one of Daredevil's deadliest and most complex foes, returned in this issue, with Alex Maleev providing a sensual new interpretation of the villain for the cover. Bendis and Maleev managed to create a series of stories that broke new ground for the Man Without Fear—without turning their backs on the character's rich history.

◄ *DAREDEVIL #1*

September 2011
Artist: Paolo Rivera

After years of dark stories, Daredevil's adventures took a new direction with this relaunch. Artist Paolo Rivera and writer Mark Waid brought back a sense of daring adventure to the Man Without Fear. Rivera's simple yet effective cover shows a smiling Daredevil in motion. The artist also found a clever new way of illustrating Daredevil's radar sense by surrounding the hero with words instead of images.

◄ *DAREDEVIL #7*

February 2012
Artist: Paolo Rivera

The image of Daredevil making a snow angel hints at the hero's near-death during an attempt to save a group of children caught in a snowstorm. Rivera's bold use of color—especially black and white—resulted in another eye-catching cover for one of the title's most critically acclaimed runs. The comic received a prestigious Eisner Award in 2012 for Best Single Issue.

ELEKTRA #1 ▶

September 2001
Artist: Greg Horn

Elektra regained her own book in 2001 with Greg Horn providing many beautifully painted covers for the series. His artwork often featured Elektra in a combative pose—this first cover shows her wielding her deadly sai. Horn's realistic approach to the work added a layer of cold beauty to the complex character.

THUNDERBOLTS #1 ▶

February 2013
Artist: Julian Tedesco

Julian Tedesco was inspired by the look of the Thunderbolts' leader, the Red Hulk, on this eye-catching cover. The book saw the Red Hulk joining forces with some of Marvel's deadliest heroes—Elektra, Punisher, Venom, and Deadpool. The anti-heroes are tinted red on the covers to reflect the color of their leader, the Red Hulk.

◀ ELEKTRA: ASSASSIN #1

August 1986
Artist: Bill Sienkiewicz

The cover to the first issue of *Elektra: Assassin* saw artist Bill Sienkiewicz at the top of his game, creating a unique vision of the femme fatale and using a white background to give Elektra's red costume maximum impact. The series, written by Frank Miller, was published by Marvel's Epic imprint, which offered an outlet for more adult-oriented material, often featuring experimental visuals.

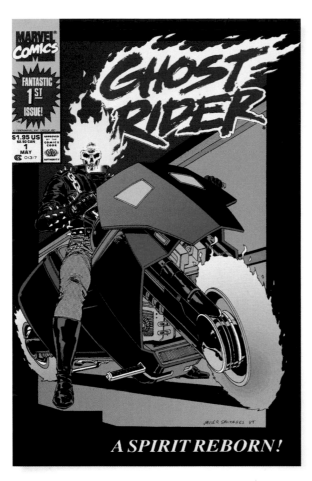

◄ GHOST RIDER #1

May 1990
Artist: Javier Saltares

A new Ghost Rider burst into action, as Javier Saltares revealed the new-look spirit of vengeance on the cover of the debut issue. The new title—featuring teenager Dan Ketch as the Ghost Rider— proved to be a smash hit, and it became one of the most popular Marvel comics of the time.

◄ SPIRITS OF VENGEANCE #1

August 1992
Artist: Adam Kubert

Adam Kubert's dramatic cover saw Johnny Blaze, the original Ghost Rider, team up with the latest incarnation. Kubert was a master of creating action scenes and dynamic movement, and he instills both characters with a sense of deadly energy in this cover portrayal.

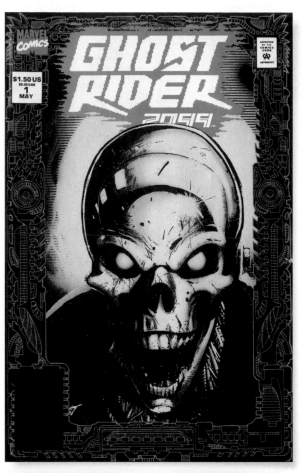

◀ *GHOST RIDER 2099* #1

May 1994
Artist: Chris Bachalo

Ghost Rider 2099's first cover was an early work by Chris Bachalo, who created a new version of the Spirit of Vengeance, set in the far future. The frame around the main image is metallic ink, reflecting the cyberpunk nature of the new hero.

◀ *EARTH X* #1

April 1999
Artist: Alex Ross

Alex Ross' beautiful, painted art graced the cover of *Earth X*, a new series set in a dark future of the Marvel Universe. The cover for the debut issue showcases some of the strange alternate versions of the Marvel characters seen in the series, with the Earth X version of Captain America at the center.

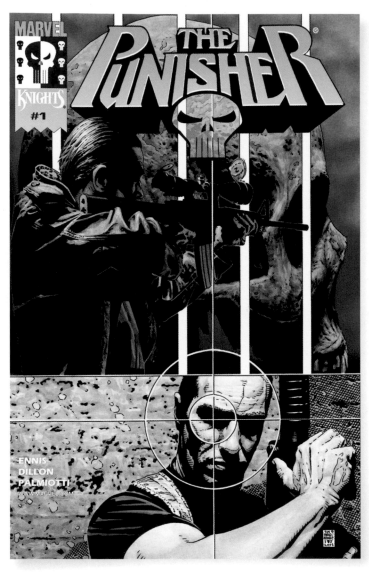

▲ *PUNISHER #1*

August 2001
Artist: Tim Bradstreet

This Tim Bradstreet cover was the perfect piece of art to help launch a new series of Frank Castle's adventures. Skulls and guns were big recurring themes for the vigilante hero and both were present here, as an assassin put the Punisher in his sights.

▲ *PUNISHER #4*

May 2004
Artist: Tim Bradstreet

While most of Tim Bradstreet's covers focused solely on the Punisher, this chilling visual selected the terrifying moment Frank caught up with a victim. Bradstreet's realistic art brought a sense of grim emptiness to the Punisher, making the hero look more ruthless than ever.

◄ *PUNISHER #1*

March 2004
Artist: Tim Bradstreet

Writer Garth Ennis had reinvigorated Punisher as part of the Marvel Knights imprint. However, a big part of the revamped title's success was due to Tim Bradstreet's realistic covers. This artwork helped to launch a new run of the Punisher's adventures—under the banner of Marvel's Max Comics imprint, reserved for graphic content. The image of Frank Castle's armory was a chilling reminder of the hero's deadly war on crime.

November 1987
Artist: Mike Zeck

Kraven the Hunter looks his insane best on this cover for "Kraven's Last Hunt," regarded as one of Spider-Man's key stories. Artist Mike Zeck depicts the crazed state Kraven was in. His desire to prove himself superior to Spider-Man reached its shocking conclusion in this penultimate chapter.

◀ *AMAZING SPIDER-MAN #290*

July 1987
Artist: Al Milgrom

Al Milgrom's cover made pretty clear the big question Peter was going to ask inside. The use of white was perfect for focusing the attention on Peter and Mary Jane, reflecting the way a marriage proposal could make the rest of the world fade into insignificance. However, the shadow of Spidey looming over Peter and his bride-to-be adds a sinister edge to the piece.

◀ *AMAZING SPIDER-MAN ANNUAL #21*

1987
Artist: John Romita Sr.

It was the wedding of the year—Peter Parker and Mary Jane—and Marvel put their top artist, John Romita Sr., on art duty for the cover. Central to the image is the happy couple, but with Spidey's foes facing off against his allies in the background, it looked like the wedding might not go according to plan.

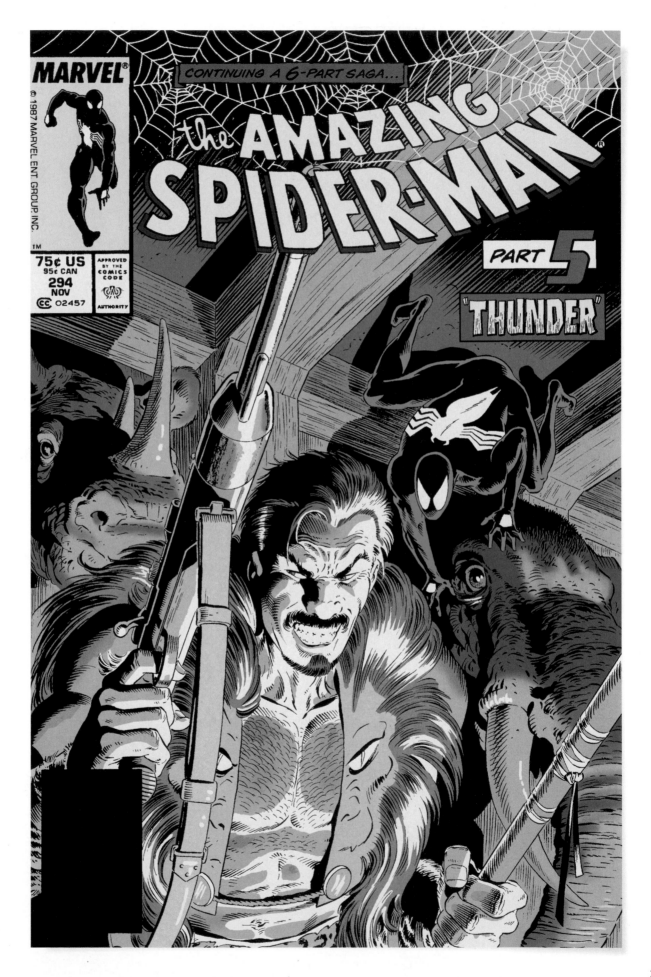

▲ *AMAZING SPIDER-MAN* #312

February 1989
Artist: Todd McFarlane

This Todd McFarlane cover features the Hobgoblin and the Green Goblin slugging it out with the webslinger caught in the middle. McFarlane's style makes the Green Goblin look crazier and more nightmarish than ever, while giving the fight scene a feeling of chaotic danger.

▲ *AMAZING SPIDER-MAN* #313

March 1989
Artist: Todd McFarlane

Todd McFarlane used his highly detailed technique to bring the Lizard to life on this cover. The close-up of the Lizard with its razor-sharp teeth, holding a seemingly beaten Spider-Man in his claws, creates a real sense of danger.

SPIDER-MAN #1 ▶

August 1990
Artist: Todd McFarlane

Following his huge success on *Amazing Spider-Man*, Marvel created a new Spidey title for Todd McFarlane to write and illustrate. McFarlane's debut cover illustration really adds the "spider" to Spider-Man, placing the hero in spider-like poses and adding intricate webbing detail. It became one of the most memorable modern-day images of Spider-Man and one of the biggest-selling Marvel comics of the decade.

▲ *SPECTACULAR SPIDER-MAN #213*

June 1994
Artist: Joe Madureira

A young Joe Madureira produced truly stunning Typhoid Mary artwork for this issue. The frowning and smiling masks at either side of the villain reflect her split personality: On one side the deadly villain Typhoid Mary, on the other the mild-mannered Mary Walker. One of the villain's original creators, Ann Nocenti, was the writer on this issue.

▲ *AMAZING SPIDER-MAN #410*

April 1996
Artist: Mark Bagley

Carnage was one of the most popular Spider-Man villains of the 1990s, so when the alien symbiote possessed Spider-Man, the result was one of the most shocking covers of the year. Approaching the end of his five-and-a-half-year run on Spidey, Mark Bagley surpassed himself with an attention-grabbing fusion of the blood-red Carnage and a crazed-looking webslinger.

▲ *SPIDER-MAN #68*

May 1996
Artist: John Romita Jr.

The mid-1990s saw a lot of changes in Spider-Man's comics. Many characters—including the webslinger—were given makeovers. This John Romita Jr. cover of a new-look Hobgoblin debuted a more menacing version of the villain, who now had cybernetic modifications. The reflection of Spidey in the pumpkin bomb is a nice touch, too.

▲ *UNTOLD TALES OF SPIDER-MAN #1*

September 1995
Artist: Pat Oliffe

Writer Kurt Busiek and artist Pat Oliffe masterminded one of the most exciting new Spidey titles of the decade. The cover established what the new title was all about: Spider-Man is shown bursting out of an old book, revealing that this series would tell new stories of Spidey, set during his first few months as a hero.

▲ *PETER PARKER: SPIDER-MAN #75*

December 1996
Artist: John Romita Jr.

The "Clone Saga," one of the most controversial Spider-Man epics of all time, came to a shocking conclusion in this issue, with John Romita Jr. producing an action-packed wraparound cover. Fans had been split when Ben Reilly (Peter Parker's clone) had become Spider-Man, but this issue saw the old order restored. The cover revealed some of the dramatic changes within, as Peter Parker returned as Spider-Man to face the original Green Goblin—a villain he had thought was long dead.

AMAZING SPIDER-MAN #30 ▶

June 2001
Artist: J. Scott Campbell

J. Scott Campbell's striking image heralded the start of a bold new era for *Amazing Spider-Man* as shocking secrets of Spidey's origin were revealed. Writer J. Michael Straczynski and artist John Romita Jr. took over the title, with Campbell creating a number of stylish covers. As the hero learned that his powers were linked to an ancient spider-god, Campbell's artwork put the "spider" back into Spider-Man.

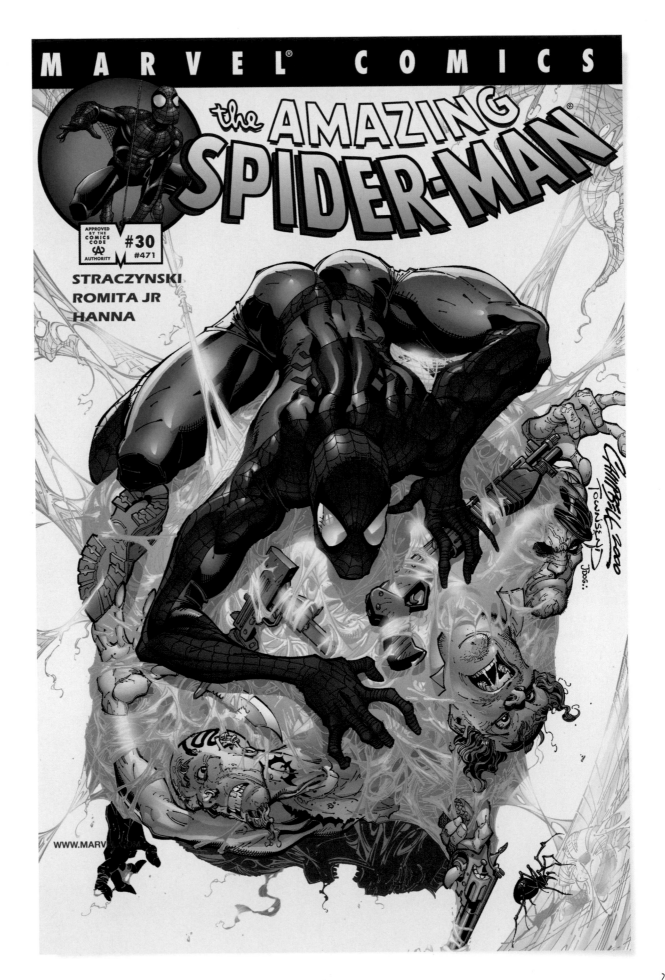

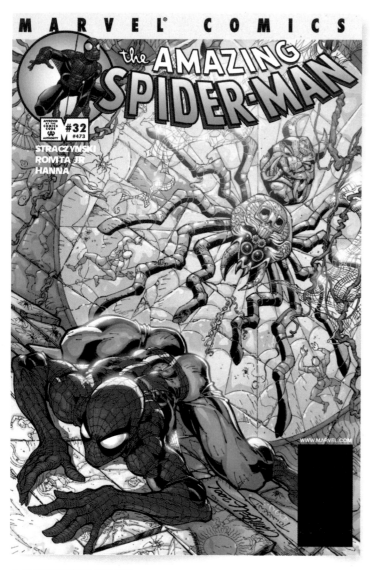

▲ *AMAZING SPIDER-MAN #32*

August 2001
Artist: J. Scott Campbell

J. Scott Campbell continued his run as cover artist on *Amazing Spider-Man* with another stunning piece. Campbell's cover hinted at the new, totemistic aspects of Spidey's origins that writer J. Michael Straczynski and artist John Romita Jr. were bringing to the title as they redefined Spidey's world.

▲ *AMAZING SPIDER-MAN #33*

September 2001
Artist: J. Scott Campbell

Ezekiel, the man who had changed Spidey's life by telling him of his links to an ancient arachnid deity, appeared beside him on this cover. Campbell's depiction of Ezekiel looking like another, older "spider-man" was a sign that things were changing as one of the most original runs in the title's history continued.

AMAZING SPIDER-MAN #500 ▶

December 2003
Artist: J. Scott Campbell

Amazing Spider-Man went back to its original numbering for the 500th issue, with Campbell creating a truly dynamic cover featuring Spidey's most iconic enemies. The artist had burst onto the comic scene with his work for WildStorm, but his *Amazing Spider-Man* covers remain some of his best-known work. For this issue, he got to convey all the classic chaos and action that had made Spidey so popular.

▲ *MARVEL KNIGHTS SPIDER-MAN* #1

June 2004
Artist: Terry Dodson

With the stellar creative team of writer Mark Millar
and artist Terry Dodson at the helm, the launch of *Marvel
Knights Spider-Man* was bound to be something special.
Terry Dodson produced a wraparound cover for the first
issue, featuring Spidey and the Black Cat on the front with
four deadly foes pursuing them on the rear of the cover.
Dodson gave Spidey's enemies a spectacular menacing edge.

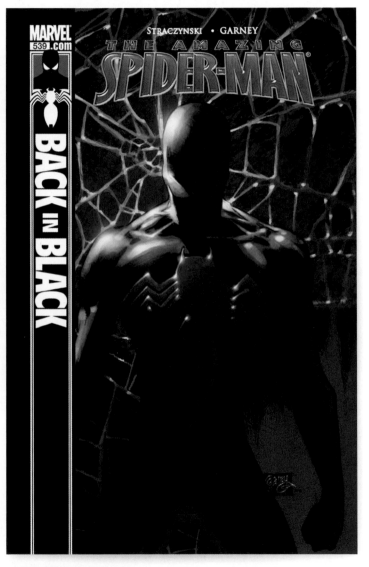

▲ *AMAZING SPIDER-MAN* #529

April 2006
Artist: Bryan Hitch

Spider-Man graced the cover of this issue in a shiny, new armored costume. Created for Spidey by Tony Stark, the suit would come to be known as the Iron Spider costume. Meanwhile, the strapline at the top also brings a sense of foreboding as the Civil War—when Super Hero would fight Super Hero—drew ever closer...

▲ *AMAZING SPIDER-MAN* #539

April 2007
Artist: Ron Garney

Following the events of the Civil War, the world knew that Peter Parker was Spider-Man. Aunt May had also been shot, as Kingpin sought revenge on anyone who knew Spider-Man. Garney's cover image captures the webslinger's dark and vengeful mood perfectly.

AMAZING SPIDER-MAN #560 ▶

July 2008
Artist: Marcos Martin

The experimentation with cover design continued with a fun layout by Marcos Martin. The background image has strong echoes of pop artist Roy Lichtenstein's work, and revealed a new villain: Piper Dali, a.k.a. Paper Doll. This mutant villain possessed the novel ability to make her body as thin as paper.

AMAZING SPIDER-MAN #561 ▶

August 2008
Artist: Marcos Martin

Paper Doll's eyes stare out at the reader from Marcos Martin's high-concept, collage-style cover, reflecting the villain's obsession with movie star Bobby Carr. The cover also hints at the idea of Mary Jane Watson (Bobby Carr's girlfriend in this story) being the Super Hero Jackpot, although this would later be revealed as a case of mistaken identity.

◀ AMAZING SPIDER-MAN #544

November 2007
Artist: Joe Quesada

"One More Day" was one of the most shocking storylines in Marvel's history as Spider-Man's marriage to Mary Jane was wiped out of existence. Quesada's powerful cover shows Spidey trapped by his own webbing—and torn between his love for Mary Jane and Aunt May. Spidey faced the hardest decision—to save Aunt May's life, he had to sacrifice his marriage to Mary Jane in a deal with Mephisto.

AMAZING SPIDER-MAN #555

June 2008
Artist: Chris Bachalo

It was, as the strapline stated, a "Brand New Day" for Spider-Man, whose adventures took an upward swing following the events of "One More Day." New villains and characters appeared while artists experimented with cover design. Bachalo's image of Spidey and Wolverine fighting Mayan warriors, with only the heroes in color, was an example of this fresh and exciting new direction.

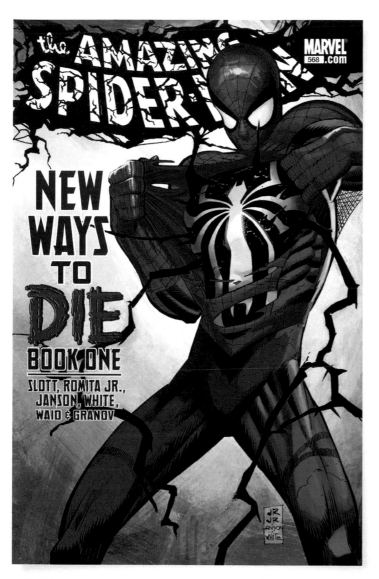

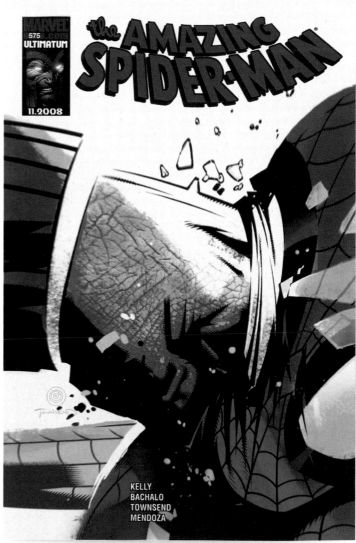

▲ *AMAZING SPIDER-MAN #568*

October 2008
Artist: John Romita Jr.

"The Brand New Day" era of Spider-Man saw Marvel experimenting with cover design, often employing interesting styles of typography, too. This cover, with "New Ways to Die" a prominent part of the artwork, reflected that trend. The dramatic image of Spidey revealing a Venom costume under his own clothes plays on a classic Super-Hero image, while the alien tendrils attacking the logo highlights the danger Venom represents.

▲ *AMAZING SPIDER-MAN #575*

December 2008
Artist: Chris Bachalo

It was a great time for artistic experimentation on *Amazing Spider-Man*, as this striking cover demonstrated. Bachalo's close-up of Spidey being punched in the face by Hammerhead is a strong image, especially with Bachalo's own, stark coloring work. The image has an even greater impact when seen in conjunction with the cover of the following issue.

▲ *AMAZING SPIDER-MAN #576*

January 2009
Artist: Chris Bachalo

The second part of the Hammerhead story
had the webslinger's response to the
previous issue's cover—Spidey punched
Hammerhead right back! Over the coming
months, other linking themes would appear
on the covers, but this black, white, and red
two-image punch-up was one of the most
dramatic—and amusing.

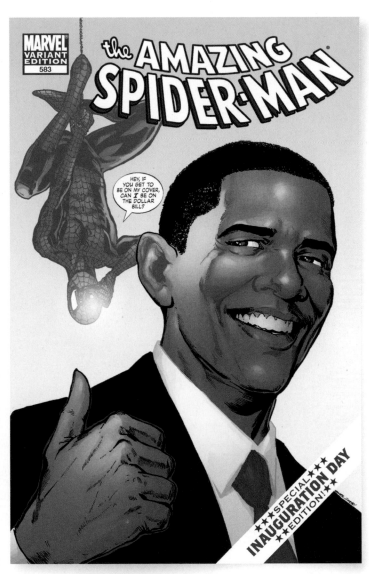

▲ *AMAZING SPIDER-MAN #583*

January 2009
Artist: Phil Jimenez

Every now and again a cover comes along that sums
up the mood of a particular moment in time. This
"Inauguration Day" variant cover did just that.
Phil Jimenez put US President Barack Obama
(a self-confessed comic fan) on the front of *Amazing
Spider-Man* to commemorate his inauguration.
President Obama also guest-starred inside the issue
as Marvel celebrated a key moment in US history.

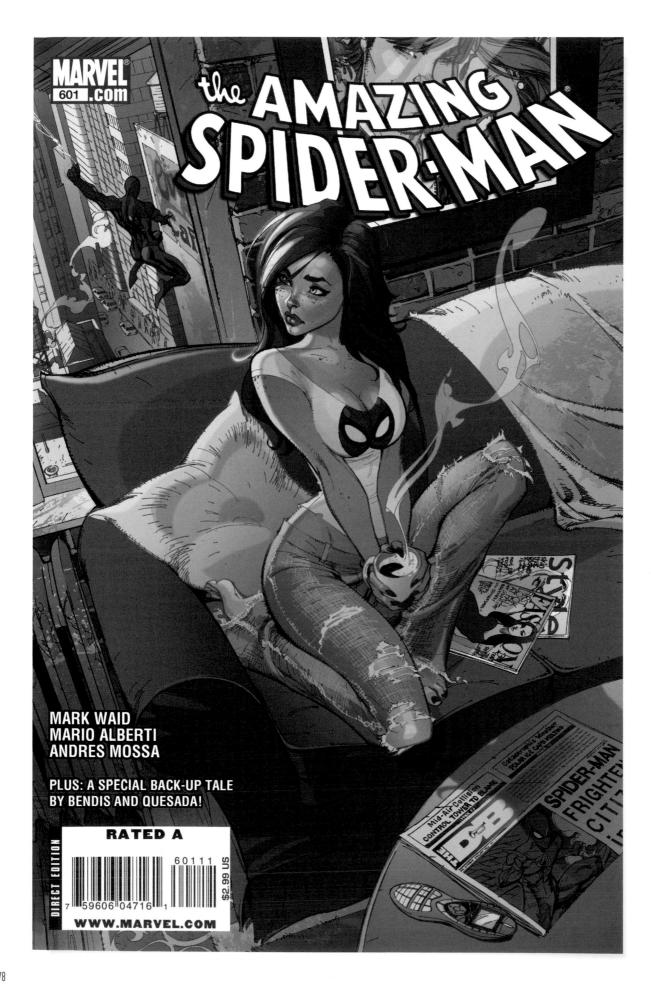

◄ *AMAZING SPIDER-MAN* #601

October 2009
Artist: J. Scott Campbell

J. Scott Campbell had always had a knack for drawing a great Mary Jane Watson, but this cover was something special. However, its appeal wasn't simply Campbell's winsomely pensive version of Spidey's ex. Readers were also thrilled by the inference that they were about to witness Peter and Mary Jane's first face-to-face meeting since "One More Day" had wiped their marriage from existence.

AMAZING SPIDER-MAN #607 ►

November 2009
Artist: J. Scott Campbell

Spidey and the Black Cat teamed up again this issue. Campbell's alluring cover hints that Felicia Hardy (the Black Cat) hadn't quite given up her criminal ways or her obsessional love of Spider-Man. It also suggests that the hero and Spidey might be a little more than friends in this issue...

AMAZING SPIDER-MAN #619 ►

March 2010
Artist: Marcos Martin

Marcos Martin proved himself to be one of the most inventive artists in the business with this striking cover. As red ink dripped from the slanted logo, it seemed that Spidey's life was about to take a deadly turn. But the story inside involved master of illusion Mysterio, so, of course, nothing was as it seemed.

▲ *AMAZING SPIDER-MAN #642–647*

September–November 2010
Artist: Marko Djurdjevic

The five-part "Origin of the Species" story saw Spider-Man
and a host of villains trying to find a baby that Lily Hollister
(aka Menace) had with Norman Osborn. There was a twist in the
tale too, when Norman's son, Harry, was revealed as the baby's
true father. This five-part series arc, and an epilogue to the end
of Spidey's "Brand New Day" era, featured six interconnected
covers by concept artist Marko Djurdjevic, showcasing the
numerous villains appearing in the story. The covers were
specially designed so they could be joined together to create
one enormous, action-packed image.

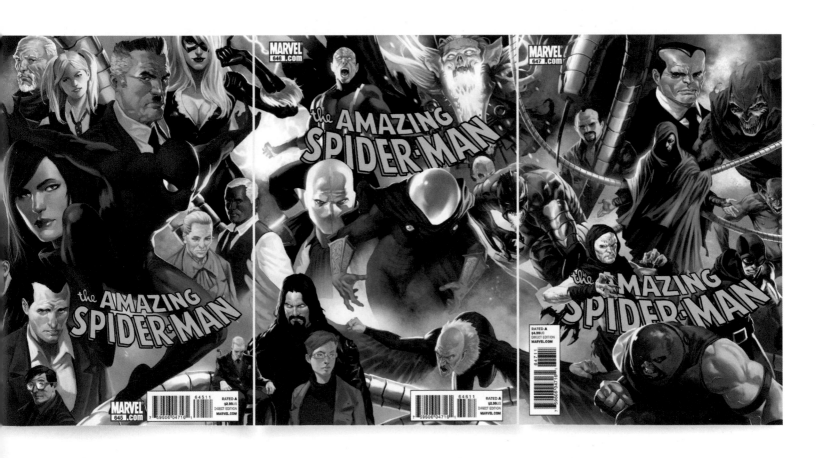

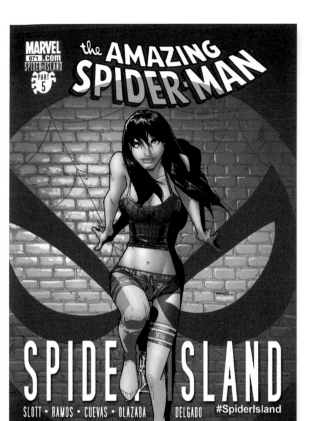

AMAZING SPIDER-MAN #700 ▶

February 2013
Artist: Mr Garcin

Marvel used this fantastic collage from Mr Garcin (an artist who specializes in collages made from Marvel comics) for what, at the time, was going to be the last-ever issue of *Amazing Spider-Man*. Garcin's work was the perfect choice for the final issue, honoring the changing styles of the wall-crawling hero since his debut in 1963.

◀ AMAZING SPIDER-MAN #671

December 2011
Artist: Humberto Ramos

The "Spider-Island" epic crossover saw the entire population of Manhattan gain Spidey-like powers before transforming into giant spiders, thanks to the machinations of the Jackal and the Queen. This cover focuses on a new role for Mary Jane in the saga as she temporarily gained spider powers to rival those of Peter Parker.

◀ AMAZING SPIDER-MAN #678

March 2012
Artist: Mike Del Mundo

Mike Del Mundo's cover makes it clear that something bad happened, as Spidey's battered hand reaches toward a *Daily Bugle* bearing the headline "New York Destroyed" and a strapline altered to read "The World's Worst Super Hero." In the time-travel story inside, Spidey was convinced that something was going to destroy New York in the next 24 hours, unless he could stop it.

June 2014
Artist: Alex Ross

Marvel released a number of variant covers to celebrate Peter Parker's return as Spider-Man. Alex Ross painted this masterpiece as a variant for issue #1—it was one of several covers he created that also celebrated Marvel's 75th anniversary. Ross' image was a celebration of Peter Parker as Spider-Man and features all of the most important things in Peter's life.

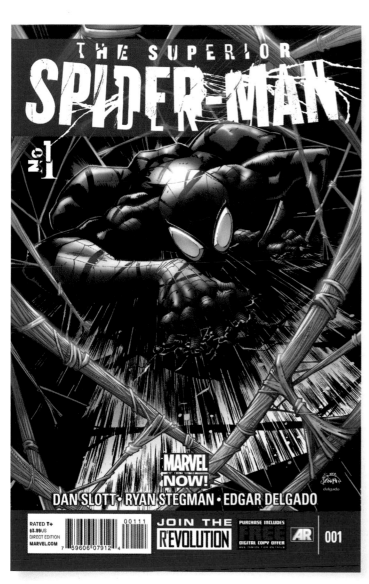

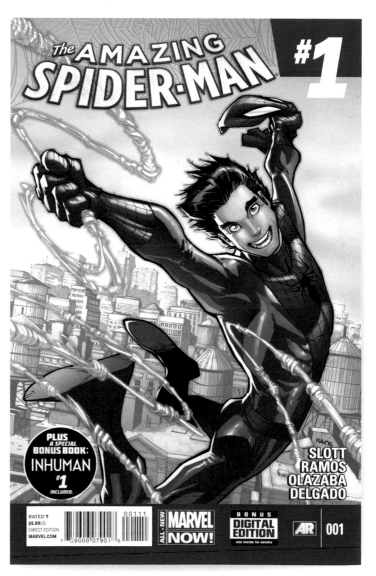

▲ *SUPERIOR SPIDER-MAN #1*

March 2013
Artist: Ryan Stegman

The old Peter Parker was dead—long live the new Peter Parker! With Doctor Octopus now masquerading as Peter, it was a time of great change for *Spider-Man* as *Superior* replaced *Amazing*. Ryan Stegman's cover showcases the new Doc Ock/Spidey as a different kind of webslinger, not just with a new costume but with a new superior—and deadly—attitude.

▲ *AMAZING SPIDER-MAN #1*

June 2014
Artist: Humberto Ramos

While it might appear as just a simple image of Spider-Man swinging through the city, the grin says it all—the real Peter Parker was back as Spider-Man. A whole new era of Spider-Man adventures was about to begin. It was one of the most upbeat Spidey covers in a long time.

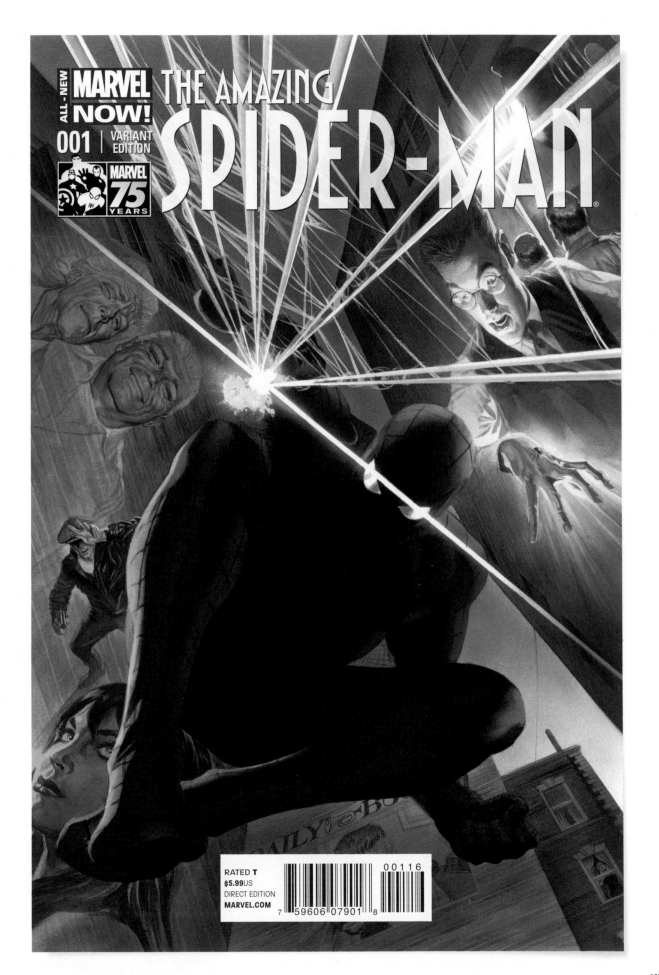

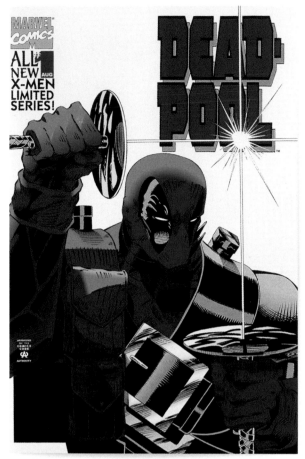

◄ DEADPOOL #1

August 1994
Artist: Ian Churchill

Ian Churchill illustrated the first cover to Deadpool's debut miniseries, focusing on a stylish body shot of the Merc with a Mouth. This early image is from a period when Deadpool was still more of an action star—albeit a slightly crazed one—in the style of Wolverine. In later years, Deadpool's style and stories would take a far more bizarre turn.

◄ DEADPOOL #11

December 1997
Artist: Pete Woods

By the time of his new ongoing series, Deadpool's adventures were starting to take a more humorous slant—as seen in this Pete Woods cover. The image is a homage to *Amazing Fantasy* issue #15 (August 1962), but it also reflects the story inside as Deadpool travels back in time to Spidey's early days. He even replaced the webslinger in an adventure that was a reworked version of *Amazing Spider-Man* issue #47 (April 1967).

◄ *DEADPOOL* #29

January 2011
Artist: Dave Johnson

This issue harked back to *Howard the Duck* with the return of one of his old enemies, Doctor Bong. Dave Johnson's cover uses soundwaves emitting from Doctor Bong's helmet to maximum design effect. He also included a somewhat kitsch Steve Rogers' image, reflecting the way the title often satirized its stablemates.

◄ *DEADPOOL KILLUSTRATED* #1

March 2013
Artist: Mike Del Mundo

This cover followed Deadpool's shocking "realization" that he was just a fictional character and as such could never really die—unless he killed the literary archetypes of modern-day heroes and villains. Cue Deadpool literally hitting the classics. Each of the four issues took on the form of an old *Classics Illustrated* comics series cover (but humorously renaming them Deadpool "Killustrated"), starting with this *Moby Dick* homage.

X-MEN: PHOENIX—ENDSONG #1 ▶

March 2005
Artist: Greg Horn

Greg Horn cleverly portrayed Phoenix's deadly power in this image, as well as capturing the alien nature of the Phoenix Force. The red costume also indicates that this is the more deadly Dark Phoenix incarnation, while the flames behind reflect Phoenix's cycle of death and rebirth. A variant cover showed Phoenix in her original green costume.

◀ *ROGUE* #1

September 2004
Artist: Carlo Pagulayan

Carlo Pagulayan painted a number of beautiful covers for *Rogue's* third series, starting with this highly effective portrait. Pagulayan managed to capture not only Rogue's beauty, but also her aloofness and the alienation caused by her inability to touch anyone without harming them.

◀ *STORM* #1

April 2006
Artist: Mike Mayhew

Storm's second series focused on Ororo Munroe's relationship with the Black Panther. The headshots of Storm and the Black Panther above a romanticized heart-shaped tree and their younger selves suggest that this series would reveal the previously untold story of their first meeting.

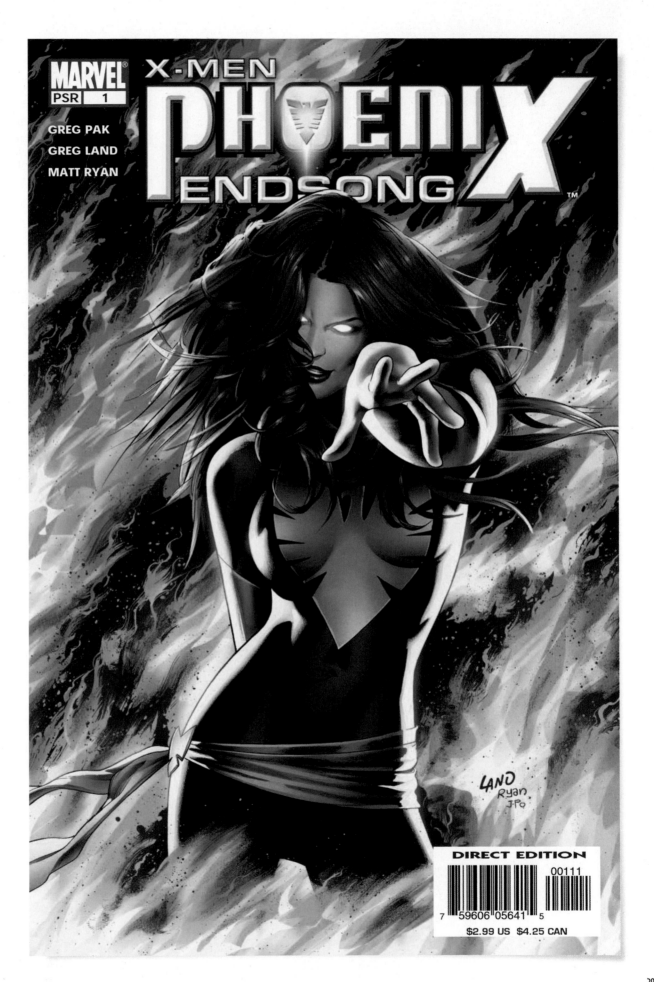

▲ *WOLVERINE #24*

May 1990
Artist: Jim Lee

Few artists can be said to have defined
Wolverine as much as Jim Lee. While drawing
the X-Men's own adventures, Lee also
provided the occasional cover for Wolverine's
solo title. This neon-lit masterpiece showing
the hero in the far eastern island of Madripoor
was one such cover. Lee's Wolverine looks
truly deadly in this dark and dangerous image.

▲ *MARVEL COMICS PRESENTS #72*

March 1991
Artist: Barry Windsor-Smith

Barry Windsor-Smith provided covers
for each of the 12 chapters of his epic
"Weapon X" story, which was serialized
in the *Marvel Comics Presents* anthology.
This dramatic first cover hinted that the
saga would reveal one of the biggest
secrets from Wolverine's past—how he
gained his Adamantium skeleton.

▲ *MARVEL COMICS PRESENTS #84*

September 1991
Artist: Barry Windsor-Smith

The wraparound cover to the final chapter of the
"Weapon X" storyline features a close-up of Wolverine
with blood seeping from his Adamantium claws as
they pierce his own skin. Windsor-Smith's image
combines the wildness of Wolverine with a sense of
the character's humanity, while the story itself was
a big influence on the *Wolverine* and *X-Men* movies.

◄ *WOLVERINE* #35

January 1991
Artist: Marc Silvestri

Marc Silvestri illustrated one of the most critically acclaimed runs in *Wolverine*'s history and produced a number of action-packed covers during that time. This early Lady Deathstrike image is a prime example of Silvestri's dynamism and the gritty feel he brought to Wolverine's adventures.

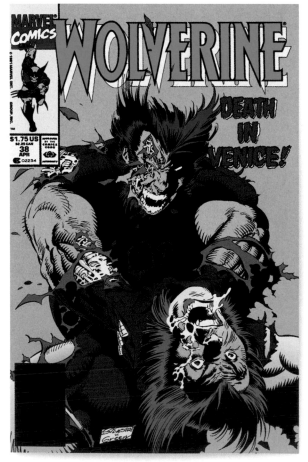

◄ *WOLVERINE* #38

April 1991
Artist: Marc Silvestri

"Albert" was one of the more interesting additions to the Wolverine mythos. He started life as a simple android duplicate of Wolverine, programmed to kill the mutant, but soon became an interesting character in his own right. This dramatic cover depicts an early showdown between Wolverine and his duplicate.

◀ *WOLVERINE #43*

August 1991
Artist: Marc Silvestri

This atmospheric Marc Silvestri cover is all about color and texture. Here Silvestri used a rain effect and a strong red to create eye-catching artwork. The central pose reflects the story inside, with Wolverine seeking revenge on an insane killer who had tortured a wolverine in the Central Park Zoo.

◀ *WOLVERINE #77*

January 1994
Artist: Adam Kubert

Adam Kubert produced many outstanding images of Wolverine. This classic cover features the mutant suffering after Magneto had ripped the Adamantium from his body. The bandages around Logan's wrists, the result of his bone claws slicing through his skin with every trademark "snikt," added a new, painful dimension to the always troubled hero.

Adam Kubert's action scene of Wolverine and Gambit leaping from the rooftops is eye-catching enough, but the addition of overlaid sniper rifle sights gives the whole scene an extra sense of danger. Splitting the logo in two also cleverly helps to direct the reader's attention to the center of the action.

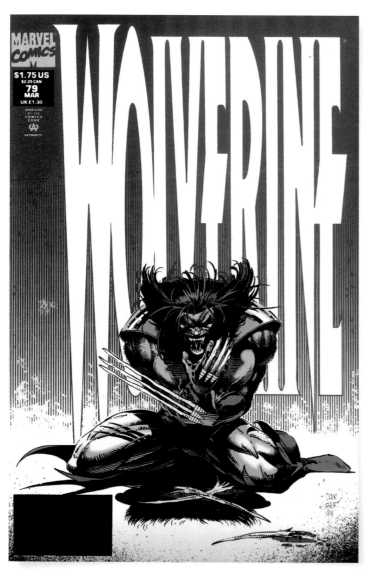

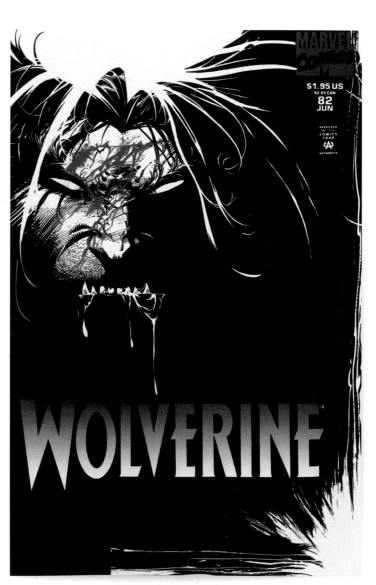

▲ *WOLVERINE #79*

March 1994
Artist: Adam Kubert

With its extended logo and shocking image of Wolverine in pain, clutching his broken claws, this classic cover shows a key moment in Wolverine's life. Kubert brought out the pain Wolverine was experiencing after his enemy Cyber snapped off three of his claws. Seeing the previously almost-indestructible Wolverine in agony was a big shock for long-term fans.

▲ *WOLVERINE #82*

June 1994
Artist: Adam Kubert

This relatively simple image was one of the most effective *Wolverine* covers that year. The stark black and white of the main image makes the blood on Wolverine's forehead and his yellow eyes even more striking. Moving the logo to the bottom of the cover was an innovative decision.

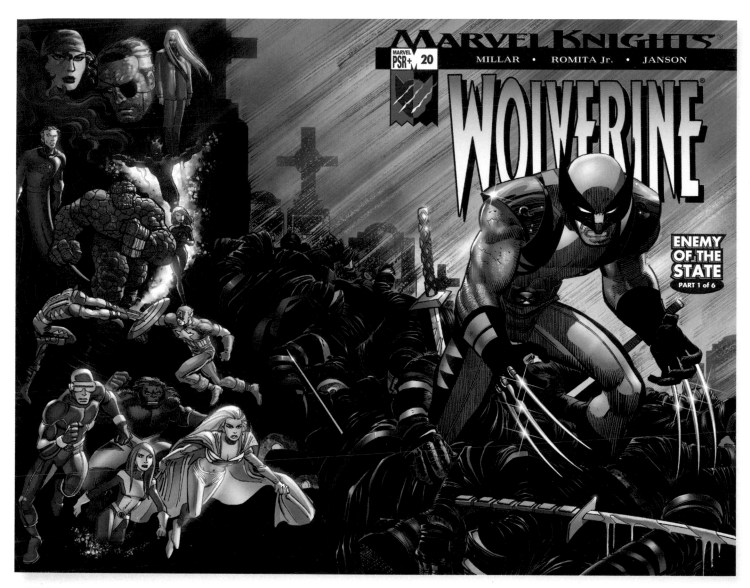

▲ *WOLVERINE #20*

December 2004
Artist: John Romita Jr.

John Romita Jr. was Marvel's leading artist when he
teamed up with one of their biggest writers, Mark Millar,
to create "Enemy of the State," a shocking story in which
Wolverine is brainwashed by ninja assassins from the
order known as the Hand. Romita Jr.'s wraparound cover
portrays a bloodthirsty Wolverine after his run-in with the
ninjas, who would soon brainwash the hero into being
their deadliest member.

◄ *ORIGIN* #1

November 2001
Artist: Joe Quesada

It was the story that some thought would never be told—the origin of Wolverine. It was up to Marvel's then Editor-in-Chief and award-winning artist, Joe Quesada, to create something special for a story this big. His atmospheric cover, with the distinctive color work of artist Richard Isanove, is reflective of the story's 19th-century setting. Separate chapter headings on each of the four covers achieves a cinematic look.

◄ *WOLVERINE* #1

July 2003
Artist: Esad Ribic

Wolverine's third series went in a grittier and darker direction than the previous run. Esad Ribic's close-up of Logan might show Wolverine's claws, but it was a more everyday image of him than his usual costumed X-Men persona. The story inside was more "thriller" than "Super Hero," as Wolverine sought vengeance for a girl who was murdered after turning to him for help.

UNCANNY X-MEN #268 ▶

September 1990
Artist: Jim Lee

Even by Jim Lee's high standards, this was a special cover—and a very special issue. The central image promised a team-up that comic book fans would love. This time it was Wolverine, Black Widow, and Captain America fighting alongside each other—and looking exceptionally heroic. The issue had a surprise in store too, as it was revealed that the three heroes had first met during World War II.

◀ *UNCANNY X-MEN* #260

April 1990
Artist: Jim Lee

Jim Lee reinvigorated the X-Men in the late 1980s. His sleek, action-packed style won him countless awards and he quickly became one of the most popular artists in the business. While Lee excelled at group shots of the X-Men, he could also produce atmospheric pieces such as this cover, showing a psychopath obsessed with Dazzler.

◀ *UNCANNY X-MEN* #269

October 1990
Artist: Jim Lee

Rogue and Ms. Marvel went way back. When Rogue was a villain, she accidentally stole Ms. Marvel's powers and memories. The two characters had met since, but this cover promised a much deadlier meeting. The image of Magneto's head at the bottom of the page, next to the words "Guess who wins!" suggested the meeting would have a surprise ending.

299

▲ *X-MEN* #1

October 1991
Artist: Jim Lee

Following the success of his work on *Uncanny X-Men*,
Jim Lee was at the helm for the launch of the first
new X-Men series since 1963. To celebrate this,
Lee created a huge fold-out cover for the first issue.
Each segment was released as a variant cover,
but another edition was released with all the
parts intact to fold out. The issue was a massive
success and became the bestselling comic of the year.

▲ *X-MEN CLASSIC* #57

March 1991
Artists: Mike Mignola and P. Craig Russell

This reprint of *Uncanny X-Men* issue #153 (January 1982) featured a beautiful new cover by Mike Mignola and P. Craig Russell. The two artists were masters of fantasy illustration and the perfect choice for this issue, which was based around a bedtime story Kitty Pryde told to the young Illyana Rasputin. While this reprint series had started as *Classic X-Men*, it changed its title to *X-Men Classic* from issue #46.

▲ *X-MEN CLASSIC* #63

September 1991
Artists: Mike Mignola and P. Craig Russell

Mike Mignola and P. Craig Russell created another masterpiece based on a classic X-Men story—*Uncanny X-Men* issue #159 (July 1982)—where the team met Dracula, who was attempting to make Storm his vampire bride. Mignola and Russell's work for these covers was so good, the series was collectible for the covers alone.

◄ *CLASSIC X-MEN* #1

September 1986
Artist: Art Adams

Classic X-Men had a series of stunning covers created by some of the best artists in the business. Each issue reprinted an old X-Men story, but also contained a second story by John Bolton. The first issue's cover, by Art Adams, was a celebration of the X-Men, with all the mutants who appeared in the classic *Giant Size X-Men* issue #1 (May 1975) brought together in one stunning image.

▲ *X-MEN: ALPHA* #1

February 1995
Artist: Joe Madureira

The "Age of Apocalypse" was one of the *X-Men* comics'
biggest storylines. Set in a reality in which Professor X
had been killed and had never formed the X-Men, it was
a massive multi-part epic the like of which had never
been seen before. Joe Madureira created an amazing
image of the alternate versions of the X-Men for the first
issue, *X-Men: Alpha*. The cover had shiny holofoil added
to the art to make it even more eye-catching.

▲ **GENERATION NEXT #1**

March 1995
Artist: Chris Bachalo

All the X-line of comics were replaced by "Age of Apocalypse" versions during the event. Chris Bachalo was already producing wonderful art for *Generation X*, a new team of teen mutants, when he created this "Age of Apocalypse" cover for its replacement title *Generation Next*. The sight of the Generation X team in their Age of Apocalypse incarnations created an intriguing and memorable image.

▲ **WEAPON X #1**

March 1995
Artist: Adam Kubert

Perhaps the most shocking image from the early "Age of Apocalypse" covers was the sight of a one-handed Wolverine. The cover for the first issue of *Weapon X* had another shock for comic fans—the image of Jean Grey with Logan. In this dark reality the two were lovers, although events in the series soon forced them apart.

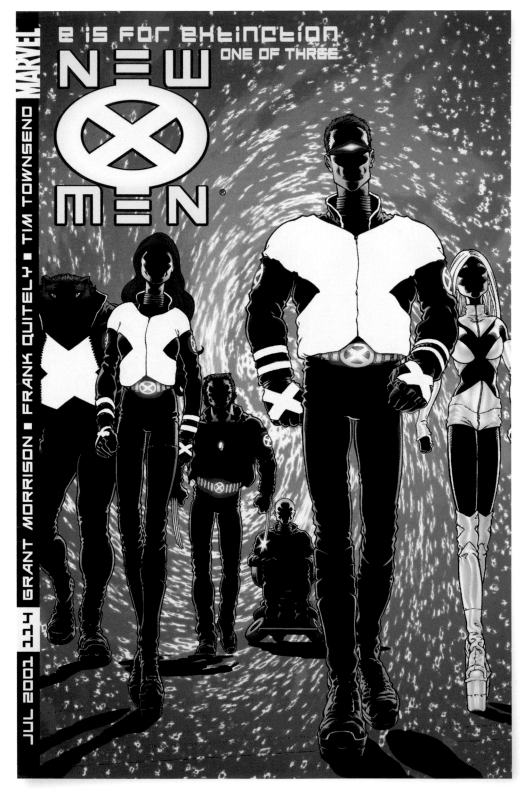

▲ *NEW X-MEN #114*

July 2001
Artist: Frank Quitely

It was all change for the X-Men in this issue as
writer Grant Morrison started his epic run on the title,
joined by artist Frank Quitely. The logo was redesigned
for the new era and the title renamed *New X-Men*.
Quitely's image of Cyclops and the X-Men moving
purposefully forward, dressed in their new paramilitary
uniforms, signified a real change in style for the heroes.

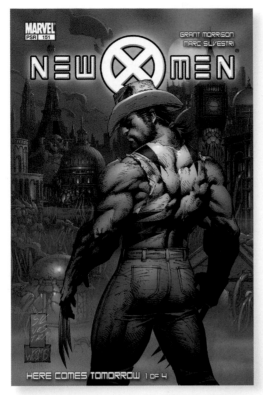

▲ *NEW X-MEN* #151—154

March 2004
Artist: Marc Silvestri

These four issues were an epic conclusion to Grant
Morrison's time as writer on *New X-Men*. Marc Silvestri,
one of the leading artists in the business at the time,
returned to Marvel for these issues and created a series of
stunning covers. The first three are futuristic incarnations
of Wolverine, Beast, and Nightcrawler, while the final shows
a dark, future version of Wolverine and his new X-Men team.

▲ *ASTONISHING X-MEN* #1

July 2004
Artist: John Cassaday

When artist John Cassaday joined forces with movie writer-director Joss Whedon, the result was one of the best X-Men comics of all time. Cassaday created a number of stylish covers for *Astonishing X-Men*, starting with this close-up of Wolverine's claws, the light shining off the middle claw providing an eye-catching flash.

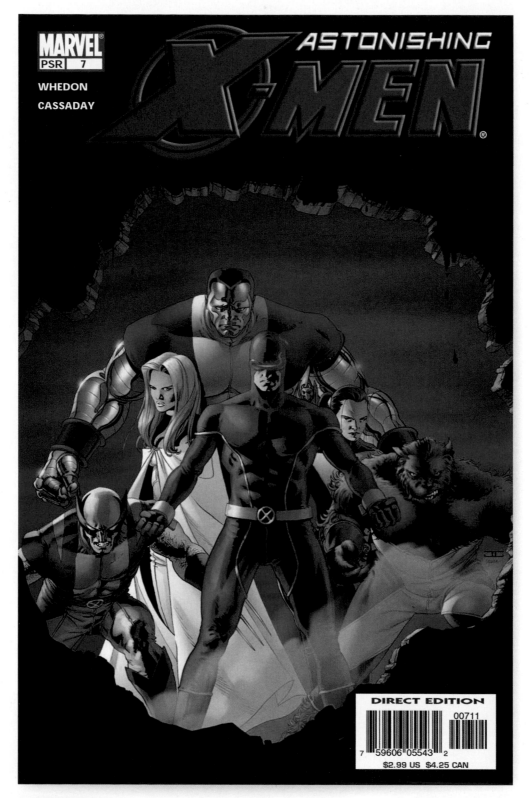

▲ *ASTONISHING X-MEN #7*

January 2005
Artist: John Cassaday

Writer Joss Whedon made Cyclops one of his star
characters during his run on *Astonishing X-Men*, with
John Cassaday portraying Cyclops in a far more heroic
light than he had in the time leading up to the series.
This issue reflects Cyclops' resurgence under this team,
with Cassaday's cover showing the team seconds after
Cyclops' optic blasts had done their job.

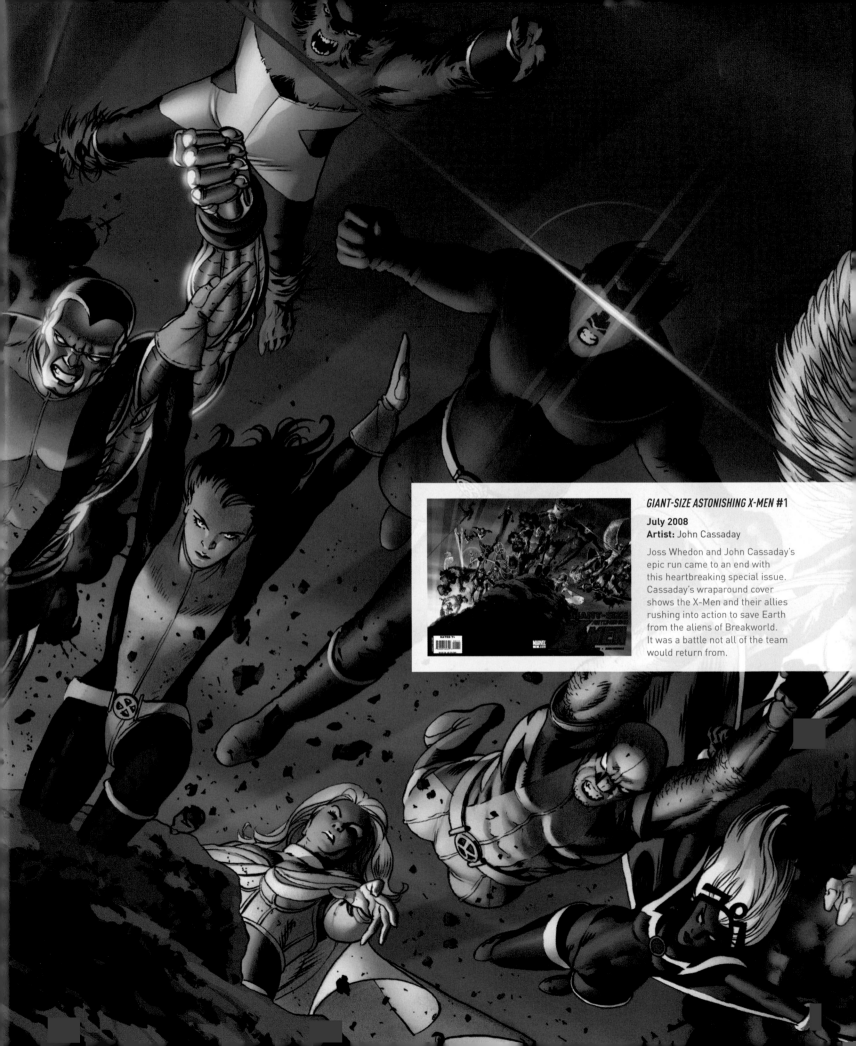

GIANT-SIZE ASTONISHING X-MEN #1

July 2008
Artist: John Cassaday

Joss Whedon and John Cassaday's epic run came to an end with this heartbreaking special issue. Cassaday's wraparound cover shows the X-Men and their allies rushing into action to save Earth from the aliens of Breakworld. It was a battle not all of the team would return from.

▲ *UNCANNY X-MEN #448*

October 2004
Artist: Greg Land

Greg Land brought his realistic style to
Uncanny X-Men to create this moody close-up
of Wolverine. It was one of the few Wolverine
covers to keep the hero's face hidden. The concealed
features, coupled with the sight of Wolverine's
claws, add an element of mystery and danger.

▲ *UNCANNY X-MEN #449*

November 2004
Artist: Greg Land

Land produced a wonderful portrait of Storm for
this issue, showing Ororo Munroe embracing her
connection to the elements. Ororo Munroe had
always been a character who seemed happiest
in wide open spaces, and this cover reflects her
pleasure at being alone with the storm-ridden sky.

UNCANNY X-MEN #466 ▶

January 2006
Artist: Chris Bachalo

Rachel Summers, the daughter
of Jean Grey and Scott Summers from
the horrifying parallel Earth of "Days
of Future Past," was the focus of this
cover. Bachalo's use of flames around
both her and the logo is symbolic
of one of the books' deadliest stories,
as Shi'ar Death Commandos were
sent to Earth to execute every
member of the Grey family.

◀ *UNCANNY X-MEN* #503

December 2008
Artist: Greg Land

Cyclops' ex-wife Madelyne Pryor made a return in this issue. A clone of Jean Grey, Madelyne had turned into the Goblin Queen years before. The X-Men believed her to be dead, but Greg Land's cover hints at her return—and her role as the new Red Queen, the opposite of Emma Frost's old position as the Hellfire Club's White Queen.

◀ *UNCANNY X-MEN* #504

January 2008
Artist: Terry Dodson

This 1920s-style cover showcases Terry Dodson's attention to detail and skill in drawing female characters. Dodson's depiction of the female X-Men wearing unusual attire turned out to be because it was an image from Cypclops' mind, as his telepathic lover, Emma Frost, entered it to find out why he had been acting so strangely.

◄ *UNCANNY X-MEN* #505

February 2008
Artist: Terry Dodson

Despite the cover showing a group pose of the X-Men, this issue focused on the individual adventures of the team, rather than one big story. Dodson created a dramatic group shot, with the leader Cyclops in the forefront and the Blackbird aircraft taking off in the background.

◄ *UNCANNY X-MEN* #535

June 2011
Artist: Terry Dodson

A follow-up to Joss Whedon's *Astonishing X-Men* series sees Kitty Pryde as the focus on the cover. With the aliens from Breakworld returning, it was only natural that Kitty would be involved—in the previous series it seemed she had given her life to save Earth. The cover, which also shows the alien Ord and the S.W.O.R.D. space station, reflected the intergalactic scope of the new story.

◄ UNCANNY X-FORCE #1

December 2010
Artist: Esad Ribic

The first issue of the new *Uncanny X-Force* series saw Wolverine again leading a team of killers—"a Black Ops" version of the X-Men. The new series had the team trying to stop one of the X-Men's deadliest enemies—Apocalypse—from returning. Ribic's dynamic and moody art was a perfect fit for this new grouping, bringing out the deadly nature of X-Force in one tough group shot.

UNCANNY X-FORCE #31 ►

November 2012
Artist: Jerome Opena

The "Final Execution" saga was the swan song for *Uncanny X-Force*. In this issue, Wolverine's son, Daken, formed a new Brotherhood of Evil Mutants to destroy the X-Force team. Jerome Opena's stylish two-tone cover reflects the dark nature and mood of the team as they prepared for their final battle with the Brotherhood.

UNCANNY X-FORCE #1 ►

March 2013
Artist: Olivier Coipel

A new X-Force team was introduced in this issue. Olivier Coipel's cover shows a group shot of the new team, which featured surprise members, such as the villain Spiral. It also promises the return of former X-Men member Bishop—shown looming in the background—without revealing whether he would return as a hero or a villain.

▲ WOLVERINE AND THE X-MEN #3

February 2012
Artist: Chris Bachalo

Wolverine and the X-Men quickly became a
favorite X-book for many fans. The stories
were set in the Jean Grey School for Higher
Learning, where Wolverine was headmaster.
Chris Bachalo provided a suitably surly image
of the popular Kid Omega (Quentin Quire) for
the cover, which captured Kid Omega's
rebellious attitude perfectly.

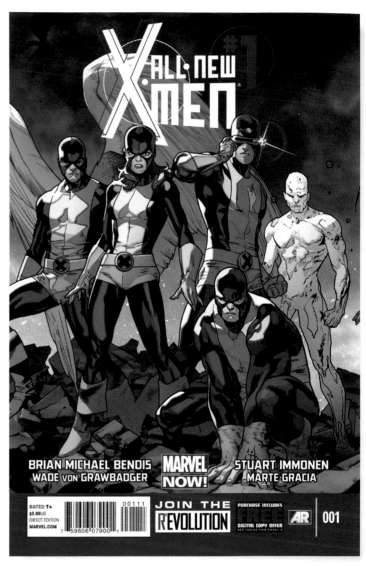

▲ ALL-NEW X-MEN #1

January 2013
Artist: Stuart Immonen

This new series reinvigorated the whole
mutant world by bringing the original five
X-Men through time into the present day.
Stuart Immonen portrayed the youth and
innocence of the young mutants on the
cover of the first issue, instantly intriguing
readers who wanted to see what would
happen when the young mutants met
their older selves.

▲ *UNCANNY X-MEN* #1

April 2013
Artist: Chris Bachalo

Bachalo's angled cover of the debut issue of a new *Uncanny X-Men* series reflects Cyclops' skewed view of the world—a world that now considered him a Super Villain. Cyclops' new visor was especially startling. The "X" represented the man Cyclops had killed while possessed by the Phoenix Force—his old mentor, Professor X.

▲ *X-MEN* #1

August 2013
Artist: Olivier Coipel

It was time for the women to take charge in the new *X-Men* series. While the *X-Men* comics had always included strong female characters, this was the first time they were featured in their own series. Coipel's eye-catching cover shows a dynamic group shot of the team, with Storm at the front, proving her leadership skills.

Editors Catherine Saunders, Heather Scott,
Julia March, Alastair Dougall, Jo Casey, Beth Davies, David Fentiman,
Gaurav Joshi, Tori Kosara, Chitra Subramanyam, Julia March and Clare Millar
Project Editor Elizabeth Dowsett
Project Art Editor Owen Bennett
Designers Hanna Ländin, Lisa Crowe, Neha Ahuja, Karan Chaudhary,
Jill Clark, Mark Richards, Dan Bunyan, Ian Midson, Gema Salamanca and Dynamo Ltd
Senior Designers Nathan Martin, Robert Perry and Mark Penfound
Pre-Production Producer Kavita Varma
Producer Naomi Green
Managing Editor Sadie Smith
Managing Art Editor Ron Stobbart
Creative Manager Sarah Harland
Art Director Lisa Lanzarini
Publisher Julie Ferris
Publishing Director Simon Beecroft

This edition published in 2016
First published in Great Britain in 2008 by
Dorling Kindersley Limited,
80 Strand, London, WC2R 0RL
A Penguin Random House Company

Originally published as two separate titles.
Contains content previously published in: *Marvel Comics 75 Years of Cover Art* (2014)
and *Marvel Year by Year A Visual Chronicle Updated and Expanded* (2013)

001—301162—Sept/2016

A CIP catalogue record for this book is available from the British Library

ISBN: 978-0-2412-9197-9

DK would like to thank David Gabriel, Jeff Youngquist, Joseph Hochstein, Mark Annunziato, Brian Overton, Sarah
Brunstad and George Beliard at Marvel; Chelsea Alon at Disney.

Alan Cowsill would like to thank Nick Abadzis, James Britnell, Glenn Dakin, Aletia and Gary Gilbert, James Hill,
Adam Levine, Dan Rachael, Richard Starkings and Dean White for answering questions, and Matt McAllister, Maggie
Calmels, Richard Jackson, Ben Robinson, John Tomlinson, Colin Williams and the folk at Eaglemoss. Special thanks
to my Mum and Dad for buying me *Mighty World of Marvel* issue #1.

Colour reproduction by Media Development and Printing Ltd, UK.
Printed and bound in China

www.dk.com

A WORLD OF IDEAS:
SEE ALL THERE IS TO KNOW